Mandarin
Chinese

A ROUGH GUIDE
PHRASEBOOK

Compiled
by Lexus

Credits

Compiled by Lexus with Julian Ward and Xu Yinong

Lexus Series Editor: Sally Davies
Rough Guides Phrasebook Editor: Jonathan Buckley
Rough Guides Series Editor: Mark Ellingham

This first edition published in 1997 by Rough Guides Ltd, 1 Mercer Street, London WC2H 9QJ.

Distributed by the Penguin Group.

Penguin Books Ltd, 27 Wrights Lane, London W8 5TZ
Penguin Books USA Inc., 375 Hudson Street, New York 10014, USA
Penguin Books Australia Ltd, 487 Maroondah Highway, PO Box 257, Ringwood, Victoria 3134, Australia
Penguin Books Canada Ltd, Alcorn Avenue, Toronto, Ontario, Canada M4V 1E4
Penguin Books (NZ) Ltd, 182–190 Wairau Road, Auckland 10, New Zealand

Typeset in Rough Serif and Rough Sans to an original design by Henry Iles.
Printed by Cox & Wyman Ltd, Reading.

©Lexus Ltd 1997
272pp.

British Library Cataloguing in Publication Data
A catalogue for this book is available from the British Library.

ISBN 1-85828-249-7

CONTENTS

Introduction   v

The BASICS: Pronunciation (3); Abbreviations (8); Nouns (9);
   Articles (9); Adjectives (10); Adverbs (12); Pronouns (12);
   Possessives (13); Measure Words (14); Verbs (17); To Be
   (18); Negatives (18); Sentence Particles (20); Questions (22);
   Prepositions (23); Yes and No (25); Imperatives (25); Dates
   (26); Days (26); Months (27); Time (27); Numbers (28); Basic
   Phrases (32); Conversion Tables (34)

English - Chinese   37

Chinese - English   203

   Signs and Notices   237

Menu Reader

   Food   251

   Drink   265

INTRODUCTION

The Rough Guide Mandarin Chinese phrasebook is a highly practical introduction to the contemporary language. Laid out in clear A-Z style, it uses key-word referencing to lead you straight to the words and phrases you want – so if you need to book a room, just look up 'room'. The Rough Guide gets straight to the point in every situation, in bars and shops, on trains and buses, and in hotels and banks.

The first part of the Rough Guide is a section called **The Basics**, which sets out the fundamental rules of the language and its pronunciation, with plenty of practical examples. You'll also find here other essentials like numbers, dates, telling the time and basic phrases.

Forming the heart of the guide, the **English-Chinese** section gives easy-to-use transliterations of the Chinese words plus the text in Chinese script, so that if the pronunciation proves too tricky, you can simply indicate what you want to say. To get you involved quickly in two-way communication, the Rough Guide also includes dialogues featuring typical responses on key topics – such as renting a room and asking directions. Feature boxes fill you in on cultural pitfalls as well as the simple mechanics of how to make a phone call, what to do in an emergency, where to change money, and more. Throughout this section, cross-references enable you to pinpoint key facts and phrases, while asterisked words indicate where further information can be found in the Basics.

The **Chinese-English** section is in two parts: a dictionary, arranged phonetically, of all the words and phrases you're likely to hear (starting with a section of slang and colloquialisms); then a compilation, arranged by subject, of all the signs, labels, instructions and other basic words you might come across in print or in public places.

Finally the Rough Guide rounds off with an extensive **Menu Reader**. Consisting of food and drink sections arranged by subject (each starting with a list of essential terms), it's indispensable whether you're eating out, stopping for a quick drink, or browsing through a local food market.

一路顺风
yílù shùnfēng!
have a good trip!

The Basics

The Basics

PRONUNCIATION

Throughout this book Chinese words have been written in the standard romanized system known as pinyin (see below). Pinyin, which was introduced in China in the 1950s, can for the most part be used as a guide to pronunciation. However, some of the syllables are not pronounced in an immediately obvious way. For this reason, a simplified transliteration is also provided in almost all instances. This transliteration should be read as though it were English, bearing in mind the notes on pronunciation below:

Vowels

ah	long 'a' as in **a**rt
ai	'i' as in **I**, **eye**
ay	as in h**ay**
eh	'e' as in b**e**d
oh	'o' as in g**o**, **oh**
ow	as in c**ow**

Consonants

ch	as in **Ch**inese
dz	like the 'ds' in hea**ds**
g	hard 'g' as in **g**et
ts	as in **ts**ar
y	as in **y**es

PINYIN

Chinese words are made up of one or more syllables, each of which is represented in the written language by a character. These syllables can be divided into initials (consonants) and finals (vowels or vowels followed by either n or ng). In spoken Chinese, the consonant finals are often not fully sounded. A full list of initials and finals, along with the closest equivalent sound in English appears below. There are, however, some sounds that are unlike anything in English. In this

pronunciation guide, words containing these sounds are given
in Chinese characters as well; ask a Chinese person to
pronounce them for you.

Initials

f, l, m, n, s, w and y	are all similar to English
b, d, g	similar to English, but a shorter sound
p, t, k	a more emphatic pronunciation as in **pop**, **tap** and **cap** (more strongly pronounced than b, d and g above)
h	slightly harsher than an **h** in English, closer to the **ch** sound in lo**ch** or Ba**ch**
j, q, x	pronounced with the lips positioned as if you were smiling:
j	'j' as in **j**eer
q	'ch' as in **ch**eer
x	'sh' as in **sh**eer
c	'ts' as in **ts**ar 菜
z	'ds' as hea**ds** 自
ch, sh, zh, r	the last group of initials is the most difficult for a non-Chinese to perfect; they are all pronounced with the tip of the tongue curled back till it touches the palate:
ch	as ch in bir**ch** 茶
sh	as sh in **sh**ower 少
zh	as ge in bu**dge** 中
r	as r in **r**ung 人

Finals

a	as in **art**
ai	as in **ai**sle
an	as in r**an**, but with a longer 'a' as in **art**
ang	as in h**ang**, but with a longer 'a' as in **art**

ao	'ow' as in c**ow**
e	like the 'e' in th**e** or the 'u' in f**u**r
ei	as in w**ei**ght
en	as in shak**en**
eng	like 'en' followed by a softly spoken 'g'
er	similar to **err**, pronounced with the tongue curled back so that it touches the palate
i	usually pronounced as in marga**ri**ne; however, after the initials c, ch, r, s, sh, z and zh it is pronounced like the 'i' in sh**i**rt or f**i**rst
ia	'ya' as in **ya**rn
ian	similar to **yen**
iang	**yang** ('i' plus 'ang', but with shorter 'a' sound)
iao	'yow' as in **yow**l
ie	'ye' as in **ye**ti
in	as in d**in**
ing	as in br**ing**
iong	**yoong** ('i' plus 'ong')
iu	'yo' as in **yo-yo**
o	as in l**o**re
ou	like **oh**
ong	**oong** ('ung' as in l**ung**, with the vowel given a longer, more rounded sound)
u	as in r**u**le; or like French **u**ne or German **ü**ber
ua	**wah** ('wa' plus 'a' as in **a**rt)
uai	similar to **why**
uan	**wahn** in most cases ('w' plus 'an'); after 'y', the second pronunciation of 'u' plus 'an'
uang	**wahng** ('w' plus 'ang')
ue	the second pronunciation of 'u' plus 'e' as in b**e**t
ui	'wai' as in **wai**t
un	as in f**un**gi
uo	similar to **war**

ü	like French une or German über
üe	'ü' followed by 'e' as in bet

Northern Chinese

In Northern Chinese, the suffix r is often placed at the end of a syllable, producing a sound reminiscent of the burr of southwest England. This is represented in pinyin by the addition of an **r** to the syllable so that **men** (door), for example, becomes **menr**, with the 'n' barely pronounced. Such pronunciation is most apparent in Beijing.

TONES

The Chinese language only uses about four hundred different sounds. The number of sounds available is increased by the use of tones: the particular pitch at which a word is pronounced determines its meaning. The same combination of letters pronounced with a different tone will produce different words. There are four tones: first tone (ˉ), second tone (ˊ), third tone (ˇ) and fourth tone (ˋ).

Not all syllables are pronounced with tones; where there is no tone, the syllable is written without a tone mark. Often when you have a word consisting of two syllables, the second syllable, for example, xuésheng (student), is written without a tone.

In Chinese, the tone is as important a part of the word as the consonant and vowel sounds. Context usually makes the meaning clear, but it is still important whenever possible to use the correct tone in order to reduce the chance of misunderstanding. The character ma [mah] has five meanings, differentiated by the tones:

mā	妈	mother
má	麻	hemp
mǎ	马	horse
mà	骂	abuse, scold
ma	吗	added to the end of a sentence to turn it into a question

To help you get a clearer idea of how the tones sound, Chinese character equivalents are given for the words in this section. Ask a Chinese speaker to read the words for you so that you can hear the tonal differences.

First tone (ˉ). High, level tone, with unchanging volume, held briefly:

gū [goo]	孤	solitary
guān [gwahn]	观	look at
kāi	开	open (verb)
yān [yahn]	烟	cigarette

Second tone (ˊ). Starting about mid-range, rising quickly and becoming louder; a shorter sound than the first tone, similar to a question showing surprise such as 'eh?':

héng [hung]	衡	balance (verb)
rén [run]	人	person
shí [shur]	十	ten
yán [yahn]	言	speech

Third tone (ˇ). Starts low and falls before rising again to slightly above the starting point; starts quietly then increases in volume; slightly longer than first tone:

běn [bun]	本	book
fǎ [fah]	法	law
qǐ [chee]	起	rise (verb)
yǎn [yahn]	掩	cover (verb)

Fourth tone (ˋ). Starts high, falling abruptly in pitch and volume; shorter than the second tone:

bèn [bun]	笨	stupid
dà [dah]	大	big
pà [pah]	怕	fear (verb)
yàn [yahn]	雁	wild goose

The tones can be illustrated in diagram form like this:

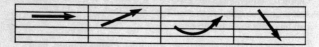

In speech, a third tone which precedes another third tone becomes a second tone. Where instances of this occur in the pinyin text of this phrasebook, the adjustment has been made.

ABBREVIATIONS

adj	adjective
pl	plural
pol	polite
sing	singular

GENERAL

The Chinese language has a number of characteristics which are very different from European languages, the most important of these being that there are no inflections for case, number or gender and that verbs do not decline. References to past, present or future are identified by context and the addition of various time words such as **míngtian** [ming-tyen] (tomorrow), **jīntian** [jin-tyen] (today), or **qùnián** [chew-nyen] (last year). In both the written and spoken language, statements are kept short and the repetition of what has already been expressed is avoided. Pronouns, both personal and impersonal, are often omitted.

NOUNS

Singular and plural forms of nouns are nearly always the same. For example, **shū** can mean either 'book' or 'books' depending on the context:

wó mǎile yíběn shū
wor mai-lur yee-bun shoo
I bought one book

wó mǎile liángběn shū
wor mai-lur lyang-bun shoo
I bought two books

The few exceptions tend to be nouns used in addressing groups of people, in which case the suffix -men is added to the end of the noun:

> **péngyoumen**
> pung-yoh-mun
> friends

> **háizimen**
> hai-dzur-mun
> children

However, -men is not used for the plural when numbers are involved as the plural is obvious from the context:

sìge péngyou
sur-gur pung-yoh
four friends

ARTICLES

There is no equivalent in Chinese for either the definite article 'the' or the indefinite articles 'a' and 'an'. The exact meaning will be clear from the context or word order. Therefore, **zázhì** (magazine) can mean 'a magazine' or 'the magazine' depending on the context.

If you want to be more precise, you can use **nèi** (that) or **zhèi** (this) with the appropriate measure word (see page 14).

(see page 14).

GRAMMAR

The number yi (one), along with the appropriate measure word (see page 14) can also be used to translate 'a/an'. But, often in such sentences, yi is either unstressed or omitted altogether, leaving just the measure word:

wó xiǎng mǎi yìběn zázhì
wor hsyang mai yee-bun dzah-jur
I am going to buy a
    magazine

or:

wó xiǎng mái běn zázhì
I am going to buy a
    magazine

ADJECTIVES

Adjectives are placed before the noun and usually the word de is added between the adjective and the noun:

piányi de shū
pyen-yee dur shoo
cheap book(s)

hěn suān de sùcài
hun swahn dur soo-tsai
very sour vegetable dish(es)

The de is frequently omitted if the adjective is monosyllabic:

gǔ huà
goo hwah
ancient paintings

hǎo bànfǎ
how bahn-fah
a good method

Some nouns can be used adjectivally:

lìshǐ
lee-shur
history

lìshǐ xiǎoshuō
lee-shur hsyow-shwor
historical novel(s)

shùxué
shoo-hsyew-eh
mathematics

shùxué jiàokēshū
shoo-hsyew-eh jyow-kur-shoo
maths textbook

Adjectival Verbs

Some verbs also function as adjectives and are known as adjectival verbs. In sentences using an adjectival verb, the word order is:

noun subject + hěn + adjectival verb

The word hěn has little meaning, unless it is stressed, when it means 'very'.

sùcài hěn suān
soo-tsai hun swahn
the vegetable dish is very
    sour

shū dōu hěn piányi
shoo doh hun pyen-yee
the books are all cheap

Suān means 'to be sour' and piányi 'to be cheap'.

For greater emphasis, add **tài** to mean 'very', 'really' or 'extremely':

tài hǎole
tai how-lur
that's really great

Comparatives

To form the comparative (more ..., ...-er) in sentences when only one thing is referred to, most often in response to a question, an adjectival verb is used by itself. In the following two examples, the adjectival verbs **hǎokàn** (attractive) and **guì** (expensive) are used:

zhèige hǎokàn
jay-gur how-kahn
this (one) is more attractive

nèige guì
nay-gur gway
that (one) is more expensive

The above phrases can also be translated as 'this one is attractive' and 'that one is expensive', but the exact meaning will be clear from the context. The following are added after the adjective or adjectival verb to indicate the degree of comparison:

... diǎnr	[dyenr]	more ...
... xiē	[hsyeh]	a bit more ...
... yìdiǎnr	[yee-dyenr]	a bit more ...
... de duō	[dur dwor]	much more ...
... duōle	[dwor-lur]	far more ...
... gèng	[gung]	even more ...

zhèige guì (yi)diǎnr/xiē
jay-gur gway (yee-)dyenr/hsyeh
this (one) is (a bit) more expensive

zhèige guì de duō
jay-gur gway dur dwor
this (one) is much more expensive

zhèige guì duōle
jay-gur gway dwor-lur
this (one) is far more expensive

zhèige gèng guì
jay-gur gung gway
this (one) is even more expensive

To compare two nouns, the word order is:

subject + **bǐ** + object of comparison + adjectival verb

Fǎguó bǐ Zhōngguó xiǎo
fah-gwor bee joong-gwor hsyow
France is smaller than China

qùnián bǐ jīnnián rè
chew-nyen bee jin-nyen rur
last year was hotter than
  this year

zhèige bǐ nèige gèng měilì
jay-gur bee nay-gur gung may-lur
this one is even more
  beautiful than that one

Superlatives

To form the superlative
(most ..., ...-est), place zuì
before the adjective or
adjectival verb:

zuì guì de zìxíngchē
dzway gway dur dzur-hsing-chur
the most expensive bicycle

zhèige fàndiàn zuì dà
jay-gur fahn-dyen dzway dah
this hotel is the largest

ADVERBS

Adverbs usually have the
same form as adjectives, but
are sometimes repeated for
emphasis (mànmàn below):

tā mànmàn de kànle nǐde xìn
tah mahn-mahn dur kahn-lur
  nee-dur hsin
he/she read your letter
  slowly

Adverbs can also be formed by
placing de after an adjective:

nǐ dàshēng de gēn tā shuō ba
nee dah-shung dur gun tah
  shwor bah
speak loudly to him/her

When de appears after a verb,
the subsequent adjective takes
on an adverbial function:

tāmen qǐde hén wǎn
tah-mun chee-dur hun wahn
they got up late

tā zúqiu tǐde hén hǎo
tah dzoo-chyew tee-dur hun how
he plays football well

PRONOUNS

Personal Pronouns

wǒ	[wor]	I; me
nǐ	[nee]	you (sing)
nín	[nin]	you (sing, pol)
tā	[tah]	he; him; she; her; it
wǒmen	[wor-mun]	we; us
nǐmen	[nee-mun]	you (pl)
nínmen	[nin-mun]	you (pl, pol)
tāmen	[tah-mun]	they; them

There are no different forms for subject and object in Chinese:

wǒ rènshi tā
wor run-shur tah
I know him/her

tā rènshi wǒ
tah runshur wor
he/she knows me

zhèi shì géi nǐ de
jay shur gay nee dur
this is for you

Tā can also mean 'it', though
this is not a common usage.
Generally, there is no need to
refer to 'it' in a sentence as
the context usually makes it
clear:

shū hěn wúqù – wó bú
xǐhuan
shoo hun woo-choo – wor boo
hshee-hwahn
the book is boring – I don't
like it

wó xǐhuan nèibén shū – hén
yǒu yìsi
wor hshee-hwahn nay-bun shoo
– hun yoh yee-sur
I like that book – it's very
interesting

wǒde	[wor-dur]	my; mine
nǐde	[nee-dur]	your; yours (sing)
nínde	[nin-dur]	your; yours (sing, pol)
tāde	[tah-dur]	his; her; hers; its; its
wǒmende	[wor-mun-dur]	our; ours
nǐmende	[nee-mun-dur]	your; yours (pl)
nínmende	[nin-mun-dur]	your; yours (pl, pol)
tāmende	[tah-mun-dur]	their; theirs

Like tā, tāmen referring to
inanimate things is rarely
used.

Demonstrative Pronouns

zhè	nà
jur	nah
this	that

zhè búshì tāde
jur boo-shur tah-dur
this is not his

nà tèbié hǎo
nah tur-byeh how
that's awfully good

In order to translate 'this one'
or 'that one' as the object of a
sentence, a measure word
(see page 14) must be added:

wǒ xǐhuan zhèige/nèige
wor hshee-hwahn jay-gur/nay-gur
I like this (one)/that (one)

POSSESSIVES

In order to form possessive
adjectives and pronouns, add
the suffix -de to the personal
pronouns on page 12:

GRAMMAR

wǒde zhuōzi
wor-dur jwor-dzur
my table

tāde péngyou
tah-dur pung-yoh
his/her friend

tāmende péngyou
tah-mun-dur pung-yoh
their friend

zhè shì nǐde
jur shur nee-dur
this is yours

De equates to 'of' or
apostrophe s in English. De
phrases always precede the
noun to be described:

Shànghǎi de fēngjǐng
shahng-hai dur fung-jing
the scenery of Shanghai

qiūtian de tiānqi
chyew-tyen dur tyen-chee
autumn weather

wǒ qīzi de yīxiāng
wor chee-dzur dur yee-hsyang
my wife's suitcase

If a relationship or possession
is obvious from the context, it
is common to omit de:

wǒ àiren
wor ai-run
my wife

tā jiā
tah jyah
his/her home

wǒ péngyou
wor pung-yoh
my friend

wǒ mǎile chēpiào le
wor mai-lur chur-pyow lur
I've bought my train ticket

Dependent Clauses and 'de'

Dependent clauses precede
the noun to be modified and
de is inserted between the
clause and the noun:

wǒ kàn de shū
wor kahn dur shoo
the book(s) (which/that) I
read

zuótian kàn de nèibù diànyǐng
dzwor-tyen kahn dur nay-boo
dyen-ying
that film I saw yesterday

tā jì de xìn
tah jee dur hsin
the letter which he sent

MEASURE WORDS

Demonstrative Adjectives and Measure Words

Nouns or groups of nouns in
Chinese have specific
measure words which are
used when counting or
quantifying the noun or
nouns, i.e. which are used

in conjunction with demonstratives and numerals. The demonstrative adjective is usually formed with the demonstrative **nèi** (that) or **zhèi** (this) followed by a measure word. Measure words, of which there are around fifty in common usage, are added to the end of the demonstrative (or numeral) and precede the noun. Some measure words can be readily translated into English while others cannot, for example:

gōngjīn
goong-jin
kilogram

mǐ
mee
metre

gōngchǐ
goong-chur
metre

píng
ping
bottle

sāngōngjīn lízi
sahng-goong-jin lee-dzur
three kilos of pears

sānmǐ miánbù
sahn-mee myen-boo
three metres of cotton

nèipíng píjiǔ
nay-ping pee-yoh
that bottle of beer

The most common measure words are:

bǎ	[bah]	chairs, knives, teapots, tools or implements with handles, stems, bunches of flowers
beī	[bay]	cups, glasses
běn	[bun]	books, magazines
fèng	[fun]	letters
ge	[gur]	general measure word
jiàn	[jyen]	things, affairs etc
kē	[kur]	trees, flowers
kuài	[kwai]	lumps, pieces
liàng	[lyang]	vehicles
pán	[pahn]	round objects
suǒ	[swor]	buildings
tiáo	[tyow]	fish and various long narrow things
wèi	[way]	polite measure word used for gentlemen, ladies, guests etc
zhāng	[jahng]	tables, beds, tickets, sheets of paper
zhī	[jur]	hands, birds, suitcases, boats

GRAMMAR

zhèiběn shū
jay-bun shoo
this book

nèijiàn lǐwù
nay-jyen lee-woo
that present

nèikē shù
nay-kur shoo
that tree

zhèiliàng zìxíngchē
jay-lyang dzur-hsing-chur
this bicycle

nèisuǒ yīyuàn
nay-swor yee-ywahn
that hospital

sāntiáo chuán
sahn-tyow chwahn
three boats

nèiwèi láibīn
nay-way lai-bin
that guest

sānzhāng piào
sahn-jahng pyow
three tickets

The most common of all measure words is ge:

zhèige shāngdiàn
jay-gur shang-dyen
this shop

nèige zhěntou
nay-gur jun-toh
that pillow

When the correct measure word is not known, the best solution is to use ge.

In a dialogue, when it is clear from the context what is being referred to, then the noun may be omitted and only the demonstrative and measure word are used:

wǒ xǐhuan nèige
wor hshee-hwahn nay-gur
I like that (one)

zhèibēi hén hǎohē
jay-bay hun how-hur
this is a lovely cup of tea

zhèiwèi shì ...
jay-way shur
this is ... (introducing people)

Numbers and Measure Words

As is the case with demonstrative adjectives, you must use a measure word with numbers when they are linked with nouns:

sìkē shù
sur-kur shoo
four trees

sānshíwǔběn shū
sahn-shur-woo-bun shoo
thirty-five books

sìshíge rén
sur-shur-gur run
forty people

See page 30 for the use of liǎng (two) with measure words.

Similarly, when ordinal numbers are linked with a noun, it is necessary to include a measure word:

> dìsānsuǒ fángzi
> dee-sahn-swor fahng-dzur
> the third house

> dìsìtiáo lù
> dee-sur-tyow loo
> the fourth road

Demonstratives and Numbers

If a demonstrative and a number are used together in a sentence, the word order is:

demonstrative + number + measure word + noun

> nèi sānběn shū
> nay sahn-bun shoo
> those three books

> zhèi bāwèi láibīn
> jay bah-way lai-bin
> these eight guests

> nèi liùge
> nay lyoh-gur
> those six

VERBS

There is no change in Chinese verbs for first, second or third person subjects, both singular and plural:

> wó zǒu
> wor dzoh
> I walk, I am walking

> tā zǒu
> tah dzoh
> he/she walks, he/she is walking

> tāmen zǒu
> tah-mun dzoh
> they walk, they are walking

Chinese verbs also have no tenses:

> wǒ míngtian zǒu
> wor ming-tyen dzoh
> I will go for a walk tomorrow

> wǒ zuótian zǒu de shíhou, tiānqi hén hǎo
> wor dzwor-tyen dzoh dur shur-hoh tyen-chee hun how
> when I was walking yesterday, the weather was lovely

The future and past are indicated in the above sentences by the time words míngtian (tomorrow) and zuótian (yesterday), while the form of the verb zǒu does not change.

The meaning of verbs is also influenced by a number of suffixes and sentence particles (see pages 20-21).

A verb used by itself, usually implies either a habitual action:

> **Zhōngguórén chī mǐfàn**
> joong-gwor-run chur mee-fahn
> Chinese people eat rice

or an imminent action:

> **nǐ qù nǎr?**
> nee chew nar
> where are you going?

TO BE

The verb 'to be', when followed by a noun, is **shì**, which corresponds to all the forms of the verb 'to be' in English ('am', 'are', 'is', 'were' etc):

> **tā shì wǒde péngyou**
> tah shur wor-dur pung-yoh
> she is my friend

> **zhè shì shénme?**
> jur shur shun-mur
> what is this?

> **tāmen shì xuésheng**
> tah-mun shur hway-shung
> they are students

The verb **shì** is not required when adjectival verbs are used (see page 10).

The preposition **zài** (in, at) is used as a verb to convey the meaning of 'to be in or at' a particular place (see page 23).

NEGATIVES

To form a negative sentence, use the word **bù** (not); when **bù** precedes a word with a fourth tone, the tone changes to a second tone (**bú**):

> **wǒ búyào nèiběn shū**
> wor boo-yow nay-bun shoo
> I do not want that book

> **tā bú qù**
> tah boo chew
> he's not going

> **nà wǒ bù zhīdao**
> nah wor boo jur-dow
> I didn't know that

Bù is also the negative used with adjectives/adjectival verbs:

> **bùmǎn**
> boo-mahn
> dissatisfied, discontented

> **fángzi bú dà**
> fahng-dzur boo dah
> the building isn't big

With the verb **yǒu** (to have), **méi** is used as a negative rather than **bù**:

tā yǒu kòng
tah yoh koong
he/she has time

wǒ méiyǒu kòng
wor may-yoh koong
I don't have time

Méi can also be used on its own to mean 'have not':

wǒ méishìr
wor may-shur
I have nothing to do

Yǒu also means 'there is/are':

shāngdiànli méiyǒu niúnǎi
shahng-dyen-lee may-yoh nyoh-nai
there's no milk in the shop

méiyǒu bànfǎ
may-yoh bahn-fah
there's nothing to be done, there's nothing you can do about it

yǒu rén
yoh run
there is someone there; engaged, occupied (on a toilet door)

Verb Suffixes

Suffixes are added to Chinese verbs to modify their meaning.

The addition of the suffix **-le** indicates a changed situation; often this means that the action of the verb has been completed:

wó mǎile sānge píngguǒ
wor mai-lur sahn-gur ping-gwor
I bought three apples

tā yǐjing líkāile
tah yee-jing lee-kai-lur
he/she has left already

wǒ zài nàr zhùle jiǔnián
wor dzai nar joo-lur jyoh-nyen
I lived there for nine years

hēwánle chá wǒ jiù kàn diànshì
hur-wahn-lur chah wor jyoh kahn dyen-shur
when I have finished my tea, I am going to watch television

As the fourth example shows, the completed action need not necessarily be in the past.

In order to express the negative form of a completed action, either **méi** or **méi yǒu** is placed before the verb and **-le** is omitted:

wǒ méi(yǒu) kàn diànshì
wor may(-yoh) kahn dyen-shur
I didn't watch television

tā méi(yǒu) líkāi
tah may(-yoh) lee-kai
he hasn't left

Continuous or prolonged action is expressed by the suffix **-zhe**:

tā chōuzhe yān
tah choh-jur yahn
he/she is smoking a
  cigarette

tā zài shāfāshang zuòzhe
tah dzai shah-fah-shahng
  dzwor-jur
he/she is sitting on the sofa

The suffix -zhe can also be
used to convey the idea of
doing more than one thing at
the same time:

tā hēzhe chá kàn shū
tah hur-jur chah kahn shoo
he read a book while
  drinking tea

When the -zhe suffix is used,
méi is placed before the verb
to form the negative:

tā méi chuānzhe
  zhōngshānzhuāng
tah may chwahn-jur
  joong-shahn-jwahng
he/she isn't wearing a Mao
  suit

Note that -zhe has no
connection with tense.
Depending on the context,
the above sentences could be
translated as: 'he/she was
smoking a cigarette', 'he/she
wasn't wearing a Mao suit'.

Another way of indicating
continuous action is to place
the word zài in front of the
verb:

tā zài chōuyān
tah dzai choh-yahn
he is smoking

nǐ zài kàn shénme?
nee dzai kahn shun-mur
what are you reading?

The suffix -guo is used to
indicate a past experience:

wǒ qùguo Zhōngguó
wor chew-gwor
I have been to China

wǒ kànguo nèiběn shū
wor kahng-gwor nay-bun shoo
I have read that book

When the suffix -guo is used,
méi is placed before the verb
to form the negative:

wǒ méi qùguo Shànghǎi
wor may chew-gwor shahng-hai
I have never been to
  Shanghai

tā méi hēguo Yìndù chá
tah may hur-gwor yin-doo chah
he/she's never drunk Indian
  tea

SENTENCE PARTICLES

The particle le at the end of a
sentence either indicates that
something happened in the
past which is still relevant to
the present or implies a
change of circumstances in
the present or future:

tā mǎi bàozhǐ qù le
tah mai bow-jur chew lur
he/she has gone to buy a
paper

**wǒ zài Lúndūn zhùle liùnián
le**
wor dzai lun-dun joo-lur
lyoh-nyen lur
I have been living in
London for six years

gūafēng le
gwah-fung lur
it's windy (now)

wǒ xiànzai bú è le
wor hsyahn-dzai boo ur lur
I'm not hungry any more

píngguǒ dōu huài le
ping-gwor doh hway lur
the apples have all gone
bad

wǒmen zǒu le
wor-mun dzoh lur
we are leaving (now)

The particle **ne** adds emphasis
to what is said:

tā hái méi líkāi ne
tah hai may lee-kai nur
he still hasn't gone

**zuò chángtú qìchē kě bù
fāngbiàn ne**
dzwor chahng-too chee-chur kur
boo fahng-byen nur
(but) it's so inconvenient to
go by bus

nǐ zuò shénme ne?
nee dzwor shun-mur nur
well, what are you going
to do?

On its own, often in
response to an earlier
question, **ne** can be used to
express the idea 'and what
about ...?':

**zhèishuāng xié tài guì –
nèishuāng ne?**
jay-shwahng hsyeh tai gway –
nay-shwahng nur
this pair of shoes is too
expensive – what about
that pair?

The particle **ba** indicates a
suggestion:

zǒu ba!
dzoh bah
let's go!

ní kǎolǜ yíxià ba
nee kow-lyew yee-syah bah
think about it, consider it

It can also mean 'I suggest'
or 'I suppose':

nǐ shì lǎo Zhāng ba?
nee shur low jahng bah
I suppose you must be
old Zhang?

nǐmen dōu hěn lèi ba?
nee-mun doh hun lay bah
you are all very tired,
aren't you?

QUESTIONS

There are a number of ways
of forming questions in
Chinese. One way is to add
the particle ma to the end of a
sentence to turn it into a
question without changing
the word order:

tā shì Rìběrén ma?
tah shur ree-bur-run mah
is he/she Japanese?

nǐ è ma?
nee ur mah
are you hungry?

nǐ mǎi zhèifèn bàozhǐ ma?
nee mai jay-fun bow-jur mah
are you buying this
newspaper?

nǐ qùguo Běijing ma?
nee choo-gwor bay-jing mah
have you ever been to
Beijing?

nǐ yǒu háizi ma?
nee yoh hai-dzur mah
do you have any children?

Alternatively, the verb is
repeated along with the
negative bù or méi:

tāmen shì búshì Yīngguórén?
tah-mun shur boo-shur
ying-gwor-run
are they British?

nǐ è búè?
nee ur bway
are you hungry?

jīntian rè bú rè?
jin-tyen rur boo rur]
is it hot today?

tā chīguo Zhōngcān méiyǒu?
tah chur-gwor joong-tsahn
may-yoh
has he/she ever eaten
Chinese food?

nǐ yǒu méiyou háizi?
nee yoh may-yoh hai-dzur
do you have any children?

Shéi (who?) and shénme
(what?) are the main
interrogative pronouns.
Interrogative pronouns are
placed in the same position in
the sentence as the noun in
the answer that is implied:

tā shì shéi?
tah shur shay
who is he?

tā shì wǒ péngyou
tah shur wor pung-yoh
he's my friend

shéi fù qián?
shay foo chyen
who is going to pay?

tā fùqián
tah foo-chyen
he is going to pay

nǐ mǎi shénme?
nee mai shun-mur
what are you going to buy?

wó mǎi yìjié diànchí
wor mai yee-jyeh dyen-chur
I'm going to buy a battery

The other common interrogatives are:

nǎr/nǎli?	[nar/nah-lee]	where?
duōshao?	[dwor-show]	how many?, how much?
nèi?	[nay]	which?
shéide?	[shay-dur]	whose?
zěnme?	[dzun-mur]	how?
wèishénme?	[way-shun-mur]	why?

shàngdiàn zài nǎr?
shahng-dyen dzai nar
where is the shop?

duōshao qián?
dwor-show chyen
how much is that?

něige fàndiàn zuì guì?
nay-gur fahn-dyen dzway gway
which hotel is most
  expensive?

ní xǐhuan něige?
nee hshee-hwahn nay-gur
which one would you like?

zhè shì shéide?
jur shur shay-dur
whose is this?

ní shì zěnme láide?
nee shur dzun-mur lai-dur
how did you get here?

tāmen wèishénme bú shàng
  huǒchē?
tah-mun way-shun-mur goo
  shahng hwor-chur
why aren't they getting on
  the train?

Háishi (or) is used in
questions posing alternatives:

ní xiáng mǎi zhèige háishi
  nèige?
nee hsyahng mai jay-gur
  hai-shur nay-gur
do you wish to buy this one
or that one?

PREPOSITIONS

Chinese prepositions are usually placed in front of the verb.
Some common prepositions are:

cóng	[tsoong]	from
dào	[dow]	to
duì	[dway]	towards, with regard to
gěi	[gay]	for
gēn	[gun]	with
lí	[lee]	from/to (in expressions of distance)
wèi	[way]	because of
yòng	[yoong]	with, by means of,
zài	[dzai]	in, at (see page 24)

wǒmen míngtian dào
Shànghǎi qù

wor-mun ming-tyen dow
shahng-hai chew

we're going to Shanghai
tomorrow

cóng sāndiǎnbàn dào sìdiǎn

tsoong sahn-dyen-bahn dow
sur-dyen

from three thirty to four
o'clock

Yīngguó lí Fǎguó bù yuǎn

ying-gwor lee fah-gwor boo
ywahn

Britain is not far from
France

wǒmen shì zuò chuán láide

wor-mun shur dzwor chwahn
lai-dur

we came by boat

wó géi ní mǎile yìxiē píngguǒ

wor gay nee mai-lur yee-hsyeh
ping-gwor

I've bought some apples
for you

qǐng gēn wǒ lái

ching gun wor lai

please come with me

tā wèi tā háizi hěn zháojí

tah way tah hai-dzur hun jow-jee

she was very worried about
her son

Zài (in, at) is also used as a
verb meaning 'to be in/at':

tā zài nǎr?

tah dzai nar

where is he/she?

tāmen zài Shànghǎi

tah-mun dzai shahng-hai

they are in Shanghai

zhuōzi zài wàibiānr

jwor-dzur zai wai-byenr

the table is outside

wǒ zài Shànghǎi méiyǒu qīnqi

wor dzai shahng-hai may-yoh
ching-chee

I don't have any relatives in
Shanghai

Place Word Suffixes

Various suffixes are added to
nouns to indicate location and
are nearly always used in
conjunction with the
preposition zài. The most
important are:

lǐ	[lee]	inside, in
shàng	[shahng]	above, on
wài	[wai]	outside
xià	[hsyah]	below
zhōng	[joong]	in the middle, between

nǐde bàozhǐ zài dàizili

nee-dur bow-jur dzai
dai-dzur-lee

your newspaper is in your
bag

chéngwài yǒu fēijīchǎng

chung-wai yoh fur-jee-chahng

there's an airport outside
the town

**nǐde zhàoxiàngjī zài
  chuángshàng**
nee-dur jow-hsyahng-jee dzai
  chwahng-shahng
your camera is on the bed

nǐde yīxiāng zài chuángxià
nee-dur yee-hsyahng dzai
  chwahng-hsyah
your suitcase is under the
  bed

zài shānzhōng
dzai shahn-joong
in the mountains

YES AND NO

Chinese has no standard
words for 'yes' and 'no', but
you can often use shì(de) (yes,
it is the case), duìle (yes,
that's right) and bú shì (no, it
is not the case).

The most common way of
saying 'yes' is to repeat the
verb of the question; to say
'no', repeat the verb of the
question together with bù or
méi as required:

ní yǒu kòng ma?
nee yoh koong mah
do you have any free time?

yǒu	**méi yǒu**
yoh	may yoh
yes	no

tā shì xuésheng ma?
tah shur hsyeh-shung mah
is he a student?

shì	**bú shì**
shur	boo shur
yes	no

**nǐ qùguo Chángchéng méi
  yǒu?**
nee chew-gwor chahng-chung
  may yoh
have you been to see the
  Great Wall?

| **qùguo** | **méi yǒu/
méi qùguo** |
|--------|-------------|
| chew-gwor | may yoh/
may chew-gwor |
| yes | no |

IMPERATIVES

To make an imperative in
Chinese, pronounce the verb
in an emphatic way:

> **zhànzhù!**
> jahn-joo
> stop!

> **gǔnchūqu!**
> gun-choo-chew
> get out!

Imperatives are rarely used
because they sound too
abrupt. The verb is more
likely to be preceded by qǐng
(please) or followed by ba
(see page 21) to make the
command sound more polite:

qǐng zuò ba
ching dzwor bah
please sit down

Negative imperatives are
formed using either **bié** or **bú
yào** (don't):

bié zǒule
byeh dzoh-lur
don't go

bú yào zài shuō
boo yow dzai shwor
say no more

DATES

Dates in Chinese are written
in the following order:

year + month + number

To write the year, place the
relevant numbers in front of
nián (year); this is followed by
the month and then the
number of the day plus **hào**:

九月一号
jiǔyuè yīhào
[jyoh-yew-eh yee-how]
the first of September

十二月二号
shíèryuè èrhào
[shur-er-yew-eh er-how]
the second of December

五月三十号
wǔyuè sānshíhào
[woo-yew-eh sahn-shur-how]
the thirtieth of May

一九九七年五月三十一
号
**yījiǔ jiǔqī nián wǔyuè
sānshíyīhào**
[yee-jyoh jyoh-chee nyen woo-yew-
eh sahn-shur-yee-how]
the thirty-first of May, 1997

一九四二年
yījiǔ sìèr nián
[yee-jyoh sur-er nyen]
1942

DAYS

Sunday xīngqītiān [hsing-chee-
tyen] 星期天

Monday xīngqīyī [hsing-chee-
yee] 星期一

Tuesday xīngqīèr [hsing-chee-
er] 星期二

Wednesday xīngqīsān [hsing-
chee-sahn] 星期三

Thursday xīngqīsì [hsing-chee-
sur] 星期四

Friday xīngqīwǔ [hsing-chee-
woo] 星期五

Saturday xīngqīliù [hsing-chee-
lyoh] 星期六

MONTHS

January yīyuè [yee-yew-eh]
一月

February èryuè [er-yew-eh]
二月

March sānyuè [sahn-yew-eh]
三月

April sìyuè [sur-yew-eh] 四月

May wǔyuè [woo-yew-eh] 五月

June liùyuè [lyoh-yew-eh] 六月

July qīyuè [chee-yew-eh] 七月

August bāyuè [bah-yew-eh]
八月

September jiǔyuè [jyoh-yew-eh]
九月

October shíyuè [shur-yew-eh]
十月

November shíyīyuè [shur-yee-
yew-eh] 十一月

December shíèryuè [shur-er-
yew-eh] 十二月

TIME

When telling the time, the
word **diǎn** is added to the
number to indicate the hours.
Zhōng (clock) is optional and
is placed at the end of most
time expressions. The word
fēn (minutes) is added to the
number of minutes.

what time is it? jídiǎn le? [jee-
dyen lur] 几点了?

o'clock diǎn zhōng [dyen joong]
点钟

one o'clock yīdiǎn (zhōng)
[yee-dyen] 一点(钟)

two o'clock liángdiǎn (zhōng)
[lyang-dyen]
两点(钟)

at one o'clock yīdiǎn (zhōng)
[yee-dyen] 一点(钟)

it's one o'clock yīdiǎn (zhōng)
一点(钟)

it's two o'clock liǎngdiǎn
(zhōng) [lyang-dyen]
两点(钟)

it's ten o'clock shídiǎn (zhōng)
[shur-dyen]
十点(钟)

five past one yīdiǎn wǔfēn
[yee-dyen woo-fun] 一点五分

ten past two liángdiǎn shífēn
[lyang-dyen shur-fun]
两点十分

quarter past one yīdiǎn yíkè
[yee-dyen yee-kur] 一点一刻

quarter past two liángdiǎn yíkè
[lyang-dyen yee-kur]
两点一刻

half past two liángdiǎn bàn
[bahn] 两点半

half past ten shídiǎn bàn
[shur-dyen] 十点半

twenty to one yīdiǎn chà
èrshífēn [yee-dyen chah
er-shur-fun] 一点差二十分

twenty to ten shídiǎn chà
èrshífēn [shur-dyen]
十点差二十分

quarter to one yīdiǎn chà yíkè
[yee-dyen chah yee-kur]
一点差一刻
quarter to two liángdiǎn chà
yíkè [lyang-dyen]
两点差一刻
a.m. (early morning up to about 9)
zǎoshang [dzow-shahng] 早上
(from about 9 til noon) shàngwǔ
上午
p.m. (afternoon) xiàwǔ
[hsyah-woo] 下午
(evening) wǎnshang
[wahn-shahng] 晚上
(night) yèli [yur-lee] 夜里
2 a.m. zǎoshang liángdiǎn
[dzow-shahng lyang-dyen]
早上两点
2 p.m.(14.00) xiàwǔ liángdiǎn
[hsyah-woo] 下午两点
6 a.m. zǎoshang liùdiǎn
[dzow-shahng lyoh-dyen]
早上六点
6 p.m. (18.00) wǎnshang
liùdiǎn [wahn-shahng]
晚上六点
10 a.m. shàngwǔ shídiǎn
[shahng-woo shur-dyen]
上午十点
10 p.m. wǎnshang shídiǎn
[wahn-shahng] 晚上十点
noon zhōngwǔ [joong-woo]
中午
midnight bànyè [bahn-yur]
半夜

hour xiǎoshí [hsyow-shur]
小时
minute fēn [fun] 分
two minutes liǎng fēnzhōng
[lyang fun-joong] 两分钟
second miǎo [myow] 秒
quarter of an hour yí kèzhōng
[kur-joong] 一刻钟
half an hour bàn xiǎoshí [bahn
hsyow-shur] 半小时
three quarters of an hour sān
kèzhōng [sahn kur-joong]
三刻钟
nearly three o'clock kuài sān
diǎn le [kwai sahn dyen lur]
快三点了

NUMBERS

See **MEASURE WORDS** on page
14.

0	líng	零
1	yī [yee]	一
2	èr, liǎng [lyang]	二
3	sān [sahn]	三
4	sì [sur]	四
5	wǔ	五
6	liù [lyoh]	六
7	qī [chee]	七
8	bā [bah]	八
9	jiǔ [jyoh]	九
10	shí [shur]	十
11	shíyī [shur-yee]	十一
12	shíèr [shur-er]	十二
13	shísān [shur-sahn]	十三
14	shísì [shur-sur]	十四

15	shíwǔ [shur-woo]	十五
16	shíliù [shur-lyoh]	十六
17	shíqī [shur-chee]	十七
18	shíbā [shur-bah]	十八
19	shíjiǔ [shur-jyoh]	十九
20	èrshí [er-shur]	二十
21	èrshíyī [er-shur-yee]	二十一
22	èrshíèr [er-shur-er]	二十二
30	sānshí [sahn-shur]	三十
31	sānshíyī [sahn-shur-yee]	三十一
32	sānshíèr [sahn-shur-er]	三十二
40	sìshí [sur-shur]	四十
50	wǔshí [woo-shur]	五十
60	liùshí [lyoh-shur]	六十
70	qīshí [chee-shur]	七十
80	bāshí [bah-shur]	八十
90	jiǔshí [jyoh-shur]	九十
100	yìbǎi	一百
101	yìbǎi líng yī	一百零一
102	yìbǎi líng èr	一百零二
110	yìbǎi yìshí [yee-shur]	一百一十
111	yìbǎi shíyī [shur-yee]	一百十一
200	èrbǎi	二百
201	èrbǎi líng yī	二百零一

202	èrbǎi líng èr	二百零二
210	èrbǎi yìshí [yee-shur]	二百一十
300	sānbǎi [sahn-bai]	三百
1,000	yìqiān [yee-chyen]	一千
2,000	liǎngqiān [lyang-chyen]	两千
3,000	sān qiān [sahn chyen]	三千
4,000	sìqiān [sur-chyen]	四千
5,000	wǔqiān [woo-chyen]	五千
10,000	yíwàn [yee-wahn]	一万
50,000	wǔwàn	五万
100,000	shíwàn [shur-wahn]	十万
1,000,000	bǎiwàn	百万
10,000,000	qiānwàn [chyen-wahn]	千万
100,000,000	yí yì	一亿

When counting 'one, two, three' and so on, yī (one) is written and said with the first tone. In other situations, the fourth tone is used:

yī, èr, sān
yee er sahn
one, two, three

yìtiáo yú
yee-tyow yoo
a fish

yìkē shū
yee-kur shoo
a tree

The exception to the above is if yì is followed by a fourth tone, in which case it changes to second tone:

yíjiàn dōngxi
yee-jyen doong-hshee
an object

In number sequences yāo is used for 'one' instead of yī, as in the two examples below:

sān-èr-wǔ-yāo-bā
sahn-er-woo-yow-bah
32518 (phone number)

yāoyāojiǔ
yow-yow-jyoh
number one hundred and nineteen (room number)

There are two words for two in Chinese: èr and liǎng. Ér is used in counting or for phone, room or bus numbers:

yī, èr, sān ...
yee er sahn
one, two three ...

èr hào
er how
number two (room, house etc)

èr lù chē
er loo chur
number two bus

Ér also occurs in compound numbers:

sānshí'èr
sahn-shur-er
thirty-two

Liǎng is similar to 'a couple' in English, is used with measure words (see page 14):

liǎngwèi péngyou
lyang-way pung-yoh
two friends

liǎngsuǒ fángzi
lyang-swor fahng-dzur
two buildings

The numbers 11-19 are made up of shí (ten) followed by the numbers yī (one) to jiǔ (nine):

shíyī	eleven
shí'èr	twelve
shísān	thirteen

Multiples of ten are formed by adding the numbers two to nine to shí (ten):

èrshí	twenty
sānshí	thirty
sìshí	forty

The numbers 21 to 29, 31-39 etc are formed by adding one to nine to the above numbers èrshí, sānshí and so on:

èrshíyī	twenty-one
sìshíqī	forty-seven
bāshíwǔ	eighty-five

A similar pattern is used with bǎi (hundred), qiān (thousand) and wàn (ten thousand):

sibǎi
sur-bai
four hundred

sibǎi jiǔshí
sur-bai jyoh-shur
four hundred and ninety

bābǎi sìshí liù
bah-bai sur-shur lyoh
eight hundred and forty-six

jiǔqiān sìbǎi qīshí
jyoh-chyen sur-bai chee-shur
nine thousand four hundred
and seventy

qīwàn sìqiān bābǎi
chee-wahn sur-chyen bah-bai
seventy-four thousand eight
hundred

For numbers in the thousands
and millions, shí, bǎi, qiān and
wàn are added to wàn:

shíwàn
shur-wahn
a hundred thousand

bǎiwàn
bai-wahn
a million

qiānwàn
chyah-wahn
ten million

yí yì
hundred million

Líng (zero) is used when there
are zeros in the middle of a
number sequence:

yìbǎi líng sān
yee-bai ling sahn
one hundred and three

yìqiān líng sān
yee-chyen ling sahn
one thousand and three

yìqiān líng bāshí
yee-chyen ling bah-shur
one thousand and eighty

Ordinals

1st	dì yī	第一
2nd	dì èr	第二
3rd	dì sān [sahn]	第三
4th	dì sì [sur]	第四
5th	dì wǔ	第五
6th	dì liù [lyoh]	第六
7th	dì qī [chee]	第七
8th	dì bā	第八
9th	dì jiǔ [jyoh]	第九
10th	dì shí [shur]	第十

BASIC PHRASES

yes	**goodbye/see you!**
shìde	zàijiàn
shur-dur	dzai-jyen
是的	再见
no	**see you later**
bù	huítóujiàn
boo	hway-toh-jyen
不	回头见
OK	
hǎo	
how	
好	
	please
	qǐng
	ching
	请
hello	**yes, please**
ní hǎo	hǎo, xièxie
nee how	how hsyeh-hsyeh
你好	好谢谢
good morning	**could you please ...?**
ní zǎo	qǐng nín ..., hǎo ma?
nee dzow	ching nin ... how mah
你早	请您..., 好吗？
good evening	**thank you**
ní hǎo	xièxie
ni how	hsyeh-hsyeh
你好	谢谢
good night	**thank you very much**
wǎn'ān	duōxiè
wahn-ahn	dwor-hsyeh
晚安	多谢

no, thank you
xièxie, wǒ bú yào
hsyeh-hsyeh wor boo yow
谢谢我不要

don't mention it
búyòng kèqi
boo-yoong kur-chee
不用客气

how do you do?
ní hǎo
ni how
你好?

how are you?
ní hǎo ma?
mah
你好吗?

fine, thanks
hén hǎo, xièxie
hun how hsyeh-hsyeh
很好谢谢

nice to meet you
jiàndào nǐ hěn gāoxìng
jyen-dow nee hun gow-hsing
见到你很高兴

excuse me (to get past)
máfan nín
mah-fahn nin
麻烦您

(to get attention)
máfan nín, qǐng wèn ...
ching wun
麻烦您请问

excuse me/sorry
duìbuqǐ
dway-boo-chee
对不起

sorry?/pardon me?
nǐ shuō shenme?
shwor shun-mur
你说什么?

I see/I understand
wǒ míngbai le
wor ming-bai lur
我明白了

I don't understand
wǒ bù dǒng
我不懂

do you speak English?
nín huì jiǎng Yīngyǔ ma?
hway jyang ying-yew mah
您回讲英语吗?

I don't speak Chinese
wǒ búhuì jiǎng Hànyǔ
wor boo-hway hahn-yew
我不回讲汉语

could you speak more slowly?
qǐng shuō màn yìdiǎnr
ching shwor mahn yee-dyenr
请说慢一点儿

could you repeat that?
qíng nǐ zài shuō yíbiàn, hǎo ma?
ching nee dzai shwor yee-byen how
  mah
请你再说一边好吗?

CONVERSION TABLES

1 centimetre = 0.39 inches

1 inch = 2.54 cm

1 metre = 39.37 inches = 1.09 yards

1 foot = 30.48 cm

1 yard = 0.91 m

1 kilometre = 0.62 miles = 5/8 mile

1 mile = 1.61 km

km	1	2	3	4	5	10	20	30	40	50	100
miles	0.6	1.2	1.9	2.5	3.1	6.2	12.4	18.6	24.8	31.0	62.1

miles	1	2	3	4	5	10	20	30	40	50	100
km	1.6	3.2	4.8	6.4	8.0	16.1	32.2	48.3	64.4	80.5	161

1 gram = 0.035 ounces

1 kilo = 1000 g = 2.2 pounds

g	100	250	500
oz	3.5	8.75	17.5

1 oz = 28.35 g

1 lb = 0.45 kg

kg	0.5	1	2	3	4	5	6	7	8	9	10
lb	1.1	2.2	4.4	6.6	8.8	11.0	13.2	15.4	17.6	19.8	22.0

kg	20	30	40	50	60	70	80	90	100
lb	44	66	88	110	132	154	176	198	220

lb	0.5	1	2	3	4	5	6	7	8	9	10	20
kg	0.2	0.5	0.9	1.4	1.8	2.3	2.7	3.2	3.6	4.1	4.5	9.0

1 litre = 1.75 UK pints / 2.13 US pints

1 UK pint = 0.57 l

1 UK gallon = 4.55 l

1 US pint = 0.47 l

1 US gallon = 3.79 l

centigrade / Celsius

$C = (F - 32) \times 5/9$

C	-5	0	5	10	15	18	20	25	30	36.8	38
F	23	32	41	50	59	65	68	77	86	98.4	100.4

Fahrenheit

$F = (C \times 9/5) + 32$

F	23	32	40	50	60	65	70	80	85	98.4	101
C	-5	0	4	10	16	18	21	27	29	36.8	38.3

English-Chinese

A

a, an* yíge [yee-gur]
一个

about: about 20 èr shí zuǒyòu
[dzwor-yoh]
二十左右

it's about 5 o'clock wǔdiǎn
(zhōng) zuǒyòu
五点钟左右

a film about China guānyú
Zhōngguó de diànyǐng
[gwahn-yew – dur dyen-ying]
关于中国的电影

above* (zài) ... shàng
[(dzai) ... shahng]
在...上

abroad guówài [gwor-wai]
国外

absorbent cotton yàomián
[yow-myen]
药棉

accept jiēshòu [jyeh-shoh]
接受

accident shìgù [shur-goo]
事故

there's been an accident
chūle ge shìgù [choo-lur gur]
出了个事故

accommodation
see room and hotel

accurate zhǔnquè [jun-chew-eh]
准确

ache téng [tung]
疼

my back aches wǒ bèijǐ téng
[wor bay-jee]
我背脊疼

acrobatics zájì [dzah-jee]
杂技

across: across the road zài
mǎlù duìmiànr [dzai mah-loo
dway-myenr]
在马路对面儿

acupuncture zhēnjiǔ [jun-jyoh]
针灸

adapter duōyòng chātóu
[dwor-yoong chah-toh]
多用插头

address dìzhǐ [dee-jur]
地址

what's your address? nín zhù
nǎr? [joo]
您住哪儿?

Addresses are written in the reverse order to the way they are written in the West, beginning with the country, followed by the province, town, street number and ending with the addressee's name. For example:

People's Republic of China
Shanxi Province
Taiyuan
Donglu (East Road) 15
Wang Shixing

People's Republic of China is sometimes shortened to PRC.

address book tōngxùnlù
[toong-hsyewn-loo]
通讯录

**admission charge: how much is
the admission charge?**
rùchǎng fèi shì duōshao
qián? [roo-chahng fay shur
dwor-show chyen]
入场费是多少？

Virtually all tourist sites have
some kind of admission charge.
This will often come to no more
than a few yuan, but discrimi-
natory pricing policies usually
mean that foreigners are
charged more than locals. In
some extreme cases, such as visiting the Forbidden City in
Beijing or the Terracotta Warri-
ors in Xi'an, foreigners may find
themselves paying many times
more than the locals. At the Forbidden City, however, the price
for foreigners includes a re-
corded commentary in English.
If you have a student card you
can occasionally get in for the
Chinese price.

adult dàrén [dah-run]
大人

advance: in advance tíqián
[tee-chyen]
提前

aeroplane fēijī [fay-jee]
飞机

after yǐhòu [yee-hoh]
以后

after you nǐ xiān qù ba [nee
hsyen chew bah]
你先去吧

after lunch chīle wǔfàn yǐhòu
[chur-lur]
吃了午饭以后

afternoon xiàwǔ [hsyah-
woo]
下午

in the afternoon xiàwǔ
下午

this afternoon jīntiān xiàwǔ
[jin-tyen]
今天下午

aftershave xūhòushuǐ
[hsyew-hoh-shway]
须后水

afterwards yǐhòu [yee-hoh]
以后

again zài [dzai]
再

age niánjì [nyen-jee]
年纪

ago: a week ago yíge xīngqī
yǐqián [yee-gur hsing-chee
yee-chyen]
一个星期以前

an hour ago yíge xiǎoshí
yǐqián [hsyow-shur]
一个小时以前

agree: I agree wǒ tóngyì [wor

toong-yee]
我同意

AIDS àizìbìng [ai-dzur-bing]
爱滋病

air kōngqì [koong-chee]
空气

by air zuò fēijī [dzwor fay-jee]
坐飞机

air-conditioning kōngtiáo
[koong-tyow]
空调

airmail: by airmail
hángkōng(xìn)
[hahng-koong(-hsin)]
航空

airmail envelope hángkōng
xìnfēng [hsin-fung]
航空信封

airplane fēijī [fay-jee]
飞机

airport fēijīchǎng [–chahng]
飞机场

to the airport, please qǐng dài
wǒ dào fēijīchǎng ba [ching
dai wor dow – bah]
请带我到飞机场吧

airport bus jīchǎng bānchē
[jee-chahng bahn-chur]
机场班车

alarm clock nàozhōng
[now-joong]
闹钟

alcohol (drink) jiǔ [jyoh]
酒

all: all of it quánbù

[chew-ahn-boo]
全部

that's all, thanks gòule,
xièxie [goh-lur hsyeh-hsyeh]
够了谢谢

allergic: I'm allergic to ... wǒ
duì ... guòmǐn [wor dway ...
gwor-min]
我对...过敏

allowed: is it allowed? zhè
yúnxǔ ma? [jur
yun-hsyew mah]
这允许吗？

all right hǎo [how]
好

I'm all right wǒ méi shìr [wor
may shur]
我没事儿

are you all right? nǐ méi shìr
ma? [nee may-shur mah]
你没事儿吗？

(greeting) ní hǎo ma? [nee
how]
你好吗？

almost chàbuduō
[chah-boo-dwor]
差不多

alone yíge rén [yee-gur run]
一个人

already yǐjing
已经

also yě [yur]
也

although suīrán [sway-rahn]
虽然

altogether yígòng [yee-goong]
一共

always zǒng [dzoong]
总

am*: I am shì [shur]
是

a.m.: at seven a.m. shàngwǔ qī
diǎn [chee dyen]
上午七点

amazing (surprising) méi
xiǎngdào [may hsyang-dow]
没想到
(very good) liǎobùqǐ
[lyow-boo-chee]
了不起

ambulance jiùhùchē
[jyoh-hoo-chur]
救护车

call an ambulance! (kuài)
jiào jiùhùchē! [(kwai) jyow]
(快)叫救护车

The number for the ambulance
service is 120.

America Měiguó [may-gwor]
美国

American (adj) Měiguó
美国

I'm American wǒ shì Měiguó
rén [wor shur – run]
我是美国人

among zài ... zhī zhōng
[dzai ... jur joong]
在...之中

amp: a 13-amp fuse shísān
ānpéi de bǎoxiǎnsī [shur-
sahn ahn-pay dur bow-hsyen-
sur]
十三安培的保险丝

and hé [hur]
和

angry shēngqì [shung-chee]
生气

animal dòngwù [doong-woo]
动物

ankle jiǎobózi [jyow-bor-dzur]
脚脖子

annoying: how annoying! zhēn
tǎoyàn! [jun tow-yahn]
真讨厌

another (different) lìng yíge
[yee-gur]
另一个
(one more) yòu yíge [yoh]
又一个

can we have another room?
wó xiǎng huàn lìngwài yíge
fángjiān [wor hsyang hwahn
ling-wai]
我想换另外一个房间

another beer, please qǐng zài
lái yì bēi píjiǔ [ching dzai lai
yee]
请再来一杯啤酒

antibiotics kàngjūnsù
[kahng-jyewn-soo]
抗菌素

antique: is it a genuine antique?
shì zhēn gǔdǒng ma? [shur

jurn goo-doong mah]

是真古董吗?

antique shop wénwù
shāngdiàn [wun-woo
shahng-dyen]

文物商店

antiseptic fángfǔjì
[fahng-foo-jee]

防腐剂

any: do you have any ...? ní
yǒu ... ma? [nee yoh ... mah]

你有...吗?

sorry, I don't have any
duìbuqǐ, wǒ méiyǒu
[dway-boo-chur wor may-yoh]

对不起我没有

anybody shéi [shay]

谁

does anybody speak English?
shéi huì shuō Yīngyǔ? [hway
shwor ying-yoo]

谁会说英语?

there wasn't anybody there
zàinàr shénme rén dōu
méiyou [zai-nar shun-mur run
doh may-yoh]

在那儿什么人都没有

anything shénme [shun-mur]

什么

•••••• DIALOGUES ••••••

anything else? hái yào shénme?
[hai yow]

nothing else, thanks bú yào,
xièxie [hsyeh-hsyeh]

would you like anything to drink?
nǐ yào hé diǎnr shénme? [hur
dyenr]

I don't want anything, thanks wǒ
shénme dōu bú yào, xièxie [wor –
doh]

apart from chúle ... yǐwài
[choo-lur]

除了...以外

apartment dānyuán
[dahn-yew-ahn]

单元

aperitif kāiwèijiǔ [kai-way-jyoh]

开胃酒

appendicitis lánwěiyán
[lahn-way-yen]

阑尾炎

appetizer lěngpánr [lung-pahnr]

冷盘儿

apple píngguǒ [ping-gwor]

苹果

appointment yuēhuì
[yew-eh-hway]

约会

•••••• DIALOGUE ••••••

good morning, how can I help you?
nín zǎo, wǒ néng bāng shénme
máng ma? [dzow wor nung bahng
shun-mur mahng mah]

I'd like to make an appointment
wó xiǎng dìng ge yùehuì [hsyang
ding gur]

what time would you like? nín
xiǎng yuē shénme [yew-eh]

three o'clock sān diǎn (zhōng) [dyen (joong)]

I'm afraid that's not possible, is four o'clock all right? duìbùqǐ sān diǎn bù xíng, sì diǎn (zhōng) xíng ma? [dway-boo-chee – hsing – mah]

yes, that will be fine xíng, kěyǐ [kur-yee]

the name was? nín guì xìng ma? [gway]

apricot xìngzi [hsing-dzur]
杏子

April sìyuè [sur-yew-eh]
四月

are*: we are wǒmen shì [wor-mun shur]
我们是

you are (sing) nǐ shì
你是

(pl) nǐmen shì [nee-mun]
你们是

they are tāmen shì [tah-mun]
他们是

area (measurement) miànjì [myen-jee]
面积

(region) dìqū [dee-chew]
地区

arm gēbo [gur-bor]
胳膊

arrange: will you arrange it for us? nǐ néng tì wǒmen ānpái yí xià ma? [nung tee wor-mun ahn-pai yee hsyah mah]
你能替我们安排一下吗？

arrive dào [dow]
到

when do we arrive? wǒmen shénme shíhou dàodá? [wor-mun shun-mur shur-hoh dow-dah]
我们什么时候到达？

has my fax arrived yet? wó géi nǐ fā de chuánzhēn dàole ma? [wor gay nee fah dur chwahn-jun dow-lur mah]
我给你发的传真到了吗？

we arrived today wǒmen jīntiān gāng dàole [jin-tyen gahng]
我们今天刚到了

art yìshù [yee-shoo]
艺术

art gallery měishùguǎn [may-shoo-gwahn]
美术馆

as: as big as... gēn ... yíyàng dà [gun ... yee-yang dah]
跟...一样大

as soon as possible jǐnkuài [jin-kwai]
尽快

ashtray yānhuī gāng [yahn-hway gahng]
烟恢缸

ask (someone to do something) qǐng

[ching]
请
(a question) **wèn** [wun]
问
could you ask him to ...? nǐ
néng bù néng qǐng tā ...?
[nung – tah]
你能不能请他...?
asleep: she's asleep tā
shuìzháole [tah shway-jow-
lur]
他睡着了
aspirin āsīpǐlín [ah-sur-pee-lin]
阿斯匹林
asthma qìchuǎn [chee-chwahn]
气喘
at*: at my hotel zài wó zhù de
fàndiàn [dzai wor joo dur]
在我住的饭店
at the railway station zài
huǒchē zhàn
在火车站
at six o'clock liùdiǎn zhōng
[lyoh-dyen joong]
六点中
at Li Zhen's zài Lǐ Zhēn jiā
[jyah]
在李真家
ATM zìdòng qǔkuǎnjī
[dzur-doong chew-kwahn-jee]
自动取款机
attendant (on train)
chéngwùyuán
[chung-woo-yew-ahn]
乘务员

August bāyuè [bah-yew-eh]
八月
aunt (father's sister, unmarried)
gūgu
姑姑
(father's sister, married) gūmǔ
姑母
(mother's sister, unmarried) yímǔ
姨母
(mother's sister, married) yímā
[yee-mah]
姨妈
Australia Àodàlìyà
[or-dah-lee-yah]
澳大利亚
Australian (adj) Àodàlìyà
澳大利亚
I'm Australian wǒ shi
Àodàlìyà rén [wor shur – run]
我是澳大利亚人
automatic (adj) zìdòng
[dzur-doong]
自动
autumn qiūtian [chyoh-tyen]
秋天
in the autumn qiūtian
秋天
average (ordinary) yíbàn
[yee-bahn]
一半
on average píngjūn
[ping-jyewn]
平均
awake: is he awake? tā
xǐngle ma? [tah hsing-lur

mah]

他醒了吗？

away: is it far away? yuǎn ma?
[yew-ahn]

远吗？

awful zāogāole [dzow-gow-lur]

糟糕了

B

baby yīng'ér [ying-er]

婴儿

baby food yīng'ér shíwù
[shur-woo]

婴儿食物

baby's bottle nǎipíng

奶瓶

**baby-sitter línshí kān xiǎoháir
de** [lin-shur kahn hsyow-hair
dur]

临时看小孩儿的

back hòu [hoh]

后

(of body) **bèi** [bay]

背

at the back zài hòumian [dzai
hoh-myen]

在后面

**can I have my money back?
qǐng ba qián huán gěi wǒ ba**
[ching bah chyen hwahn gay wor
bah]

请把钱还给我吧

to come back huílai [hway–]

回来

to go back huíqu [–chew]

回去

backache bèitòng [bay-toong]

背痛

bad huài [hwai]

怀

**a bad headache tóu téng
de lìhai** [toh tung dur lur-
hai]

头疼得利害

bag dàizi [dai-dzur]

带子

(handbag) **shǒutíbāo**
[shoh-tee-bow]

手提包

(suitcase) **shǒutíxiāng**
[shoh-tee-hsyang]

手提箱

baggage xíngli [hsing-lee]

行李

baggage check (US) **xíngli
jìcúnchù** [jee-tsun-choo]

行李寄存处

baggage claim xíngli tíqǔchù
[tee-chew-choo]

行李提取处

bakery miànbāodiàn
[myen-bow-dyen]

面包店

balcony yángtái

阳台

**a room with a balcony dài
yángtái de fángjiān** [dur
fahng-jyen]

带阳台的房间

ball qiú [chyoh]
球

ballet bāléiwǔ [bah-lay-woo]
芭蕾舞

ballpoint pen yuánzhūbǐ
[yew-ahn-joo-bee]
圆珠笔

bamboo zhúzi [joo-dzur]
竹子

bamboo shoots zhúsǔn
[joo-sun]
竹笋

banana xiāngjiāo [hsyang-jyow]
香蕉

band (musical) yuèduì
[yew-eh-dway]
乐队

bandage bēngdài [bung-dai]
绷带

Bandaid® xiàngpí gāo
[hsyang-pee gow]
橡皮膏

bank (money) yínháng
[yin-hahng]
银行

Banks in major Chinese cities
are sometimes open seven days
a week, though foreign exchange
is usually only available from
Monday to Friday, approximately from 9 a.m. to noon and
from 2 to 5 p.m. All banks are
closed for the first three days of
→

the Chinese New Year (Spring
Festival), with reduced hours
for the following eleven days.

bank account zhànghù
[jahng-hoo]
帐户

banquet yànhuì [yen-hway]
宴会

bar jiǔbājiān [jyoh-bah-jyen]
酒吧间
a bar of chocolate yí kuàir
qiǎokèlì [yee kwair
chyow-kur-lee]
一块儿巧克力

Increasingly, bars are found in
China's major cities, both within
large hotels and as individual
enterprises. There are even a
few karaoke bars. Substantial
mark-ups are to be expected
in such places, especially on
foreign spirits.

barber's lǐfàdiàn [lee-fah-dyen]
理发店

bargaining
Bargaining is common practice
in markets, but isn't generally
pursued with the same enthusi-
asm as in other Asian countries.
Most taxi cars have meters but
→

be prepared to negotiate a price before hiring a motorized or cycle rickshaw or a motorbike taxi.

•••••• DIALOGUE ••••••

how much is this? zhèi ge duōshao qián? [jay gur dwor-show chyen]

30 yuan sān shí kuài qián [kwai chyen]

that's too expensive, how about 20? tài guì le, èr shí kuài, zénme yàng? [gway lur – dzun-mur]

I'll let you have it for 25 èr shí wǔ kuài ba [bah]

can you reduce it a bit more? zài jiǎn yí diǎnr ba [dzai jyen yee dyenr]

OK, it's a deal hǎo ba [how]

basket kuāng [kwahng]
筐

bath xízǎo [hshee-dzow]
洗澡

can I have a bath? wǒ néng xǐ ge zǎo ma? [wor nung hshee gur dzow mah]
我能洗个澡吗？

bathroom yùshì [yew-shur]
浴室

with a private bathroom dài xízǎojiān de fángjiān [dai hshee-dzow-jyen dur fahng-jyen]
带洗澡间的房间

bath towel yùjīn [yew-jin]
浴锦

bathtub zǎopén [dzow-pun]
澡盆

battery diànchí [dyen-chur]
电池

bay hǎiwān [hai-wahn]
海湾

be* shì [shur]
是

beach hǎitān [hai-tahn]
海滩

on the beach zài hǎitānshang [dzai – shahng]
在海滩上

bean curd dòufu [doh-foo]
豆腐

beans dòu [doh]
豆

French beans sìjìdòu [sur-jee-doh]
四季豆

broad beans cándòu [tsahn-doh]
蚕豆

string beans jiāngdòu [jyang-doh]
豇豆

soya beans huángdòu [hwahng-doh]
黄豆

bean sprouts dòu yár
豆芽儿

beard húzi [hoo-dzur]
胡子

beautiful (object) **měilì** [may-lee]
美丽
(woman) **piàoliang**
[pyow-lyang]
漂亮
(view, city, building) **měi**
美
(day, weather) **hǎo** [how]
好
because yīnwèi [yin-way]
因为
because of … yóuyú …
[yoh-yew]
由于
bed chuáng [chwahng]
床
**I'm going to bed now wǒ yào
shuì le** [wor yow shway lur]
我要睡了
bed and breakfast
see **hotel**
bedroom wòshì [wor-shur]
卧室
beef niúròu [nyoh-roh]
牛肉
beer píjiǔ [pee-jyoh]
啤酒
**two beers, please qǐng lái
liǎng bēi píjiǔ** [ching]
请来两杯啤酒

The popularity of beer in China
rivals that of tea, and for men it
is the preferred mealtime beverage. (Drinking alcohol in
→

public is considered improper
for Chinese women, though not
for foreigners.) Chinese beer is
produced and drunk throughout
the country and closely resem-
bles some European lagers
though it is usually served at
room temperature. The excellent **Tsingtao** label, established
in the eastern city of Qingdao
during the time of German juris-
diction, is widely available and
just about every province produces at least one brand of 4%
pilsner. Sold in litre bottles, it's
always drinkable, often pretty
good, and is actually cheaper
than bottled water. A number
of foreign brands, notably
San Miguel and Carlsberg, are
available in bigger cities.

before: before … … yīqián
[yee-chyen]
… 以前
begin kāishǐ [kai-shur]
开始
**when does it begin? shénme
shíhou kāishǐ?** [shun-mur
shur-hoh]
什么时候开始？
beginner chūxuézhě
[choo-yew-eh-jur]
初学者
behind zài … hòumian

[dzai ... hoh-myen]

在...后面

behind me zài wǒ hòumian

[wor]

在我候面

believe xiāngxìn [hsyang-hsin]

相信

below* zài ... xiàmian [dzai ... hsyah-myen]

在...下面

(less than) zài ... yǐxià [yee-hsyah]

在...以下

belt yāodài [yow-dai]

腰带

bend (in road) lùwánr [loo-wahnr]

路弯儿

berth (on train) wòpù [wor-poo]

卧铺

beside: beside the ... zài ... pángbiān [dzai ... pahng-byen]

在...旁边

best zuìhǎo [dzway-how]

最好

better: even better gèng hǎo [gung how]

更好

a bit better hǎo yì diǎnr [dyenr]

好一点儿

are you feeling better? háo diǎnr le ma? [lur mah]

好点儿了吗?

between zài ... zhī jiān

[dzai ... jur-jyen]

在...之间

bicycle zìxíngchē

[dzur-hsing-chur]

自行车

China has the highest number of bicycles of any country in the world, with about a quarter of the population owning one. Private car ownership is beyond all but the most affluent. Few cities have any hills, and all have **zǔchēbù** (bike rental shops or booths), especially near the train stations, where you can rent a set of wheels for a couple of yuan a day. To do this, you will need to leave a deposit and show some form of ID. You're fully responsible for anything that happens to the bike while it's in your care, so check brakes, tyre pressure and gears before renting. Most rental bikes are very basic old models. Cheap **xiūchēbù** (repair shops) are all over the place should you need a tyre patched or a chain fixed. Note that there is little in the way of private insurance in China, so if the bike sustains any serious damage it's up to the parties involved to sort out responsibility and payment on →

the spot. To avoid theft always use a bicycle chain or lock – they're available everywhere – and in cities, leave your vehicles in one of the ubiquitous designated parking areas, where it will be guarded by an attendant for a few mao.

An alternative to renting is to buy a bike, a sensible option if you're going to be based anywhere for a while. All department stores stock them and demand is so high that there should be little problem reselling the bike when you leave.

As in virtually the whole of Asia, restaurant bills are never shared in China and people go to great lengths to claim the honour of paying the whole bill by themselves. Normally that honour falls to the person perceived as the most senior, and if you are a foreigner dining with Chinese you should make some effort to stake your claim, though it is most likely that someone else will grab the bill before you do. Attempting to pay your 'share' of the bill will cause embarrassment.

big dà [dah]

大

  too big tài dà le [lur]

太大了

  it's not big enough búgòu dà [boo-goh]

不够大

bill zhàngdānr [jahng-dahnr]

帐单儿

  (US: money) chāopiào [chow-pyow]

钞票

  could I have the bill, please? qǐng bāng wǒ jiézhàng, hǎo ma? [ching bahng wor jyeh-jahng how mah]

请帮我结帐好吗？

bin lājī xiāng [lah-jee hsyang]

垃圾箱

bird niǎo [nyow]

鸟

birthday shēngrì [shung-rur]

生日

  happy birthday! zhù nǐ shēngrì kuàilè! [joo – kwai-lur]

祝你生日快乐

biscuit bǐnggān [bing-gahn]

饼干

bit: a little bit yìdiǎnr [yee-dyenr]

一点儿

  a big bit yídàkuàir [yee-dah-kwair]

一大块儿

a bit expensive yì diǎnr guì
一点儿贵

bite (by insect) yǎo [yow]
咬

bitten by a dog ràng gǒu gěi yǎoshāng le [rahng goh gay yow-shahng]
让狗给咬伤了

bitter (taste etc) kǔ
苦

black hēi [hay]
黑

blanket tǎnzi [tahn-dzur]
毯子

blind xiā [hsyah]
瞎

blocked dǔzhùle [doo-joo-lur]
堵住了

blond (adj) jīnhuángsè [jin-hwahng-sur]
金黄色

blood xiě [hsyeh]
血

high blood pressure gāo xuèyā [gow hsyew-eh-yah]
高血压

blouse nǚchènshān [nyew-chun-shahn]
女衬衫

blow-dry: I'd like a cut and blow-dry wó xiǎng lǐfà hé chuīfēng [wor hsyang lee-fah hur chway-fung]
我想理发和吹风

blue lánsè [lahn-sur]
蓝色

blue eyes lán yǎnjing [lahn yahn-jing]
蓝眼睛

boarding pass dēngjì zhèng [dung-jee zhung]
登记证

boat chuán [chwahn]
船

(for passengers) kèchuán [kur-chwahn]
客船

body shēntǐ [shun-tee]
身体

boiled egg zhǔ jīdàn [joo jee-dahn]
煮鸡蛋

boiled rice mǐfàn [mee-fahn]
米饭

boiled water kāishuǐ [kai-shway]
开水

bone gǔ [goo]
骨

book (noun) shū
书

(verb) dìng
定

can I book a seat? wǒ néng dìng ge zuòwei ma? [wor nung – gur dzwor-way mah]
我能定个座位吗？

• • • • • DIALOGUE • • • • •

I'd like to book a table for two/three wǒ xiǎng dìng liǎng/sān ge rén yi zhùo de wèizi [wor hsyang – gur run yee jwor dur way-dszur]

what time would you like it booked for? nín yào jǐdiǎn zhōng? [yow jee-dyen joong]

half past seven qī diǎn bàn

that's fine xíng [hsing]

and your name? nín guì xìng? [gway]

bookshop, bookstore shūdiàn [shoo-dyen]
书店

boot (footwear) xuēzi [hsyew-eh-dzur]
靴子
(of car) xínglixiāng [hsing-lee-hsyang]
行李箱

border (of country) biānjiè [byen-jyeh]
边界
border region biānjìng
边境

bored: I'm bored fán sǐ le [fahn sur-lur]
烦死了

boring méi jìnr [may]
没劲儿

born: I was born in Manchester wǒ shì zài Mànchéng shēng de [wor shur dzai – shung dur]
我是在曼城生的

I was born in 1960 wǒ shì yí jiǔ liù líng nián shēng de
我是一九六零年生的

borrow jiè [jyeh]
借
may I borrow ...? wǒ kéyi jiè yíxia … ma? [wor kur-yee jyeh yee-hsyah ... mah]
我可以借一下...吗?

both liǎngge dōu [lyang-gur doh]
两个都

bother: sorry to bother you duìbuqǐ dájiǎo nín le [dway-boo-chee dah-jyow nin lur]
对不起打搅您了

bottle píngzi [ping-dzur]
瓶子
a bottle of beer yì píng píjiǔ
一瓶啤酒

bottle-opener kāi píng qì [chee]
开瓶器

bottom dǐr [deer]
底儿
(of person) pìgu
屁股
at the bottom of the road lù de jìntóu [loo dur jin-toh]
路的尽头

box hézi [hur-dzur]
盒子
a box of chocolates yí hé qiǎokèlì [hur chyow-kur-lee]
一盒巧克力

box office shòupiào chù
[shoh-pyow]
售票处

boy nánhái [nahn-hai]
男孩

boyfriend nán péngyou [nahn pung-yoh]
男朋友

bra xiōngzhào [hsyoong-jow]
胸罩

bracelet shǒuzhuó [shoh-jwor]
手镯

brandy báilándì [bai-lahn-dee]
白兰地

bread (baked) miànbāo
[myen-bow]
面包

(steamed) mántou [mahn-toh]
馒头

white bread bái miànbāo
白面包

brown bread hēi miànbāo
[hay]
黑面包

wholemeal bread
quánmài miànbāo
[chew-ahn-mai]
全麦面包

Western-style bread is available in bigger cities but it is usually very light and lacking in flavour. Chinese eat **mántou**, a heavy steamed bread, with their →

meals. In Xinjiang, wonderful unleavened bread can be found in street markets.

break (verb) dǎpò [dah-por]
打破

I've broken the ... wó dǎpòle ... [wor dah-por-lur]
我打破了...

I think I've broken my ... wǒde ... kěnéng duànle [wor-dur ... kur-nung dwahn-lur]
我的 ... 可能断了

breakdown gùzhàng [goo-jahng]
故障

breakfast zǎofàn [dzow-fahn]
早饭

break-in: I've had a break-in (in room) wǒde fángjiān ràng rén gěi qiàole mén le
[wor-dur fahng-jyen rahng run gay chyow-lur mun lur]
我的房间让人给撬了门了

breast xiōng [hsyoong]
胸

breeze wēifēng [way-fung]
微风

bridge (over river) qiáo [chyow]
桥

brief duǎn [dwahn]
短

briefcase gōngwénbāo
[goong-wun-bow]
公文包

bright (light etc) **míngliàng**
[ming-lyang]
明亮

brilliant (idea, person) **gāomíng**
[gow-ming]
高明

bring dàilái
带来

I'll bring it back later wǒ guò
xiē shíhou dàihuílái [wor gwor
hsyeh shur-hoh dai-hway-lai]
我过些时侯带回来

Britain Yīngguó [ying-gwor]
英国

British Yīngguó
英国

brochure shuōmíng shū
[shwor-ming]
说明书

broken (object) **pòle** [por-lur]
破了

(leg etc) **duànle** [dwahn-lur]
断了

(not working) **huàile** [hwai-lur]
怀了

brooch xiōngzhēn [hsyoong-
jun]
胸针

brother xiōngdì [hsyoong-dee]
兄弟

(older) **gēge** [gur-gur]
哥哥

(younger) **dìdi**
弟弟

brother-in-law (elder sister's

husband) **jiěfū** [jyeh-foo]
姐夫

(younger sister's husband) **mèifu**
[may-foo]
妹夫

(wife's elder brother) **nèixiōng**
[nay-hsyoong]
内兄

(wife's younger brother) **nèidì**
[nay-dee]
内弟

(husband's elder brother) **dàbó**
[dah bor]
大伯

(husband's younger brother)
xiǎoshū [hsyow-shoo]
小叔

brown zōngsè [dzoong-sur]
棕色

brush shuāzi [shwah-dzur]
刷

bucket tǒng [toong]
桶

Buddha Fó [for]
佛

Buddhism Fójiào [for-jyow]
佛教

Buddhist (adj) **Fójiàotú**
佛教徒

buffet car cānchē [tsahn-chur]
餐车

building fángzi [fahng-dzur]
房子

(multi-storey) **dàlóu** [dah-loh]
大楼

bunk: bottom bunk xià pù
[hsyah]
下铺
middle bunk zhōng pù [joong]
中铺
top bunk shàng pù [shahng]
上铺
bureau de change wài huì
duìhuàn bù [hway dway-hwahn]
外汇对换部
see **bank**
burglary dàoqiè [dow-chyeh]
盗窃
Burma Miǎndiàn [myen-dyen]
缅甸
burn (noun) shāoshāng
[show-shahng]
烧伤
(verb) ránshāo [rahn-show]
燃烧
burnt: this is burnt (food)
shāojiāole [show-jyow-lur]
烧焦了
bus (public transport) gōnggòng
qìchē [goong-goong chee-chur]
公共汽车
(limited stop) shìqūchē
[shur-chew-chur]
市区车
(in suburbs) jiāoqūchē
[jyow-chew-chur]
郊区车
(long-distance) chángtú qìchē
[chahng-too chee-chur]
长途汽车

what number bus is it to ...?
dào ... qù zuò jǐ hào chē?
[dow ... chew dzwor jee how chur]
到...去坐几号车？
when is the next bus to ...?
dào ... qù de xià (yì) bān
chē shì jídiǎn? [dow ... chew
dur hsyah (yee) bahn chur shur
jee-dyen]
到...去的下一班车是
几点？
what time is the last bus?
mòbānchē shì jǐ diǎn?
[mor-bahn-chur shur jee dyen]
末班车是几点？

All Chinese cities have a very
extensive public transport system. Beijing and Shanghai have
efficient underground railways,
with Guangzhou's still being
constructed. Elsewhere in cities,
buses are the main form of
transport. These are cheap and
run from around 6 a.m. to 9 p.m.
or later, but are usually slow and
crowded. Pricier private minibuses often run the same routes
in similar comfort and at greater
speed.
The bus is the cheapest (and
often only) way of getting from
town to town. However, bus
travel is very slow: there are
breakdowns from time to time
→

and stops every few minutes to pick up or set down passengers. There are a few new expressways, but poor surfaces and maintenance mean that country roads can be downright dangerous, as is the habit of saving fuel by coasting down hills or mountainsides with the engine off. Take some food along because though buses usually pull up at inexpensive roadhouses at mealtimes, they have been known to take two drivers and plough on for 24 hours without stopping.

The standard Chinese long-distance bus is fairly ramshackle, with wooden or lightly padded seats, and is neither heated nor air-conditioned. Luggage racks are tiny, and you'll have to put anything bulkier than a satchel on the roof, on your lap, or beside the driver. On popular routes you'll also find more comfortable options, although these are more expensive than an ordinary bus. Luxury buses have larger and better padded seats which often recline; sometimes there's even air-conditioning and a video. Sleeper buses have basic bunks →

instead of seats, and can be comfortable if a little cramped; they tend to be harder to book, however, and road travel at night is always more dangerous. Minibuses are common on routes of less than 100km or so, and can be immensely useful. If you've missed the only bus to where you're going, you can usually hop there in stages by minibus. All are privately run and prices vary around the country, but they typically cost a little more than the same journey by public bus.

Tickets are sold at the point of departure, whether this is a proper bus station or just a kerb stop – in which case you'll pay on board; you'll do this too if you hail a bus in passing. Destinations are always displayed (in Chinese characters) on the front of the vehicle. It's best to buy your ticket a day or two in advance if possible.

•••••• DIALOGUE ••••••

does this bus go to ...? zhèi liàng chē qù ... ma? [jay lyang chur chew ... mah]

no, you need a number ... bú qù, nǐ yào zùo ... hào chē [chew nee yow zwor ... how chur]

business shēngyi [shung-yee]
生意
(firm, company) gōngsī
[goong-sur]
公司
bus station gōnggòng qìchē
zǒngzhàn [goong-goong
chee-chur dzoong-jahn]
公共汽车总站
bus stop gōnggòng qìchē
zhàn [jahn]
公共汽车站
busy (road etc) rènào [rur-now]
热闹
(person) hěn máng [hun
mahng]
很忙
I'm busy tomorrow wǒ
míngtiān hěn máng [wor
ming-tyen hun mahng]
我明天很忙
but kěshi [kur-shur]
可是
butcher's ròu shāng [roh
shahng]
肉商
butter huángyóu [hwahng-
yoh]
黄油
button niǔkòu [nyoh-koh]
纽扣
buy mǎi
买
where can I buy ...? zài nǎr
néng mǎidào ...? [dzai nar

nung mai-dow]
在哪儿能买到...?
by: by bus zuò gònggōng
qìchē [dzwor]
坐公共汽车
written by ... shì ... xiě de
[shur ... sheh dur]
是...写的
by the window zài chuānghu
pángbiān [dzai]
在窗户旁边
by the sea zài hǎibiān
在海边
by Thursday xīngqī sì zhī
qián [jur chyen]
星期四之前
bye zàijiàn [dzai-jyen]
再见

C

cabbage báicài [bai-tsai]
白菜
cabin (on ship) chuáncāng
[chwahn-tsahng]
船舱
cake dàngāo [dahn-gow]
蛋糕
cake shop gāodiǎndiàn
[gow-dyen-dyen]
糕点店
call (verb: to phone) dǎ diànhuà
[dah dyen-hwah]
打电话

what's it called? zhèige jiào shénme? [jay-gur jyow shun-mur]

这个叫什么？

he/she is called ... (given name) tā jiào ... [tah jyow]

他叫...

(surname) tā xìng ... [hsing]

他姓 . . .

please call the doctor qǐng bǎ yīshēng jiào lái [ching bah yee-shung jyow]

请把医生叫来

please give me a call at 7.30 a.m. tomorrow qǐng míngtiān zǎoshàng qī diǎn bàn géi wó dǎ diànhuà [ching ming-tyen dzow-shahng chee dyen bahn gay wor dah dyen-hwah]

请明天早上七点半给我打电话

please ask him to call me qǐng tā dǎ diànhuà géi wǒ [tah dah – gay]

请他打电话给我

call back: I'll call back later (phone back) wǒ guò yí huìr zài dǎ lái [gwor yee hwayr dzai dah]

我过一回儿再打来

call round: I'll call round tomorrow wǒ míngtiān lái zháo nǐ [jow]

我明天来找你

camcorder shèxiàngjī [shur-hsyang-jee]

摄相机

camera zhàoxiàngjī [jow-hsyang-jee]

照相机

---

camping

Camping rough for foreigners is officially not allowed. Camping is only really feasible in the wildernesses of western China, where you are not going to wake up under the prying eyes of local villagers. In parts of Tibet, Qinghai, Xinjiang, Gansu and Inner Mongolia there are places within reach for hikers or cyclists where camping is possible. All equipment would have to be brought in from outside the country. There are no official campsites.

---

can (noun) guàntou [gwahn-toh]

罐头

a can of beer yí guànr píjiǔ

一罐儿啤酒

can: can you ...? nǐ néng ... ma? [nung ... mah]

你能...吗？

can I have ...? qíng géi wǒ ...? [ching gay wor]

请给我...？

I can't ... wǒ bù néng ...

我不能...

Canada Jiānádà [jyah-nah-dah]

加拿大

Canadian (adj) Jiānádà

加拿大

I'm Canadian wǒ shì Jiānádàrén [wor shur – run]

我是加拿大人

canal yùnhé [yewn-hur]

运河

cancel (reservation etc) tuì [tway]

退

candies tángguǒ [tahng-gwor]

糖果

candle làzhú [lah-joo]

蜡烛

can-opener kāiguàn dāojù [kai-gwahn dow-joo]

开罐刀具

Cantonese (adj) Guǎngdōng [gwahng-doong]

广东

(language) Guǎngdōnghuà [–hwah]

广东话

(person) Guǎngdōng rén [run]

广东人

cap (hat) màozi [mow-dzur]

帽子

(of bottle) pínggài [ping-gai]

瓶盖

car qìchē [chee-chur]

汽车

by car zuò qìchē [dzwor]

坐汽车

card kǎpiàn [kah-pyen]

卡片

here's my (business) card zhèi shì wǒde míngpiàn [jay shur wor-dur ming-pyen]

这是我的名片

Christmas card shèngdàn kǎ [shung-dahn kah]

圣诞卡

birthday card shēngrì kǎ [shung-rur kah]

生日卡

cardphone cíkǎ diànhuà [tsur-kah dyen-hwah]

磁卡电话

careful: be careful! xiǎoxīn! [hsyow-hsin]

小心

car ferry lúndù [lun-doo]

轮渡

car park tíngchēchǎng [ting-chur-chahng]

停车场

carpet dìtǎn [dee-tahn]

地毯

car rental qìchē chūzū [chee-chur choo-dzoo]

汽车出租

carriage (of train) chēxiāng [chur-hsyang]

车厢

carrot húluóbo [hoo-lwor-bor]

胡萝卜

carry ná [nah]

拿

cash (noun) xiànqián
[hsyen-chyen]

现钱

will you cash this for me? nǐ
néng tì wǒ huàn chéng xiàn
qián ma? [nung tee wor hwahn
chung – mah]

你能替我换成现钱吗?

cash desk jiāokuǎnchù
[jyow-kwahn-choo]

交款处

cash dispenser zìdòng
qúkuǎnjī [dzur-doong
chew-kwahn-jee]

自动取款机

cassette cídài [tsur-dai]

磁带

cassette recorder lùyīnjī
[loo-yin-jee]

录音机

castle chéngbǎo [chung-bow]

城堡

casualty department jíjiùshì
[jee-jyoh-shur]

急救室

cat māo [mow]

猫

catch (verb) zhuā [jwah]

抓

where do we catch the bus
to ...? qù ... zài nǎr shàng

chē? [chew ... dzai – chur]

去...在哪儿上车?

cathedral dà jiàotáng [dah
jyow-tahng]

大教堂

Catholic (adj) tiānzhǔjiào
[tyen-joo-jyow]

天主教

cauliflower càihuā [tsai-hwah]

菜花

cave shāndòng [shahn-doong]

山洞

(dwelling) yáodòng [yow-
doong]

窑洞

cemetery mùdì

墓地

centigrade shèshì [shur-shur]

摄氏

centimetre límǐ [lee-mee]

厘米

central zhōngyāng [joong-yang]

中央

central heating nuǎnqì
[nwahn-chee]

暖气

centre zhōngxīn [joong-hsin]

中心

how do we get to the city
centre? qù shì zhōngxīn
zénme zuǒ? [chew shur
joong-hsin dzun-mur dzwor]

去市中心怎么走?

certainly dāngrán [dahn-grahn]

当然

certainly not dāngrán bù
当然不

chair yǐzi [yee-dzur]
椅子

Chairman Mao Máo zhǔxí [mow jyew-hshee]
毛主席

change (noun: money) língqián [ling-chyen]
零钱

(verb: money) duìhuàn [dway-hwahn]
对换

can I change this for ...? nǐn néng bāng wǒ duìhuàn chéng ... ma? [nung bahng wor dway-hwahn chung ... mah]
您能帮我对换成...吗?

I don't have any change wǒ yìdiǎnr língqián yě méi yǒu [wor yee-dyenr ling-chyen yur may yoh]
我一点儿零钱也没有

can you give me change for a hundred-yuan note? yí bǎi kuài nín zhǎodekāi ma? [kwai nin jow-dur-kai mah]
一百块您找得开吗?

••••• DIALOGUE •••••

do we have to change (trains)? zhōngtú yào huàn chē ma? [joong-too yow hwahn chur mah]

yes, change at Hangzhou yào zài Hángzhōu huàn chē [yow dzai

no, it's a direct train bú yòng huàn chē, zhè shì zhídáchē [yoong – jur shur jur-dah-chur]

changed: to get changed huàn yīfu [hwahn yee-foo]
换衣服

character (in Chinese writing) zì [dzur]
字

charge (noun) shōufèi [shoh-fay]
收费

charge card see credit card

cheap piányi [pyen-yee]
便宜

do you have anything cheaper? yǒu piányi diǎnr de ma? [yoh pyen-yee dyenr dur mah]
有便宜点儿的吗?

check: could you check the bill, please? qǐng ba zhàngdān jiǎnchá yíxià, hǎo ma? [ching bah jahng-dahn jyen-chah yee-syah how mah]
请把帐单检查一下好吗?

check (US: bill) zhàngdānr [jahng-dahnr]
帐单儿

check in dēngjì [dung-jee]
登记

where do we have to check in? wǒmen zài nǎr yào dēngjì? [wor-men dzai nar yow]
我门在哪儿要登记?

cheerio! zàijiàn! [dzai-jyen]
再见

cheers! (toast) gānbēi!
[gahn-bay]
干杯

cheese nǎilào [nai-low]
奶酪

chemist's yàofáng [yow-fahng]
药房

cherry yīngtao [ying-tow]
樱桃

chess guójì xiàngqí [gwor-jee hsyang-chee]
国际象棋

to play chess xià qí [hsyah chee]
下棋

Chinese Chess xiàngqí [hsyang-chee]
象棋

chest (body) xiōng [hsyoong]
胸

chicken (meat) jīròu [jee-roh]
鸡肉

child háizi [hai-dzur]
孩子

Anyone taking children into China should be aware that they will attract a great deal of friendly interest. Care should taken with hygiene, food etc.
see **health**

---

child minder báomǔ [bow-moo]
保母

chin xiàba [hsyah-bah]
下巴

china cíqì [tsur-chee]
瓷器

China Zhōngguó [joong-gwor]
中国

China tea Zhōngguo chá
[chah]
中国茶

Chinese (adj) Zhōngguó
[joong-gwor]
中国
(person) Zhōngguó rén
[run]
中国人
(spoken language) Hànyǔ
[hahn-yew]
汉语
(written language) Zhōngwén
[joong-wun]
中文
the Chinese Zhōngguó
rénmín [run-min]
中国人民

Chinese leaf báicài [bai-tsai]
白菜

Chinese-style Zhōngshì
[joong-shur]
中式

chips zhá tǔdòu tiáo [jah too-doh tyow]
炸土豆条
(US) (zhá) tǔdòupiànr

[too-doh-pyenr]

（炸）土豆片儿

chocolate qiǎokèlì

[chyow-kur-lee]

巧克力

milk chocolate niúnǎi qiǎokèlì [nyoh-nai]

牛奶巧克力

plain chocolate chún qiǎokèlì

纯巧克力

a hot chocolate yì bēi rè qiǎokèlì (yǐnliào) [bay rur – (yin-lyow)]

一杯热巧克力(饮料)

choose xuǎn [hsyew-ahn]

选

chopsticks kuàizi [kwai-dzur]

筷子

Christmas Shèngdàn jié [shung-dahn jyeh]

圣诞节

Christmas Eve Shèngdànqiányè [–chyen-yur]

圣诞前夜

Merry Christmas! Shèngdàn jié kuàilè! [kwai-lur]

圣诞节快乐

church jiàotáng [jyow-tahng]

教堂

cigar xuějiā [hsyew-eh-jyah]

雪茄

cigarette xiāngyān [hsyang-yen]

香烟

Smoking is an almost universal habit among Chinese men. In the few places where non-smoking stickers have been posted (soft-seat train compartments for example), the signs are rarely observed. Handing out cigarettes is one of the most basic ways to establish trust and non-smokers should be apologetic about turning down cigarettes. Many foreign brands are on sale, with Marlboro being by some way the most popular.

cinema diànyǐng yuàn [dyen-ying yew-ahn]

电影院

circle yuánquān [ywahn-kwahn]

圆圈

(in theatre) lóutīng [loh-ting]

楼厅

city chéngshì [chung-shur]

城市

city centre shì zhōngxīn [shur joong-hsin]

市中心

clean (adj) gānjìng [gahn-jing]

干净

can you clean these for me?

nǐ néng ti wó xǐyixǐ, hǎo ma? [nung tee wor hshee-yee-hshee how mah]

你能替我洗一洗好吗？

clear (water) qīngchè
[ching-chur]

清澈

(speech, writing) qīngxī
[ching-hshee]

清晰

(obvious) míngxiǎn [–hsyen]

明显

clever cōngming [tsoong-ming]

聪明

cliff xuányá [hsyew-ahn-yah]

悬崖

climbing páshān [pah-shahn]

爬山

clinic zhénsuǒ [jun-swor]

诊所

cloakroom yīmàojiān
[yee-mow-jyen]

衣帽间

clock zhōng [joong]

钟

close (verb) guān [gwahn]

关

• • • • • • DIALOGUE • • • • • •

what time do you close? nǐmen
shénme shíhou guān mén?
[nee-mun shun-mur shur-hoh – mun]

we close at 8 p.m. on weekdays
and 6 p.m. on Saturdays zhōurì
xiàwǔ bā diǎn, xīngqī liù xiàwǔ
liù diǎn [joh-rur]

do you close for lunch? chī wǔfàn
de shíhou guān mén ma? [chur
woo-fahn dur shur-hoh – mah]

yes, between 1 and 3.30 p.m.
shì de, cóng yī diǎn dào sān
diǎn bàn yě guān mén [shur dur
tsoong – dow – yur]

closed guānménle
[gwahn-mun-lur]

关门了

cloth (fabric) bùliào [bool-yow]

布料

(for cleaning etc) mābù
[mah-boo]

抹布

clothes yīfu [yee-foo]

衣服

clothes line shàiyīshéng
[shai-yee-shung]

晒衣绳

clothes peg yīfu jiāzi [yee-foo
jyah-dzur]

衣服袈子

cloudy yīntiān [yin-tyen]

阴天

coach (bus) chángtú qìchē
[chahng-too chee-chur]

长途汽车

(tourist bus) lǚyóu chē
[lyew-yoh chur]

旅游车

(on train) kèchē [kur-chur]

客车

coach station chángtú
qìchēzhàn [chang-too
chee-chur-jahn]

长途汽车站

coach trip zuò chángtú qìchē lǚxíng [dzwor chahng-too chee-chur lyew-hsing]
坐长途汽车旅行

coast hǎibīn
海滨

coat (long coat) dàyī [dah-yee]
大衣

coathanger yījià [yee-jyah]
衣架

cockroach zhāngláng [jahng-lahng]
蟑螂

code (for phoning) diànhuà qūhào [dyen-hwah chew-how]
电话区号

what's the (dialling) code for Beijing? Běijīng de diànhuà qūhào shì duōshao? [dur – shur dwor-show]
北京的电话区号是多少？

coffee kāfēi [kah-fay]
咖啡

two coffees, please qǐng lái liǎng bēi kāfēi [ching]
请来两杯咖啡

Coffee is grown and drunk in Yunnan and Hainan, and available as instant powder elsewhere; Hainan produces a nice instant variety with coconut

essence. Jars of Nescafé are on sale throughout the country. Milk is generally sold in powder form as baby food, though you sometimes find cartons of UHT in supermarket fridges.

coin yìngbì [ying-bee]
硬币

Coke® Kěkǒukělè [kur-koh-kur-lur]
可口可乐

cold lěng [lung]
冷

I'm cold wó juéde hén lěng [wor jyew-eh-dur hun lung]
我觉得很冷

I have a cold wǒ gǎnmào le [gahn-mow lur]
我感冒了

collapse: he's collapsed tā kuǎle [tah kwah-lur]
他垮了

collar yīlǐng
衣领

collect qǔ ... [chew]
取

I've come to collect ... wǒ lái qǔ ... [wor]
我来取

collect call duìfāng fùkuǎn [dway-fahng foo-kwahn]
对方付款

college xuéyuàn
[hsyew-eh-yew-ahn]
学院

colour yánsè [yahn-sur]
颜色
do you have this in other
colours? yǒu biéde yánsè de
ma? [yoh byeh-dur – dur mah]
有别的颜色吗?

colour film cǎisè jiāojuǎnr
[tsai-sur jyow-jyew-ahnr]
彩色胶卷儿

comb shūzi [shoo-dzur]
梳子

come lái
来

•••••• DIALOGUE ••••••

where do you come from? nǐ shì
cóng nǎr láide? [shur tsoong nar
lai-dur]

I come from Edinburgh wǒ shì
cóng Àidīngbǎo lái de [wor]

come back huílai [hway-lai]
回来
I'll come back tomorrow wǒ
míngtiān huílai [ming-tyen]
我明天回来

come in qǐng jìn [ching jin]
请进

comfortable shūfu [shoo-foo]
舒服

communism gòngchǎnzhǔyì
[goong-chahn-joo-yee]
共产主义

Communist Party
Gòngchándǎng [–dahng]
共产党

Communist Party member
gòngchándǎngyuán
[–dahng-yew-ahn]
共产党员

compact disc jīguāng
chàngpiàn [jee-gwahng
chahng-pyen]
激光唱片

company (business) gōngsī
[goong-sur]
公司

compass zhǐnánzhēn
[jur-nahn-jun]
指南针

complain mányuàn
[mahn-yew-ahn]
埋怨

complaint bàoyuàn
[bow-yew-ahn]
抱怨
I have a complaint to make
wó xiǎng tí yí ge yìjiàn [wor
hsyang tee yee gur yee-jyen]
我想提一个意见

completely wánwánquánquán
[wahn-wahn-chahn-chahn]
完完全全

computer diànnǎo [dyen-now]
电脑

concert yīnyuèhuì
[yin-yew-eh-hway]
音乐会

concussion nǎozhèndàng
[now-jun-dahng]
脑震荡

conditioner (for hair) hùfàsù
[hoo-fah-soo]
护发素

condom bìyùntào
[bee-yewn-tow]
避孕套

conference huìyì [hway-yee]
会议

congratulations! gōngxǐ!
gōngxǐ! [goong-hshee]
恭喜恭喜

connecting flight xiánjiē de
bānjī [hsyen-jyeh dur bahn-jee]
衔接的班机

connection (in travelling) liányùn
[lyen-yewn]
联运

(rail) zhōngzhuǎn
[joong-jwahn]
中转

constipation biànbì [byen-bee]
便秘

consulate lǐngshìguǎn
[ling-shur-gwahn]
领事馆

contact (verb) liánxi [lyen-
hshee]
联系

contact lenses wēixíng yǎnjìng
[way-hsing yahn-jing]
微型眼镜

contraceptive bìyùn yòngpǐn

[bee-yewn yoong-pin]
避孕用品

convenient fāngbiàn
[fahng-byen]
方便

that's not convenient bù
fāngbiàn
不方便

cooker lúzào [loo-dzow]
炉灶

cookie xiáo bǐnggān [hsyow
bing-gahn]
小饼干

cool liángkuai [lyang-kwai]
凉快

corner: on the corner jiējiǎor
[jyeh-jyowr]
街角儿

in the corner qiángjiǎor
[chyang-jyowr]
墙角儿

correct (right) duì [dway]
对

corridor zǒuláng [dzoh-lahng]
走廊

cosmetics huàzhuāngpǐn
[hwah-jwahng-pin]
化妆品

cost (noun) jiàqián [jyah-
chyen]
价钱

how much does it cost?
duōshao qián? [dwor-show
chyen]
多少钱？

cotton miánhuā [myen-hwah]
棉花

cotton wool yàomián
[yow-myen]
药棉

couchette wòpù [wor-poo]
卧铺

cough késou [kur-soh]
咳嗽

cough medicine zhǐké yàoshuǐr
[jur-kur yow-shwayr]
止咳药水儿

could: could you ...? nín
kěyi ... ma? [kur-yee ... mah]
您可以...吗?

I couldn't ... wǒ bù néng ...
[wor boo nung]
我不能

country (nation) guójiā
[gwor-jyah]
国家

(countryside) xiāngcūn
[hsyang-tsun]
乡村

couple (two people) fūfù
[foo-foo]
夫妇

a couple of ... liǎngge ...
[lyang-gur]
两个...

courier xìnshǐ [hsin-shur]
信使

course: of course dāngrán
[dahn-grahn]
当然

of course not dāngrán bù
当然不

cousin (son of mother's brother:
older than speaker) biǎogē
[byow-gur]
表哥

(younger than speaker) biǎodì
表弟

(son of father's brother: older than
speaker) tángxiōng
[tahng-hsyoong]
堂兄

(younger than speaker) tángdì
堂弟

(daughter of mother's brother: older
than speaker) biáojiě [byow-jyeh]
表姐

(younger than speaker) biǎomèi
[byow-may]
表妹

(daughter of father's brother: older
than speaker) tángjiě
[tahng-jyeh]
堂姐

(younger than speaker) tángmèi
[tahng-may]
堂妹

cow nǎiniú [nain-yoh]
奶牛

crab pángxiè [pahng-hsyeh]
螃蟹

craft shop gōngyìpǐn
shāngdiàn [goong-yee-pin
shahng-dyen]
工艺品商店

crash (noun) **zhuàng chē**
[jwahng chur]
撞车

crazy shénjīngbìng
[shun-jing-bing]
神经病

credit card xìnyòng kǎ
[hsin-yoong kah]
信用卡

**do you take credit cards? kěyǐ
yòng xìnyòng kǎ ma?**
[kur-yee yoong – mah]
可以用信用卡吗？

Visa, American Express, and
Mastercard are accepted at big
tourist hotels, and you can obtain a cash advance with a Visa
card within an hour at many
Chinese banks. Wiring money
through the Bank of China
will take weeks even in Beijing,
Shanghai, or Guangzhou, and
rates charged at both ends make
it a poor option except as a last
resort. In cases of dire emergency, you will either have to
rely on the good will of fellow
travellers or get in touch with
your embassy.

• • • • • • DIALOGUE • • • • • •

**can I pay by credit card? wǒ kéyǐ
yòng xìnyòng kǎ jiāo kuǎn ma?**
[wor kur-yee yoong hsin-yoong kah

jyow kwahn mah]

which card do you want to use?
nín yóng de shì shénme kǎ? [dur
shur shun-mur kah]

Mastercard/Visa

yes, sir kěyǐ [kur-yee]

**what's the number? duōshao
hàomǎ?** [dwor-show how-mah]

and the expiry date? jǐ shí guòqī?
[jee shur gwor-chee]

crisps (zhá) **tǔdòupiànr** [(jah)
too-doh-pyenr]
(炸)土豆片儿

crockery cānjù [tsahn-jew]
餐具

crossing (by sea) **guòdù**
[gwor-doo]
过渡

crossroads shízì lùkǒu
[shur-dzur loo-koh]
十字路口

crowd rénqún [run-chewn]
人群

crowded yōngjǐ [yoong-jee]
拥挤

crown (on tooth) **yáguàn**
[yah-gwahn]
牙冠

cruise zuò chuán lǚxíng [dzwor
chwahn lyew-sing]
坐船旅行

crutches guǎizhàng [gwai-
jahng]
拐杖

cry (verb) **kū**
哭

Cultural Revolution **wénhuà dà gémìng** [wun-hwah dah gur-ming]
文化大革命

cup **bēizi** [bay-dzur]
杯子

a cup of tea/coffee, please **yì bēi chá/kāfēi** [bay]
一杯茶/咖啡

cupboard **guìzi** [gway-dzur]
柜子

cure (verb) **zhìyù** [jur-yew]
治愈

curly **juǎnqūde** [jwahn-chew-dur]
卷曲的

---

currency

Chinese currency is formally called **yuán**, more colloquially known as **kuài**, and breaks down into units of ten **máo** or **jiǎo**, and one hundred **fēn**. The last are effectively worthless and you'll only ever be given them in official currency transactions, or see the tiny yellow or green notes folded up into little twists and used to build model dragons or boats. Paper money was invented in China and is still the main form of exchange, available in 100, 50, 20, 10, 5, and 1 yuan notes, with a similar →

selection of mao; you occasionally come across tiny mao or fen coins, and rare brass 1 yuan pieces.

Tourist hotels in Beijing, Shanghai and Guangzhou also sometimes accept, or even insist on, payment in Hong Kong or US dollars. Yuan are not available overseas, though they can be obtained in Hong Kong.

---

current (electric) **diànliú** [dyen-lyoh]
电流

(in water) **shuǐliú** [shway-lyoh]
水流

curry **gālì** [gah-lee]
咖喱

curtains **chuānglián** [chwahng-lyen]
窗帘

cushion **diànzi** [dyen-dzur]
垫子

custom **fēngsú** [fung-soo]
风俗

Customs **hǎiguān** [hai-gwahn]
海关

You are allowed to import up to six hundred cigarettes, two litres of alcohol and twenty fluid ounces of perfume. It's illegal to →

import printed matter, tapes or videos of a politically sensitive nature. There is no restriction on the amount of foreign currency you are allowed to bring into China.

Export restrictions apply to items more than a hundred years old, for which you require an export form available from a friendship store in Beijing or another major city. You could be asked to show receipts for any cultural relics you have.

cut (noun) dāoshāng [dow-shahng]
刀伤
I've cut myself wó bǎ zìjǐ gēshāng le [wor bah dzur-jee gur-shahng lur]
我把自己割伤了
cutlery dāochā cānjù [dow-chah tsahn-jyew]
刀叉餐具
cycling qí zìxíngchē [chee dzur-hsing-chur]
骑自行车
cyclist qí zìxíngchē de rén [dur run]
骑自行车的人

D

dad bàba [bah-bah]
爸爸
daily měi tiān [may tyen]
每天
damage (verb) sǔnhuài [syewn-hwai]
损坏
damaged sǔnhuài le
损坏了
I'm sorry, I've damaged this duìbùqǐ, wó bǎ zhèi ge nòng huài le [dway-boo-chee wor bah jay gur noong hwai lur]
对不起我把这个弄坏了
damn! zāole! [dzow-lur]
糟了
damp (adj) cháoshī [chow-shur]
潮湿
dance (noun) wúdǎo [woo-dow]
舞蹈
(verb) tiàowǔ [tyow-woo]
跳舞
would you like to dance? ní xiǎng tiàowǔ ma? [hsyang – mah]
你想跳舞吗？
dangerous wēixiǎn [way-hsyen]
危险
Danish (adj) Dānmàiyǔ [dahn-mai-yoo]
丹麦语

dark (adj) **àn** [ahn]
暗
(colour) **shēn ... sè** [shun ... sur]
深...色
it's getting dark **tiān ànxiàlái le** [tyen ahn hsyah-lai lur]
天暗下来了

date*: what's the date today? **jīntiān jǐ hào?** [jin-tyen jee how]
今天几号？
let's make a date for next Monday **zánmen xiàge xīngqīyī jiànmiàn** [zahn-mun hsyah-gur – jyen-myen]
咱门下个星期一见面

daughter nǚ'ér [nyew-er]
女儿

daughter-in-law érxífur [er-hshee-foor]
儿媳妇儿

dawn límíng
黎明
at dawn **tiān gāng liàng** [tyen gahng lyang]
天刚亮

day tiān tyen]
天
the day after **dìèr tiān**
第二天
the day after tomorrow **hòutiān** [hoh-tyen]
后天
the day before **qián yì tiān**
[chyen]
前一天
the day before yesterday **qiántiān** [chyen-tyen]
前天
every day **měitiān** [may-tyen]
每天
all day **zhěngtiān** [jung-tyen]
整天
in two days' time **liǎng tiān nèi** [nay]
两天内
have a nice day **zhù nǐ wánr de hěn gāoxìng** [joo nee wahnr dur hun gow-hsing]
祝你玩儿得很高兴
day trip **yírìyóu** [yee-rur-yoh]
一日游

dead sǐle [sur-lur]
死了
deaf ěr lóng [loong]
耳聋
deal (business) **mǎimài**
买卖
it's a deal! **yì yán wéi dìng!** [yee yahn way]
一言为定
death sǐwáng [sur-wahng]
死亡
December shí'èr yuè [shur-er yew-eh]
十二月
decide juédìng [jyew-eh-ding]
决定
we haven't decided yet

wǒmen hái méi juédìng
[wor-mun hai may]
我门还没决定

decision juédìng
决定

deck (on ship) **jiábǎn** [jyah-bahn]
甲板

deep shēn [shun]
深

definitely yídìng
一定

definitely not yídìng bù
一定不

degree (qualification) **xuéwèi**
[hsyew-eh-way]
学位

delay (noun) **wǎndiǎn**
[wahn-dyen]
晚点

deliberately gùyì [goo-yee]
故意

delicious hǎochī [how-chur]
好吃

deliver sòng [soong]
送

delivery (of mail) **sòngxìn**
[soong-hsin]
送信

Denmark Dānmài [dahn-mai]
丹麦

dentist yáyī [yah-yee]
牙医

Avoid going to the dentist in China. In many places dentists can be seen operating on street corners without the benefit of anaesthetic. If at all possible, wait until you get home, or at least to Beijing or Hong Kong, where any treatment will be extremely expensive, though it should be covered by insurance.

• • • • • • DIALOGUE • • • • •

it's this one here **zhèr zhèi kē** [jer jay kur]

this one? **zhèi kē ma?** [mah]

no that one **bù, shì nèi kē** [shur nay]

here? **zhèr?**

yes **duì** [dway]

dentures jiǎyá [jee-ah-yah]
假牙

deodorant chúchòujì
[choo-choh-jee]
除臭剂

department (administrative) **bù**
部

(academic) **xì** [hshee]
系

department store bǎihuò dàlóu
[bai-hwor dah-loh]
百货大楼

departure lounge hòujīshì
[hoh-jee-shur]
侯机室

depend: it depends on ... nà
yào kàn ... [nah yow kahn]
那要看...

deposit yājīn [yah-jin]
押金

dessert tiánpǐn [tyen-pin]
甜品

destination mùdìdì
目地地

develop (film) chōngxǐ
[choong-hshee]
冲洗

• • • • • DIALOGUE • • • • •

could you develop these films?
qǐng nín bāng wǒ chōng yíxià
zhèi xiē jiāojuǎnr, hǎo ma? [ching
nin bahng wor choong yee-hsyah jay
hsyeh jyow-jyew-ahnr how mah]
yes, certainly kěyǐ [kur-yee]
when will they be ready? shénme
shíhou néng chōng hǎo?
[shun-mur shur-hoh nung choong how]
tomorrow afternoon míngtiān
xiàwǔ [ming-tyen hsyah-woo]
how much is the four-hour service?
sì xiǎoshí fúwù duōshao qián?
[sur hsyow-shur foo-woo dwor-show]

diabetic (noun) tángniàobìng
rén [tahng-nyow-bing run]
糖尿病人

dial (verb) bōhào [bor-how]
拨号

dialling code diànhuà qūhào
[dyen-hwah chew-how]
电话区号

To call abroad from mainland
China dial 00 + country code
(see below) + area code minus
initial zero + number:

UK 44
US 1
Canada 1
Australia 61
New Zealand 64
Ireland 353

diamond zuànshí [dzwahn-shur]
钻石

diaper niàobù [nyow-boo]
尿布

diarrhoea lā dùzi [lah doo-dzur]
拉肚子
do you have something for
diarrhoea? ní yǒu yī lā dùzi
de yào ma? [nee yoh yee lah
doo-dzur dur yow mah]
你有医拉肚子的药吗?

diary rìjì [rur-jee]
日记

dictionary cídiǎn [tsur-dyen]
词典

didn't* see not

die sǐ [sur]
死

diet jìkǒu [jee-koh]
忌口
I'm on a diet wǒ zài jìkǒu
[wor dzai]
我在忌口

I have to follow a special diet
wó děi chī guīdìng de yǐnshí
[day chur gway-ding dur yin-shur]
我得吃规定的饮食

difference bùtóng [boo-toong]
不同

what's the difference? yǒu
shénme bùtóng? [yoh
shun-mur]
有什么不同？

different bùtóng
不同

difficult kùnnan [kun-nahn]
困难

difficulty kùnnan
困难

dining room cāntīng [tsahn-
ting]
餐厅

dinner (evening meal) wǎnfàn
[wahn-fahn]
晚饭

to have dinner chī wǎnfàn
吃晚饭

direct (adj) zhíjiē [jur-jyeh]
直接

(flight) zhífēi [jur-fay]
直飞

is there a direct train? yǒu
zhídá huôchē ma? [yoh
jur-dah hwor-chur mah]
有直达火车吗？

direction fāngxiàng
[fahng-hsyang]
方向

which direction is it? zài něige
fāngxiàng? [dzai nay-gur]
在哪个方向？

is it in this direction? shì
zhèige fāngxiàng ma? [shur
jay-gur – mah]
是这个方向吗？

director zhǔrén [joo-run]
主人

dirt wūgòu [woo-goh]
污垢

dirty zāng [dzahng]
脏

disabled cánfèi [tsahn-fay]
残废

is there access for the
disabled? yǒu cánfèirén de
tōngdào ma? [you –run dur
toong-dow mah]
有残废人的通道吗？

disaster zāinàn [dzai-nahn]
灾难

disco dísīkē [dee-sur-kur]
迪斯科

discount jiǎnjià [jyen-jyah]
减价

is there a discount? néng
jiǎnjià ma? [nung – mah]
能减价吗？

disease jíbìng
疾病

disgusting ěxīn [ur-hsin]
恶心

dish (meal) cài [tsai]
菜

(bowl) diézi [dyeh-dzur]

碟子

disk (for computer) ruǎnpán [rwahn-pahn]

软盘

disposable diapers/nappies (yícìxìng) niàobù [(yee-tsur-hsing) nyow-boo]

(一次性)尿布

distance jùlí

距离

in the distance zài yuǎnchù [dzai yew-ahn-choo]

在远处

district dìqū [dee-chew]

地区

disturb dárǎo [dah-row]

打扰

divorced líhūn [lee-hun]

离婚

dizzy: I feel dizzy wǒ tóuyūn [wor toh-yewn]

我头晕

do (verb) zuò [dzwor]

作

what shall we do? ní xiǎng zuò shénme? [hsyang – shun-mur]

你想作什么?

how do you do it? gāi zěnme zuò? [dzun-mur]

该怎么作?

will you do it for me? máfan nǐ bāng wǒ zuò yíxià, hǎo ma? [mah-fahn nee bahng wor dzwor yee-hsyah how mah]

麻烦你帮我作一下好吗?

•••••• DIALOGUES ••••••

how do you do? nín hǎo? [how]

nice to meet you jiàn dào nín zhēn gāoxìng [jyen dow nin jun gow-hsing]

what do you do? (work) nǐ shì zuò shénme gōngzuò de? [shur – goong-dzwor dur]

I'm a teacher, and you? wǒ shì jiàoshī, nǐ ne? [wor – nur]

I'm a student wǒ shì xuésheng

what are you doing this evening? nǐ jīnwǎn zuò shénme? [jin-wahn]

we're going out for a drink, do you want to join us? wǒmen chū qù hē jiǔ, ní xiǎng gēn wǒmen yí kuàir qù ma? [wor-mun choo chew hur jyoh nee hsyang gun – kwair chew mah]

do you want more rice? nǐ hái yào mǐfàn, ma? [yow mee-fahn]

I do, but she doesn't wǒ yào, tā bú yào [wor yow tah]

doctor yīshēng [yee-shung]

医生

please call a doctor qíng nǐ jiào ge yīshēng [ching nee jyow gur]

请你叫个医生

Medical facilities are good, at least in the big cities. Low standards of public hygiene and overcrowded conditions are to blame for most of the problems that beset visitors. If you do get ill, international clinics in Beijing, Shanghai and Guangzhou can provide diagnosis and treatment for minor complaints; also, every town has a pharmacy which can suggest remedies and doctors who can treat you with traditional Chinese or Western techniques. You canKt expect to find English-speaking medical or pharmacy staff.

Large hotels usually have a clinic offering diagnosis, advice and prescriptions and there'll be someone who speaks English. If you are seriously ill, it's best to head straight to a hospital (don't get the police involved as they are rarely helpful) – though you could try giving CITS (the state tour operator) a ring for advice on where to go. You will be expected to pay for your treatment on the spot, so keep the receipt and you can claim the money back from your insurance policy when you get home.

see **health**

• • • • • • **DIALOGUE** • • • • • •

where does it hurt? nár téng? [tung]

right here jiù zài zhèr [jyoh dzai jer]

does that hurt now? xiànzài hài téng ma? [hsyahn-dzai – mah]

yes hái téng

take this prescription to the chemist ná zhèi gè yàofāng dào yàodiàn qù pèi yào [nah jay gur yow-fahng dow yow-dyen chew pay yow]

document wénjiàn [wun-jyen]
文件

dog gǒu [goh]
狗

domestic flight guónèi hángbān [gwor-nay hahng-bahn]
国内行班

don't!* búyào! [boo-yow]
不要

don't do that! bié zhème zuò [byeh jur-mur zwor]
别这么作

see **not**

door mén [mun]
门

doorman bǎménrde [bah-munr-dur]
把门儿的

double shuāng [shwahng]
双

double bed shuāngrén chuáng [– run chwahng]
双人床

double room shuāngrén fáng(jiān) [fahng(jyen)]
双人房(间)

down xià [hsyah]
下

down here jiù zài zhèr [jyoh dzai jer]
就在这儿

put it down over there gē zài zhèr [gur]
搁在这儿

it's down there on the right jiù zài yòubian [yoh-byen]
就在右边

it's further down the road zài wǎng qián [wahng chyen]
再往前

downstairs lóuxià [loh-hsyah]
楼下

dozen yì dá [dah]
一打

half a dozen bàn dá [bahn]
半打

dragon lóng [loong]
龙

draught beer shēng píjiǔ [shung pee-jyoh]
生啤酒

draughty: it's draughty zhèr tōngfēng [jer toong-fung]
这儿通风

drawer chōuti [choh-tee]
抽屉

drawing huìhuà [hway-hwah]
绘画

dreadful zāotòule [dzow-toh-lur]
糟透了

dress (noun) liányīqún [lyen-yee-chewn]
连衣裙

Judging what clothing is appropriate is generally a matter of common sense. Shorts are OK for temples, but women should not wear anything too revealing.

---

dressed: to get dressed chuān yīfu [chwahn]
穿衣服

dressing gown chényī [chun-yee]
晨衣

drink (noun: alcoholic) jiǔ [jyoh]
酒

(non-alcoholic) yǐnliào [yin-lyow]
饮料

(verb) hē [hur]
喝

a cold drink yì bēi léngyǐn [yee bay lung-yin]
一杯冷饮

can I get you a drink? hēdiǎnr shénme ma? [dyenr shun-mur mah]
喝点儿什么吗？

what would you like (to drink)? ní xiǎng hē diǎnr shénme? [hsyang]
你想喝点儿什么？

no thanks, I don't drink bù,
xièxie, wǒ bú huì hē jiǔ
[hsyeh-hsyeh wor boo hway hur
jyoh]

不谢谢我不会喝酒

I'll just have a drink of water
wǒ hē diánr shuǐ ba [shway
bah]

我喝点儿水吧

see bar

drinking water yǐnyòngshuǐ
[yin-yoong-shway]

饮用水

is this drinking water? zhè
shuǐ kěyǐ hē ma? [jur shway
kur-yee hur ma]

这水可以喝吗？

drive (verb) kāichē [kai-chur]

开车

we drove here wǒmen kāichē
lái de [wor-mun kai-chur lai dur]

我们开车来的

I'll drive you home wǒ kāichē
sòng nǐ huíjiā [wor kai-chur
soong nee hway-jyah]

我开车送你回家

driver sījī [sur-jee]

司机

ENGLISH ◆ CHINESE | Dr

driving

Renting a car to drive yourself
is impossible for a tourist, but
it is possible to rent vehicles
with a driver for local use in
Beijing, Shanghai and Sanya,
in Hainan Island.
Prices are set by negotiating and
you'll be expected to provide
lunch for the driver. It's easiest
to arrange this type of rental
through a hotel, though some
tour operators rent out vehicles
too – which might be more useful as they often include the
services of an interpreter. In
Tibet, hiring a jeep with driver
is pretty much the only way to
get to many destinations.

driving licence jiàshǐ zhízhào
[jyah-shur jur-jow]

驾驶执照

drop: just a drop, please (of
drink) zhēn de yí diǎnr,
xièxie [jun dur yee dyen
hsyeh-hsyeh]

真的一点儿谢谢

drugs (narcotics) dúpǐn [doo-pin]

毒品

drunk (adj) hēzuìle
[hur-dzway-lur]

喝醉了

dry (adj) gān [gahn]

干

dry-cleaner gānxǐdiàn
[gahn-hshee-dyen]

干洗店

duck (meat) yā [yah]

鸭

due: he was due to arrive
yesterday tā yuán gāi shì
zuótiān dào de [tah yew-ahn
gai shur dzwor-tyen dow tah]
他原该是昨天到的
when is the train due?
huǒchē jǐ diǎn dào?
[hwor-chur jee shur]
火车几点到？

dull (pain) yínyǐn zuòtòng
[dzwor-toong]
隐隐作痛
(weather) yīntiān [yin-tyen]
阴天

during zài … de shíhou
[dzai … dur shur-hoh]
在...的时候

dust huīchén [hway-chun]
恢尘

dustbin lājīxiāng
[lah-jee-hsyang]
垃圾箱

Dutch (adj) Hélán [hur-lahn]
荷兰

duty-free (goods) miǎnshuì
[myen-shway]
勉税

duty-free shop miǎnshuì
shāngdiàn [shahng-dyen]
勉税商店

dynasty cháodài [chow-dai]
朝代

E

each (every) měi [may]
每
how much are they each? yí
ge yào duōshao qián? [yee
gur yow dwor-show chyen]
一个要多少钱？

ear ěrduo [er-dwor]
耳朵

earache: I have earache wó
ěrduo téng [wor – tung]
我耳朵疼

early zǎo [dzow]
早
early in the morning yì
zǎo
一早
I called by earlier wó zǎo xiē
shíhou láiguo [wor – hsyeh
shur-hoh lai-gwor]
我早些时候来过

earrings ěrhuán [er-hwahn]
耳环

east dōng [doong]
东
in the east dōngfāng
[doong-fahng]
东方

East China Sea Dōng Hǎi
东海

easy róngyì [roong-yee]
容易

eat chī [chur]
吃

we've already eaten, thanks
xièxie, wǒmen yǐjing chīle
[hsyeh-hsyeh wor-mun –
chur-lur]
谢谢我门已经吃了
economy class jīngjìcāng
[–tsahng]
经济舱
egg jīdàn [jee-dahn]
鸡蛋
either: either … or …
huòzhe … huòzhe …
[hwor-jur]
或着…或着…
either of them něi liǎngge
dōu kéyǐ [nay lyang-gur doh
kur-yee]
那两个都可以
elastic band xiàngpíjīnr
[hsyahng–]
橡皮筋儿
elbow gēbozhǒur [gur-bor-johr]
胳膊肘儿
electric diàn [dyen]
电
electric fire diàn lúzi [loo-dzur]
电炉子
electrician diàngōng
[dyen-goong]
电工
electricity diàn [dyen]
电
see **voltage**
elevator diàntī [dyen-tee]
电梯

else: something else biéde
dōngxi [byeh-dur doong-hshee]
别的东西
somewhere else biéde dìfāng
[dee-fahng]
别的地方

•••••• DIALOGUE ••••••

would you like anything else? hái
yào biéde ma? [yow – mah]
no, nothing else, thanks bú yào le,
xièxie [lur hsyeh-hsyeh]

embassy dàshíguǎn
[dah-shur-gwahn]
大使馆
embroidery cìxiù [tsur-hsyoh]
刺锈
emergency jǐnjí qíngkuàng
[ching-kwahng]
紧急情况
this is an emergency!
jiùmìng! [jyoh-ming]
救命
emergency exit ānquánmén
[ahn-choo-en-mun]
安全门
emperor huángdì [hwahng-dee]
皇帝
empress nǚ huángdì [nyew]
女皇帝
empty kōng [koong]
空
end (noun) mòduān
[mor-dwahn]
末端

at the end of the street zhèi tiáo jiē de jìntóu [jay tyow jyeh dur jin-toh]

这条街的尽头

when does it end? shénme shíhou jiéshù? [shun-mur shur-hoh jyeh-shoo]

什么时候结束?

engaged (toilet) yǒurén [yoh-run]

有人

(phone) zhànxiàn [jahn-hsyen]

战线

(to be married) dìnghūnle [ding-hun-lur]

定婚了

England Yīngguó [ying-gwor]

英国

English (adj) Yīngguó [ying-gwor]

英国

(language) Yīngyǔ [ying-yew]

英语

I'm English wǒ shì Yīngguó rén [wor shur – run]

我是英国人

do you speak English? ni huìbuhuì shuō Yīngyǔ? [hway-boo-hway shwor]

你会不会说英语?

enjoy: to enjoy oneself wánr de hěn kāixīn [wahnr dur hun kai-hsin]

玩儿得很开心

how did you like the film? nǐ juéde diànyǐng zěnme yàng? [jyew-eh-dur dyen-ying dzun-mur yang]

I enjoyed it very much, did you enjoy it? wǒ juéde hén hǎo, nǐ ne? [wor – hun how nee nur]

enjoyable lìng rén yúkuàide [run yew-kwai-dur]

令人愉快的

enormous dàjíle [dah-jee-lur]

大极了

enough: that's enough gòule [goh-lur]

够了

there's not enough bú gòu

不够

it's not big enough bú gòu dà

不够大

entrance (noun) rùkǒuchù [roo-koh-choo]

入口处

envelope xìnfēng [hsin-fung]

信封

equipment shèbèi [shur-bay]

设备

(for climbing, sport etc) qìxiè [chee-hsyeh]

器械

especially tèbié [tur-byeh]

特别

essential **zhòngyào** [joong-yow]

重要

it is essential that ... ... **shì juéduì bìyào de** [shur jyew-eh-dway bee-yow dur]

...是决对必要的

Europe **Ōuzhōu** [oh-joh]

欧洲

European (adj) **Ōuzhōu**

欧洲

even **shènzhi** [shun-jur]

甚至

even if ... **jìshǐ ... yě** [jee-shur ... yur]

即使...也

evening **wǎnshang** [wahn-shahng]

晚上

this evening **jīntiān wǎnshang** [jin-tyen]

今天晚上

in the evening **wǎnshang**

晚上

evening meal **wǎnfàn** [wahn-fahn]

晚饭

eventually **zuìhòu** [dzway-hoh]

最后

ever **céngjīng** [tsung-jing]

曾经

•••••• **DIALOGUE** ••••••

have you ever been to the Great Wall? **nǐ qùguo Chángchéng ma?** [chew-gwor – mah]

yes, I was there two years ago **qùguo, liǎng nián qián qùguo** [chew-gwor lyang nyen chyen chew-gwor]

every **měige** [may-gur]

每个

every day **měitiān** [may-tyen]

每天

everyone **měige rén** [may-gur run]

每个人

everything **měijiàn shìr** [may-jyen shur]

每件事儿

(objects) **suóyǒu de dōngxi** [swor-yoh dur doong-hshee]

所有的东西

everywhere **měige dìfāng** [may-gur dee-fahng]

每个地方

exactly! **duìjíle!** [dway-jee-lur]

对极了

exam **kǎoshì** [kow-shur]

考试

example **lìzi** [lee-dzur]

例子

for example **lìrú**

例如

excellent **hǎojíle** [how-jee-lur]

好极了

except chúle ... yǐwài [choo-lur]

除了...以外

excess baggage chāozhòng xíngli [chow-joong hsing-lee]

超重行李

exchange rate duìhuàn lǜ [dway-hwahn lyew]

对换率

exciting (day) cìjī [tsur-jee]

刺激

excuse me (to get past) máfan nín [mah-fahn]

麻烦您

(to get attention) máfan nín, qǐng wèn ... [ching wun]

麻烦您请问

(to say sorry) duìbuqǐ [dway-boo-chee]

对不起

exhausted (tired) lèisǐle [lay-sur-lur]

累死了

exhibition (of paintings etc) zhǎnlǎn [jan-lan]

展览

(trade fair etc) jiāoyì huì [jyow-yee hway]

交易会

exit chūkǒu [choo-koh]

出口

where's the nearest exit? zuì jìn de chūkǒu zài nǎr? [dzway jin dur choo-koh dzai]

最近的出口在哪儿?

expensive guì [gway]

贵

experienced yǒu jīngyàn [yoh jing-yen]

有经验

explain jiěshì [jyeh-shur]

解释

can you explain that? nǐ néng jiěshì yíxià ma? [nung – yee-syah mah]

你能解释一下吗?

express (mail) kuàidì [kwai-dee]

快递

(train) kuàichē [kwai-chur]

快车

extension (telephone) fēnjī [fun-jee]

分机

extension 221, please qǐng guà èr èr yāo fēnjī [ching gwah er er yow]

请挂二二一分机

extra: can we have an extra one? qǐng zài lái yíge? [dzai lai yee-gur]

请再来一个?

do you charge extra for that? hái yào qián ma? [hai yow chyen mah]

还要钱吗?

extremely fēicháng [fay-chahng]

非常

eye yǎnjing [yahn-jing]

眼睛

will you keep an eye on my

suitcase for me? máfan nín
bāng wǒ kān yíxià tíbāo, hǎo
ma? [mah-fahn nin bahng wor
kahn yee-hsyah tee-bow how
mah]
麻烦您帮我看一下提
包好吗？

eyeglasses yǎnjìng [yahn-jing]
眼镜

F

face liǎn [lyen]
脸

factory gōngchǎng
[goong-chahng]
工厂

Fahrenheit huáshì [hwah-shur]
华氏

faint (verb) yūn [yewn]
晕
she's fainted tā yūndǎole [tah
yewn-dow-lur]
她晕倒了
I feel faint wǒ juéde yóu diǎn
(tóu) yūn [wor jyew-eh-dur yoh
dyen (toh)]
我觉得有点(头)晕

fair (adj) gōngpíng [goong-ping]
公平

fake màopái [mow-pai]
冒牌

fall (verb: person) shuāidǎo
[shwai-dow]
摔倒

she's had a fall tā shuāile yì
jiāo [tah shwai-lur yee jyow]
她摔了一交

fall (US) qiūtiān [chyoh-tyen]
秋天
in the fall qiūtiān
秋天

false jiǎ [jyah]
假

family jiātíng [jyah-ting]
家庭

famous yǒumíng [yoh-ming]
有名

fan (electrical) fēngshàn
[fung-shahn]
风扇
(hand-held) shànzi [shahn-dzur]
扇子
(sports) qiúmí [chyoh-mee]
球迷

fantastic (wonderful) tàihǎole
[tai-how-lur]
太好了

far yuǎn [yew-ahn]
远

• • • • • DIALOGUE • • • • •

is it far from here? lí zhèr yuǎn
ma? [jer – mah]
no, not very far bú tài yuǎn
well how far? duō yuǎn ne? [dwor
– nur]
it's about 20 kilometres èr shí
gōnglǐ zuǒyòu [goong-lee
dzwor-yoh]

fare chēfèi [chur-fay]

车费

Far East Yuǎndōng
[yew-ahn-doong]

远东

farm nóngchǎng [noong-chahng]

农厂

fashionable shímáo [shur-mow]

时髦

fast kuài [kwai]

快

fat (person) pàng [pahng]

胖

(on meat) féiròu [fay-roh]

肥肉

father fùqīn [foo-chin]

父亲

father-in-law yuèfù [yew-eh-foo]

岳父

faucet shuǐlóngtóu
[shway-loong-toh]

水龙头

fault cuò [tswor]

错

sorry, it was my fault duìbuqǐ
shì wǒde cuò [dway-boo-chee
shur wor-dur tswor]

对不起是我的错

it's not my fault bú shì wǒde
cuò

不是我的错

faulty yǒu máobìng [yoh
mow-bing]

有毛病

favourite zuì xǐhuan de [dzway

hshee-hwahn dur]

最喜欢的

fax (noun) chuánzhēn
[chwahn-jun]

传真

to send a fax fā chuánzhēn
[fah]

发传真

February èryuè [er-yew-eh]

二月

feel gǎnjué [gahn-jyew-eh]

感觉

I feel hot wǒ juéde hěn rè
[wor jyew-eh-dur hun rur]

我觉得很热

I feel unwell wǒ juéde
bú tài shūfu [–dur – shoo-foo]

我觉得不太舒服

I feel like going for a walk wó
xiǎng qù zǒuzǒu [hsyahng
chew dzoh-dzoh]

我想去走走

how are you feeling? nǐ juéde
zěnme yàng le?
[nee jyew-eh-dur dzun-mur – lur]

你觉得怎么样了？

I'm feeling better wó háo
diǎnr le [how dyenr]

我好点儿了

fence zhàlan [jah-lahn]

栅栏

ferry bǎidù

摆渡

There are any number of river and sea journeys to make while in China, though passenger ferries are generally on the decline as new roads are built with buses providing a faster service. It might not always be the quickest or cheapest form of transport, but a boat ride can be a refreshing change from the tribulations of train or bus travel, and it's always affordable. Conditions on board are greatly variable, but on overnight trips there's always a choice of classes – sometimes as many as six – which can range from a bamboo mat on the floor, right through to the luxury of private cabins. Toilets and food can be basic, though, so plan things as best you can.

festival jiérì [jyeh-ree]
节日

Traditionally, there were a large number of festivals in China, many of which marked different stages of the agricultural year. In recent years, some have been revived.

Moon Festival Celebrations are held to mark the middle of →

autumn on the fifteenth day of the eighth lunar month; they always feature fireworks and lanterns, large mooncakes (with images of three-legged toads and rabbits and symbols of the moon carved on the top) and Maotai (a clear spirit distilled from rice or millet). Poems are composed and recited in honour of the full moon.

The birthday of Confucius on 28 September is marked by celebrations at all Confucian temples. It is a good time to visit his birthplace, Qufu, which is located in Shandong Province, elaborate ceremonies being held in the temple there.

On **Dēngjié** (Lantern Festival), which takes place on the fifteenth day of the New Year, all shops and houses display lanterns in recognition of the coming of greater light and warmth.

The **Qīngmíng** (Pure Brightness) festival, held on 5 April, is the day for honouring ancestors. Graves are swept and various paper objects, such as money and sacrificial utensils, are displayed before being burnt.

On the fifth day of the fifth →

month, the **Dragon-Boat Festival** is held in honour of the great poet Qu Yuan who drowned in a river on this day. In many towns of southern China, races are held between long dragon boats. **Zhōng Yuán**, which takes place on the fifteenth day of the seventh month, is another festival in honour of ancestors. Traditionally on this day, lanterns are lit and sutras recited in Buddhist temples in order to lead the souls of the departed through the sea of suffering. On **Chóng Yáng** (Double Yang), held on the ninth day of the ninth month, people climb hills to recite poems, drink wine and enjoy nature.

---

fetch qǔ [chew]

取

I'll fetch him wǒ qù jiào tā lái [wor – jyow tah]

我去叫他来

will you come and fetch me later? děng huìr nǐ lái jiē wǒ, hǎo ma? [dung hwayr – jyeh]

等会儿你来接我好吗?

feverish fāshāo [fah-show]

发烧

few: a few yì xiē [yee-hsyeh]

一些

a few days jǐ tiān [tyen]

几天

fiancé wèihūnfū [way-hun-foo]

未婚夫

fiancée wèihūnqī [way-hun-chee]

未婚妻

field tiándì [tyen-dee]

田地

(paddy) dàotián [dow-tyen]

稻田

fill in tián [tyen]

填

do I have to fill this in? wǒ yào tián zhèi zhāng biǎo ma? [wor yow tyen jay jahng byow mah]

我要填这张表吗?

filling (in cake, sandwich) xiànr [hsyenr]

陷儿

(in tooth) bǔ yá [byew yah]

补牙

film (movie) diànyǐng [dyen-ying]

电影

(for camera) jiāojuǎnr [jyow-jew-ahnr]

交卷儿

• • • • • DIALOGUE • • • • • •

do you have this kind of film? ní yǒu zhèi zhǒng jiāojuǎnr ma? [yoh jay-joong jyow-jyew-ahnr mah]

yes, how many exposures? yǒu, nǐ

yào duōshao zhāng de? [yow
dwor-show jahng dur]

36 sān shí liù zhāng (de)

filthy zāng [dzahng]

脏

find (verb) zhǎodào [jow-dow]

找到

I can't find it wó zhǎobúdào
[wor jow-boo-dow]

我找不到

I've found it zhǎodàole [jow-
dow-lur]

找到了

find out zhǎochū [jow-choo]

找出

could you find out for me? nǐ
néng tì wǒ diàochá yíxià
ma? [nung tee wor dyow-chah
yee-hsyah mah]

你能替我调查一下吗？

fine (weather) qínglǎng
[ching-lang]

晴朗

(punishment) fákuán
[fah-kwahn]

罚款

••••• DIALOGUES •••••

how are you? nǐ hǎo ma? [how
mah]

I'm fine, thanks hén hǎo, xièxie
[hun how hsyeh-hsyeh]

is that OK? zhèyàng xíng ma?
[jur-yang hsing mah]

that's fine, thanks xíng, xièxie

finger shóuzhǐ [shoh-jur]

手旨

finish (verb) zuò wán [dzwor
wahn]

作完

I haven't finished yet wǒ hái
méi nòng wán [wor hai may
noong wahn]

我还没弄完

when does it finish? shénme
shíhou néng wán? [shun-mur
shur-hoh nung]

什么时候能完？

fire huǒ [hwor]

火

(blaze) huǒzāi [hwor-dzai]

火灾

fire! zháohuǒle! [jow-hwor-
lur]

着火了

can we light a fire here? zhèr
néng dián huǒ ma? [jer nung
dyen hwor mah]

这儿能点火吗？

fire alarm huójǐng [hwor-jing]

火警

fire brigade xiāofángduì
[hsyow-fahng-dway]

消防队

The number for the fire brigade
is 119.

fire escape tàipíngtī

太平梯

fire extinguisher mièhuǒqì
[myeh-hwor-chee]

灭火器

first dìyī

第一

I was first wǒ dìyī [wor]

我第一

first of all shǒuxiān
[shoh-hsyen]

首先

at first qǐchū [chee-choo]

起初

the first time dìyí cì [tsur]

第一次

first on the left zuǒbian dì
yíge [zwor-byen – gur]

左边第一个

first aid jíjiù [jee-jyoh]

急救

first-aid kit jíjiùxiāng
[–hsyahng]

急救箱

first class (travel etc) yīděng
[yee-dung]

一等

first floor èr lóu [er loh]

二楼

(US) yí lóu

一楼

first name míngzi [ming-dzur]

名子

fish (noun) yú [yew]

鱼

fit: it doesn't fit me zhè duì wǒ
bù héshì [jur dway wor boo
hur-shur]

这对我不合适

fitting room shì yī shì [shur yee
shur]

试衣室

fix: can you fix this? (repair) nǐ
néng bǎ zhèige xiū hǎo ma?
[nung bah jay-gur hsyoh how
mah]

你能把这个修好吗？

fizzy yǒuqìde [yoh-chee-
dur]

有气的

flag qí [chee]

旗

flannel (xǐliǎn) máojīn
[(hshee-lyen) mow-jin]

毛巾

flash (for camera)
shǎnguāngdēng
[shahng-wahng-dung]

闪光灯

flat (noun: apartment) dānyuán
[dahn-yew-ahn]

单元

(adj) píngtǎn [ping-tahn]

平坦

I've got a flat tyre wǒde
chētāi biěle [wor-dur chur-tai
byeh-lur]

我的车胎瘪了

flavour wèidao [way-dow]

味道

flea tiàozǎo [tyow-dzow]

跳蚤

flight hángbān [hahng-bahn]
行班

flight number hángbān hào
[how]
行班号

flood hóngshuǐ [hoong-shway]
洪水

floor (of room: wooden) dìbǎn
地板

(storey) lóu [loh]
楼

(in hotel etc) céng [tsung]
层

on the floor zài dìshang [dzai
dee-shahng]
在地上

florist huādiàn [hwah-dyen]
花店

flower huā [hwah]、
花

flu liúgǎn [lyoh-gahn]
流感

fluent: he speaks fluent Chinese
tā Hànyǔ jiǎngde hěn liúlì
[tah hahn-yew jyang-dur hun
lyoh-lee]
他汉语讲得很流利

fly (noun) cāngying [tsahng-ying]
苍蝇

(verb) fēi [fay]
飞

can we fly there? dào nàr yǒu
fēijī ma? [dow nar yoh fay-jee
mah]
到那儿有飞机吗？

fog wù
雾

foggy: it's foggy yǒu wù [yoh]
有雾

folk dancing mínjiān wúdǎo
[min-jyen woo-dow]
民间舞蹈

folk music mínjiān yīnyuè
[yin-yew-eh]
民间音乐

food shíwù [shur-woo]
食物

(in shops) shípǐn [shur-pin]
食品

food poisoning shíwù zhòngdú
[joong-doo]
食物中毒

food shop, food store shípǐn
diàn [shur-pin dyen]
食品店

foot (measurement) yīngchǐ
[ying-chur]
英尺

(of person) jiǎo [jyow]
脚

to go on foot bùxíng
[boo-hsing]
步行

football (game) zúqiúsài
[dzoo-chyoh-sai]
足球塞

(ball) zúqiú [dzoo-chyoh]
足球

**for*: do you have something
for ...?** (illness) ní yǒu yī ... de

yào ma? [yoh – dur yow mah]
你有医…的药吗？

•••••• DIALOGUES ••••••

who are the dumplings for? zhèi
xiē jiǎozi shì shéi (jiào) de? [jay
hsyeh jyow-dzur shur shay (jyow) dur]
that's for me shì wǒ de [shur wor]
and this one? zhèi gè ne? [jay gur
nur]
that's for her shì tā de [shur tah]

where do I get the bus for Beijing?
qù Běijīng zài nár zuò chē? [chew
– dzai nar dzwor chur]
the bus for Beijing leaves from
Donglu Street qù Běijīng de chē
zài Dōnglù kāi [chew – dur chur
dzai]

how long have you been here? nǐ
lái zhèr duō cháng shíjiān le? [jer
dwor chahng shur-jyen lur]
I've been here for two days, how
about you? wǒ láile liǎng tiān le,
nǐ ne? [wor lai-lur lyang tyen lur nee
nur]
I've been here for a week wǒ láile
yíge xīngqī le [yee-gur hsing-chee
lur]

Forbidden City Gùgōng
[goo-goong]
故宫
foreign wàiguó [wai-gwor]
外国

foreigner wàiguó rén [run]
外国人

Foreigners are highly conspicu-
ous in China and local people
are profoundly curious to see
them, particularly in remote rural areas. When they appear,
people run up and shout **Lǎo
Wài!** ('old outside person'), and
although this is not intended to
be rude or insulting, it can give
foreigners the uncomfortable
feeling of being like an animal
in a zoo. The best way to diffuse
this sensation is to address the
onlookers in Chinese, if you can.
Visitors who speak Chinese will
encounter an endless series of
delighted and amazed people
who will invariably ask about
their age and marital status before anything else. Even if you
don't speak Chinese, you will
run into enough locals eager to
practise their English.
Surprisingly, the main gripe of
foreign travellers concerns the
widespread Chinese attitude
that foreigners should pay double. This attitude is so deeply
rooted in the Chinese sense of
justice that you would do well
to indulge it. The average rickshaw driver would consider it
→

a humiliating defeat to carry a foreigner for the same price as a local.

Foreign teachers or students may find themselves expelled from the country for talking about politics or religion. The Chinese they talk to will be treated less leniently.

forest sēnlín [sun-lin]

森林

forget wàng [wahng]

忘

I forget, I've forgotten wǒ wàngle [wor –lur]

我忘了

fork (for eating) chā [chah]

叉

(in road) chàlù [chah-loo]

岔路

form (document) biǎo [byow]

表

formal (dress) zhèngshì [jung-shur]

正式

fortnight liǎngge xīngqī [lyang-gur hsing-chee]

两个星期

fortunately xìngkuī [hsing-kway]

幸亏

forward: could you forward my mail? nín néng bāng wǒ zhuǎn yíxià xìn ma? [nung bahng wor jwahn yee-hsyah hsin mah]

您能帮我转一下信吗?

forwarding address zhuǎnxìn dìzhǐ [jwahn-hsin dee-jur]

转信地址

fountain pēnquán [pun-chew-ahn]

喷泉

foyer xiūxītīng [hsyoh-see-ting]

休息厅

fracture (noun) gǔzhé [gyew-jur]

骨折

France Fǎguó [fah-gwor]

法国

free zìyóu [dzur-yoh]

自由

(no charge) miǎn fèi [myen fay]

免费

is it free (of charge)? miǎn fèi de ma? [dur mah]

免费的吗?

French (adj) Fǎguó [fah-gwor]

法国

(language) Fáyǔ [fah-yew]

法语

French fries zhá tǔdòu tiáo [jah too-doh tyow]

炸土豆条

frequent jīngcháng [jing-chahng]

经长

how frequent is the bus to the

Forbidden City? dào Gùgōng qù de gōnggòng qìchē duōcháng shíjiān kāi yì bān? [dow goo-goong chew dur goong-goong chee-chur dwor-chahng shur-jyen kai yee bahn]

到故宫去的公共汽车多长时间开一班？

fresh (weather, breeze) qīngxīn [ching-hsin]

清新

(fruit etc) xiān [hsyen]

鲜

fresh orange juice xiān júzhī [jyew-jur]

鲜桔汁

Friday xīngqī wǔ [hsing-chee-woo]

星期五

fridge bīngxiāng [−hsyahng]

冰箱

fried (shallow-fried) jiānde [jyen-dur]

煎的

(deep-fried) zháde [jah-dur]

炸

(stir-fried) chǎode [chow-dur]

炒

fried egg jiān jīdàn [jyen jee-dahn]

煎鸡蛋

fried noodles chǎomiàn [chow-myen]

炒面

fried rice chǎofàn [chow-fahn]

炒饭

friend péngyou [pung-yoh]

朋友

friendly yóuhǎo [yoh-how]

友好

friendship yǒuyì [yoh-yee]

友谊

friendship store yǒuyì shāngdiàn [yoh-yee shahng-dyen]

友谊商店

Friendship stores are state-run shops where you can buy genuine antiques and paintings, good silks and souvenirs. Prices are high, but you may get the occasional bargain. The larger stores have a reasonable selection of Western foodstuffs.

---

from* cóng [tsoong]

从

how far is it from here? lí zhèr duō yuǎn? [jer dwor ywahn]

离这儿多远？

when does the next train from Suzhou arrive? cóng Sūzhōu lái de xià yì bān huǒchē jídiǎn dàodá? [tsoong soo-joh lai dur hsyah yee bahn hwor-chur jee-dyen dow-dah]

从苏州来的下一班火车几点到达？

from Monday to Friday cóng xīngqī yī dào xīngqī wǔ [tsoong hsing-chee-yee dow hsing-chee]

从星期一到星期五

from next Thursday cóng xià xīngqī sì qǐ [hsyah – sur chee]

从下星期四起

•••••• DIALOGUE ••••••

where are you from? nǐ shì nár rén? [shur nar run]

I'm from Slough wǒ shì Slough láide rén [wor shur – lai-dur]

front qiánmian [chyen-myen]

前面

in front, at the front zài qiánbianr [dzai chyen-byenr]

在前边儿

in front of the hotel zài fàndiàn qiánmian [dzai fahn-dyen chyen-myen]

在饭店前面

frozen bīngdòngde [bing-doong-dur]

冰冻的

fruit shuíguǒ [shway-gwor]

水果

fruit juice guǒzhī [gwor-jur]

果汁

full mǎn [mahn]

满

it's full of ... lǐmian dōu shì ... [lee-myen doh shur]

里面都是...

I'm full wó bǎole [wor bow-lur]

我饱了

full board shì zhù quán bāo [shur joo choo-en bow]

食住全包

fun: it was fun hén hǎo wánr [hun how wahnr]

很好玩儿

funeral zànglǐ [dzahng-lee]

葬礼

funny (strange) qíguài [chee-gwai]

奇怪

(amusing) yǒu yìsi [yoh yee-sur]

有意思

(comical) huájī [hwah-jee]

滑稽

furniture jiājù [jyah-jew]

家具

further: it's further down the road zài wǎng qián zǒu [dzai wahng chyen soh]

再往前走

•••••• DIALOGUE ••••••

how much further is it to the Forbidden City? dào Gùgōng hái yǒu duōshao lù? [dow – yoh dwor-show]

about 5 kilometres dàyuē wǔ gōnglǐ (lù) [dah-yew-eh woo goong-lee]

future jiānglái [jyang-lai]

将来

in future jiānglái
将来

G

game (cards etc) yóuxì
[yoh-hshee]
游戏
(match) bǐsài
比塞
(meat) yěwèi [yur-way]
野味
garage (for fuel) jiāyóu zhàn
[jyah-yoh jahn]
加油站
(for repairs) qìchē xiūlíchǎng
[chee-chur hsyoh-lee-chahng]
汽车修理场
(for parking) chēkù [chur-koo]
车库
garden huāyuán [hwah-yew-ahn]
花园
garlic dàsuàn [dah-swahn]
大蒜
gas méiqì [may-chee]
煤气
gasoline qìyóu [chee-yoh]
气油
gas station jiāyóu zhàn
[jyah-yoh jahn]
加油站
gate dàmén [dah-mun]
大门
(at airport) dēngjìkǒu
[dung-jee-koh]
登记口

gay tóngxìngliàn
[toong-hsing-lyen]
同性恋
general (adj) yì bān [yee bahn]
一般
gents' toilet nán cèsuǒ [nahn
tsur-swor]
男厕所
genuine (antique etc) zhēnzhèng
[jun-jung]
真正
German (adj) Déguó [dur-gwor]
德国
(language) Déyǔ [dur-yew]
德语
Germany Déguó
德国
get (fetch) qǔ [chew]
取
could you get me another one,
please? qíng nǐ zài géi wǒ yí
ge hǎo ma? [ching nee dzai gay
wor yee gur how mah]
情你再给我一个好吗?
how do I get to ...? qù ...
zěnme zǒu? [chew ...
dzun-mur dzoh]
去...怎么走?
do you know where I can get
them? nǐ zhīdao wó zài nǎr
néng mǎi dào ma? [jee-dow
wor dzai nar nung mai dow mah]
你知道我在哪儿能买
到吗?

•••••• DIALOGUE ••••••

can I get you a drink? hē diǎnr shénme ma? [hur dyenr shun-mur mah]

no, I'll get this one, what would you like? zhèi huí wǒ lái mǎi, ní xiǎng hē shénme? [jay hway wor – hsyahng hur]

a glass of Maotai (lái) yì bēi Máotáijiǔ [bay]

get back huílai [hway-lai]
回来

get in (arrive) dàodá [dow-dah]
到达

get off: where do I get off? wǒ zài nár xià chē? [wor dzai nar hsyah chur]
我在哪儿下车?

get on (to train etc) shàng chē [shahng chur]
上车

get out (of car etc) xià chē [hsyah-chur]
下车

get up (in the morning) qǐchuáng [chee-chwahng]
起床

gift lǐwù [lee-woo]
礼物

If you are invited to someone's home a gift might well be expected, though people will not open it in front of you, nor will →

they express profuse gratitude for it. The Chinese way is to express gratitude through reciprocal actions rather than words, and elaborate protestations of thanks can be interpreted as an attempt to avoid obligation.

gift shop lǐwù shāngdiàn [shahng-dyen]
礼物商店

ginger shēngjiāng [shung-jyang]
生姜

girl nǚ háir [nyew]
女孩儿

girlfriend nǚ péngyou [pung-yoh]
女朋友

give gěi [gay]
给

can you give me some change? qǐng géi wǒ líng qián, hǎo ma? [ching gay wor ling chyen how mah]
请给我零钱好吗?

I gave ... to him wǒ ba ... sòng gěi tā [wor bah ... soong gay tah]
我把...送给他

will you give this to ...? qǐng ba zhèige sònggěi ...? [ching bah jay-gur soong-gay]
请把这个送给...?

give back huán [hwahn]
还

glad gāoxìng [gow-sing]
高兴

glass (material) bōli [bor-lee]
玻璃
(for drinking) bōli bēi [bay]
玻璃杯
a glass of wine yì bēi jiǔ
一杯酒

glasses yǎnjìng [yahn-jing]
眼镜

gloves shǒutào [shoh-tow]
手套

glue jiāoshuǐr [jyow-shwayr]
胶水儿

go qù [chew]
去
**we'd like to go to the
Summer Palace** wǒmen
xiǎng qù Yíhéyuán [wor-mun
hsyahng]
我门想去颐和园
where are you going? nǐ qù
nǎr?
你去哪儿？
where does this bus go? zhèi
liàng chē qù nár? [jay lyang
chur]
这辆车去哪儿？
let's go! wǒmen zǒu ba!
[wor-mun dzoh bah]
我门走吧
she's gone tā yǐjing zǒule
[tah yee-ying zoh-lur]
她已经走了
where has he gone? tā dào

nǎr qù le? [dow]
他到哪儿去了？
I went there last week wǒ shì
shàng xīngqī qù nàr de [wor
shur shahng hsing-chee]
我是上星期去儿的

go away líkāi
离开
go away! zǒu kāi! [dzoh]
走开

go back (return) huí [hway]
回

go down (the stairs etc) xià
[hsyah]
下

go in jìn
进

go out (in the evening) chūqu
[choo-chew]
出去
do you want to go out tonight?
nǐ jīntiān wǎnshang xiǎng
chūqù ma? [jin-tyen
wahn-shahng hsyahng – mah]
你今天晚上想出去吗？

go through chuān [chwahn]
穿

go up (the stairs etc) shàng
[shahng]
上

God shàngdì
上帝

gold (metal) huángjīn
[hwahng-jin]
黄金

(colour) jīnsè [jin-sur]

金色

good hǎo [how]

好

good! hǎo!

好

it's no good bù hǎo

不好

goodbye zàijiàn [dzai-jyen]

再见

good evening ní hǎo [how]

你好

good morning ní zǎo [zow]

你早

good night wǎn'ān [wahn-ahn]

晚安

goose é [ur]

鹅

got: we've got to leave wǒmen déi zǒu le [wor-mun day zoh lur]

我门得走了

have you got any ...? ní yǒu ... ma? [yoh ... mah]

你有...吗？

government zhèngfǔ [jung-foo]

政府

gradually jiànjiàn de [jyen-jyen dur]

渐渐的

grammar yúfǎ [yew-fah]

语法

gram(me) kè [kur]

克

granddaughter (daughter's daughter) wàisūnnǔr [wai-sun-nyewr]

外孙女儿

(son's daughter) sūnnǔr

孙女儿

grandfather (maternal) wàigōng [wai-goong]

外公

(paternal) yéye [yur-yur]

爷爷

grandmother (maternal) wàipó [wai-por]

外婆

(paternal) nǎinai

奶奶

grandson (daughter's son) wài sūnzi [sun-dzur]

外孙子

(son's son) sūnzi

孙子

grapefruit pútáoyòu [poo-tow-yoh]

葡萄柚

grapes pútáo [poo-tow]

葡萄

grass cǎo [tsow]

草

grateful gǎnjī [gahn-jee]

感激

great (excellent) hǎojíle [how-jee-lur]

好极了

a great success **jùdà chéngjiù** [joo-dah chung-jyoh]
巨大成就

greedy (for money etc) **tānxīn** [tahn-hsin]
贪心
(for food) **chán** [chahn]
馋

green lǜsè(de) [lyew-sur(-dur)]
绿色的

greengrocer's càidiàn [tsai-dyen]
菜店

---

greetings

The Chinese do not have elaborate methods of greeting, although the shaking of hands is quite common among men. It is very common to see young men and women displaying affection for a friend of the same sex. This can involve holding hands or even stroking legs. Generally the Chinese are less physical in their affections between the sexes than Westerners and are embarrassed by over-enthusiastic displays of affection by Western couples.

---

grey huīsè(de) [hway-sur(-dur)]
灰色的

grilled kǎo [kow]
烤

grocer's záhuòdiàn [dzah-hwor-dyen]
杂货店

ground: on the ground zài dì shàng [dzai dee shahng]
在地上

ground floor yī lóu [loh]
一楼

group (tourist etc) **cānguāntuán** [tsahn-gwahn-twahn]
参观团
(study, work etc) **xiáozǔ** [hsyow-dzew]
小组

guarantee (noun) **bǎozhèng** [bow-jung]
保证
is it guaranteed? bǎo bù bǎoxiū? [bow – hsyoh]
保不保修?

guest kèrén [kur-run]
客人

guesthouse bīnguǎn [bing-wahn]
宾馆
see **hotel**

guide (tour guide) **dǎoyóu** [dow-yoh]
导游

guidebook dǎoyóu shǒucè [shoh-tsur]
导游手册

guided tour yóu dǎoyóu de yóulǎn [yoh – dur yoh-lahn]
有导游的游览

guitar jítā [jee-tah]
吉他

gum (in mouth) chǐyín [chur-yin]
齿龈

gym tǐyùguǎn [tee-yoo-gwahn]
体育馆

H

hair tóufa [toh-fah]
头发

haircut lǐfà [lee-fah]
理发

hairdresser's lǐfàdiàn
[dyen]
理发店

hairdryer diànchuīfēng
[dyen-chway-fung]
电吹风

hair spray pēnfàjì [pun-fah-jee]
喷发剂

half* (adj) bàn [bahn]
半
(noun) yí bàn
一半

half an hour bàn xiǎoshí
[hsyow-shur]
半小时

half a litre bàn shēng [shung]
半升

about half that nàme yí bàn
[nah-mur]
那么一半

half board bàn shísù [shur-soo]
半食宿

half-bottle bàn píng
半瓶

half fare bànfèi [bahn-fay]
半费

half price bànjià [bahn-jyah]
半价

ham huótuǐ [hwor-tway]
火腿

hamburger niúròubǐng [nyoh-roh-bing]
牛肉饼

hand shǒu [shoh]
手

handbag shǒutíbāo
[shoh-tee-bow]
手提包

handkerchief shǒujuànr
[shoh-jwahnr]
手绢儿

hand luggage shǒutí xíngli
[shoh-tee hsing-lee]
手提行李

happen fāshēng [fah-shung]
发生

what's happening? zěnme huí
shìr? [dzun-mur hway shur]
怎么回事儿?

what has happened? fāshēng
le shénme shìr la? [fah-shung
lur shun-mur lah]
发生了什么事儿啦?

happy kuàilè [kwai-lur]
快乐

I'm not happy about this wǒ
duì zhèige bù mǎnyì [wor

dway jay-gur boo mahn-yee]

我对这个不满意

harbour gángkǒu [gahng-koh]

港口

hard yìng

硬

(difficult) nán [nahn]

难

hardly: hardly ever hén shǎo

[hun show]

很少

hard seat yìngxí [ying-

hshee]

硬席

see **train**

hardware shop wǔjīn (shāng)

diàn [woo-jin (shahng) dyen]

五金(商)店

hat màozi [mow-dzur]

帽子

hate (verb) hèn [hun]

恨

have* yǒu [yoh]

有

can I have a ...? (asking for

something) qǐng gěi wǒ ...

hǎo ma? [ching gay wor ... how]

请给我...好吗?

(ordering food) qǐng lái ..., hǎo

ma? [ching]

请来...好吗?

(in shop) wó xiáng mǎi ...

[wor hsyahng]

我想买...

do you have ...? nímen

yǒu ... ma? [nee-mun yoh ...

mah]

你们有...吗?

what'll you have? ní xiǎng hē

shénme? [hsyahng hur

shun-mur]

你想喝什么?

I have to leave now wó déi

zǒu le [wor day dzoh lur]

我得走了

do I have to ...? wó déi ...

ma?

我得...吗?

hayfever huāfěnrè

[hwah-fun-rur]

花粉热

he* tā [tah]

他

head tóu [toh]

头

headache tóuténg [toh-tung]

头疼

health

There is no point in getting
paranoid about your health
while travelling in China but
it's worth being aware of the
dangers and taking sensible
precautions. It's advisable not
to walk around in bare feet and
to wear flip-flops in the shower.
As for food, the two most important considerations are to eat at
places which look busy and →

clean, and to stick to fresh, thoroughly cooked food. Seafood is risky as the water pollution levels in China are high. Fresh fruit you've peeled yourself is safe; other uncooked foods are risky. The other thing to watch out for is dirty chopsticks; the disposable chopsticks provided in most restaurants are fine, but if you want to be really sure, bring your own pair.

Probably the biggest hazard to your health in China is the host of flu infections that strike down a large proportion of the population, mostly in the winter months. The problem is compounded by the overcrowded conditions, chain smoking, pollution and the widespread habit of spitting.

Parts of China are tropical and here it can require a couple of weeks to acclimatize to the temperature and humidity. High humidity causes heat rashes, prickly heat and fungal infections. Prevention and cure are the same: wear loose clothes made of natural fibres, wash frequently and dry off thoroughly afterwards. Talcum powder and the use of mild antiseptic soap →

helps too. And don't underestimate the strength of the sun in tropical areas such as Hainan Island, in desert regions such as Xinjiang or very high up, for example on the Tibetan plateau. At the other extreme, there are plenty of parts of China that get very cold indeed. If you're trekking in Tibet or visiting northern China during the winter, it is essential to be prepared. Hypothermia is sometimes fatal. To prevent the condition, wear lots of layers and a hat, and try to stay dry and out of the wind.
see **water** and **mosquito**

hear tīngjian [ting-jyen]
听见

• • • • • • DIALOGUE • • • • • •

can you hear me? nǐ néng tīngjiàn ma? [nung ting-jyen mah]
I can't hear you, could you repeat that? duìbuqǐ, tīngbujiàn, nǐ néng zài shuō yí biàn ma? [dway-boo-chee ting-boo-jyen – dzai shwor yee byen]

hearing aid zhùtīngqì [joo-ting-chee]
助听器
heart xīnzàng [hsin-dzahng]
心脏

heart attack xīnzàngbìng
[–bing]
心脏病

heat rè [rur]
热

heater sànrèqì [sahn-rur-chee]
散热器

heating nuǎnqì [nwahn-chee]
暖器

heavy zhòng [joong]
重

heel (of foot) jiǎogēn [jyow-gun]
脚跟

(of shoe) xié hòugēn [hsyeh]
鞋后跟

could you heel these? qíng
géi wǒ dǎ hòugēn, hǎo ma?
[ching gay wor dah – how mah]
请给我打后跟好吗？

heelbar xiūxiépù
[hsyoh-hsyeh-poo]
修鞋铺

helicopter zhíshēng fēijī
[jur-shung fay-jee]
直升飞机

hello ní hǎo [nee how]
你好

(answer on phone) wéi [way]
喂

help bāngzhù [bahng-joo]
帮助

help! jiùmìng! [jyoh-ming]
救命

can you help me? nǐ néng bù
néng bāngzhù wǒ? [nung

bahng-joo wor]
你能不能帮助我？

**thank you very much for your
help** xièxie nǐde bāngzhù
[hsyeh-hsyeh nee-dur]
谢谢你的帮助

helpful bāngle bú shǎo máng
[bahng-lur boo show mahng]
帮了不少忙

hepatitis gānyán [gah-nyen]
肝炎

her* tā [tah]
她

that's her towel nà shì tāde
máojīn [nah shur tah-dur
mow-jin]
那是她的毛巾

herbs (for cooking) zuǒliào
[dzwor-lyow]
作料

(medicinal) cǎoyào [tsow-yow]
草药

here zhèr [jer]
这儿

here is/are ... zhèr shì ...
[shur]
这儿是...

here you are géi nǐ [gay]
给你

hers* tāde [tah-dur]
她的

that's hers zhè shì tāde [jur
shur]
这是她的

hey! hēi! [hay]
嘿

hi! (hello) ní hǎo! [how]
你好

high gāo [gow]
高

hill shān [shahn]
山

him* tā [tah]
他

hip túnbù [tun-boo]
臀部

hire (bike, car) zū [dzoo]
租

(guide, interpreter) gù
顾

for hire chūzū [choo-dzoo]
出租

where can I hire a bike? zài
nǎr néng zū dào zìxíngchē?
[dzai nar nung zoo dow
dzi-hsing-chur]
在那儿能租到自行车？

his* tāde [tah-dur]
他的

hit (verb) dǎ [dah]
打

hitch-hike dā biànchē
[byen-chur]
搭便车

hobby shìhào [shur-how]
嗜好

hole dòng [doong]
洞

holiday (public) jiàqī [jyah-chee]
假期

(festival) jiérì [jyeh-ree]
节日

on holiday dùjià [doo-jyah]
度假

home jiā
家

at home (in my house etc) zài jiā
[dzai]
在家

we go home tomorrow (to
country) wǒmen míngtiān huí
guó [wor-mun ming-tyen hway
gwor]
我们明天回国

honest chéngshí [chung-shur]
诚实

honey fēngmì [fung-mee]
蜂蜜

honeymoon mìyuè [mee-
yew-eh]
蜜月

Hong Kong Xiānggǎng
[hsyahng-gahng]
香港

hope xīwàng [hshee-wahng]
希望

I hope so wǒ xīwàng shì
zhèi yàng [wor – shur jay
yang]
我希望是这样

I hope not wǒ xīwàng bú shì
zhèi yàng
我希望不是这样

hopefully xīwàng rúcǐ
[hshee-wahng roo-tsur]
希望如此

horrible kěpà [kur-pah]
可怕

horse mǎ [mah]
马

horse riding qí mǎ [chee]
骑马

hospital yīyuàn [yee-yew-ahn]
医院

hospitality hàokè [how-kur]
好客

thank you for your hospitality
xièxie nínde shèngqíng
kuǎndài [hsyeh-hsyeh nin-dur
shung-ching kwahn-dai]
谢谢您的盛情款代

hot rè [rur]
热

(spicy) là [lah]
辣

I'm hot wǒ juéde hěn rè [wor
jyew-eh-dur hun rur]
我觉得很热

it's hot today jīntiān hěn rè
[jin-tyen]
今天很热

hotel (small) lǚguǎn
[lyew-gwahn]
旅馆

(luxury) fàndiàn [fahn-dyen]
饭店

In Chinese there are several different words for hotel, which give a vague indication of the status of the place. A more upmarket hotel might be called **dà jiǔlóu** or **dà jiǔdiàn**, which translates as something like 'big wine bar'. The far more common term **bīnguǎn** is similarly used for smart new establishments. **Fàndiàn** (literally: restaurant) is the least reliable term as it is used fairly indiscriminately for top-class hotels, as well as humble and obscure ones. Reliably downmarket – and rarely accepting foreigners – is **zhāodàisuǒ**, while the humblest of all is **lǚguǎn** (sometimes translated as 'inn'), where you might occasionally get to stay in some rural areas.

In the larger cities – including virtually all provincial capitals – you'll find upmarket four- or five-star hotels, often managed by foreigners and offering all the usual international facilities. Mid-range hotels will generally have clean, spacious, standard double rooms with attached bathroom, 24-hour hot water, TV and air-conditioning, but often have dodgy plumbing, poor
→

temperature control and insufficient lift capacity. Single rooms are rarely available.

In budget hotels, you'll notice that the local Chinese routinely rent beds rather than rooms doubling up with one or more strangers – as a means of saving money. Foreigners are only very occasionally allowed to share rooms with Chinese people, but tourist centres tend to have one or two budget hotels with special foreigners' dormitory accommodation. Cheap hotels are often perfectly comfortable, but hot water is usually available for only limited hours in the evening, and you would be advised not to leave valuables in the rooms.

Guests are not normally entrusted with keys; instead reception gives you a ticket which you hand to the floor attendant, who opens the door for you. It is normal to pay in full for the room when you check in; a refundable deposit against theft or damage is nearly always required at the same time.

Some hotels have arbitrary rules stipulating that foreigners pay as much as a hundred per cent →

extra. With polite, friendly bargaining, it is possible to reduce or eliminate such surcharges.

Whatever type of hotel you are staying in, there are two things you can rely on. One is a pair of plastic slippers under the bed that you use for walking to the bathroom, and the other is a Thermos of drinkable water that can be refilled any time by the floor attendant.

Checking into a hotel involves filling in a detailed form. Upmarket hotels have English versions of these forms, but hotels unaccustomed to foreigners usually have them in Chinese only. Filling in forms correctly is a serious business in bureaucratic China and if potential guests are unable to carry out this duty, they may not be allowed to stay.

hour xiǎoshí [hsyow-shur]
小时
house fángzi [fahng-dzur]
房子
how zěnme [dzun-mur]
怎么 ?
how many? (if answer is likely to be more than ten) duōshao?
[dwor-show]
多少 ?

(if answer is likely to be ten or less)
jǐge? [jee-gur]
几个 ?
how do you do? ní hǎo [how]
你好?

•••••• DIALOGUES ••••••

how are you? ní hǎo ma? [mah]
fine, thanks, and you? hén hǎo, nǐ ne? [hun – nur]

how much is it? duōshao qián? [chyen]
17 yuan shí qī kuài [shur chee kwai]
I'll take it wǒ mǎi [wor]

humid cháoshī [chow-shur]
潮湿
hungry è [ur]
饿
are you hungry? nǐ èle ma? [ur-lur mah]
你饿了吗?
hurry: I'm in a hurry wó hên jímáng de [wor hun jee-mahng dur]
我很急忙的
there's no hurry mànmàn lái [mahn-mahn]
慢慢来
hurry up! kuài diǎnr! [kwai dyenr]
快点儿
hurt (verb) téng [tung]
疼

it really hurts zhēn téng [jun tung]
真疼
husband zhàngfu [jahng-foo]
丈夫

I

I wǒ [wor]
我
ice bīng
冰
with ice jiā bīngkuàir [jyah bing-kwair]
加冰块儿
no ice, thanks bù jiā bīngkuàir, xièxie [boo jyah bing-kwair hsyeh-hsyeh]
不加冰块儿谢谢
ice cream bīngqílín [bing-chee-lin]
冰淇淋
ice-cream cone dànjuǎnr bīngqílín [dahn-jyew-ahnr]
蛋卷儿冰淇淋
ice lolly bīnggùnr [bing-gunr]
冰棍儿
idea zhǔyì [joo-yee]
主意
idiot shǎguā [shah-gwah]
傻瓜
if rúguǒ [roo-gwor]
如果
ill bìngle [bing-lur]
病了

I feel ill wǒ juéde bù shūfu [wor jyew-eh-dur]

我觉得不舒服

illness jíbìng

疾病

imitation (leather etc) fǎng [fahng]

仿

immediately mǎshàng [mah-shahng]

马上

important zhòngyào [joong-yow]

重要

it's very important hěn zhòngyào [hun joong-yow]

很重要

it's not important bú zhòngyào

不重要

impossible bù kěnéng [kur-nung]

不可能

impressive (building, view) xióngwěi [hsyoong-way]

雄伟

improve tígāo [tee-gow]

提高

I want to improve my Chinese wó xiǎng tígāo wǒde Hàyǔ shuǐpíng [wor hsyahng – wor-dur hah-yew shway-ping]

我想提高我的汉语水平

in*: it's in the centre zài zhōngjiān [dzai joong-jyen]

在中间

in my car zài wǒde chē lǐ [wor-dur chur lee]

在我的车里

in London zài Lúndūn

在伦敦

in two days from now liǎng tiān zhī hòu [tyen jur hoh]

两天之后

in five minutes wǔ fēn zhōng (zhī) nèi [fun joong (jur) nay]

五分钟（之）内

in May zài wǔyuè

在五月

in English yòng Yīngyǔ

用英语

in Chinese yòng Hànyǔ

用汉语

is Mr Li in? Li xiānsheng zài ma? [hsyahng-shung dzai mah]

李先生在吗？

inch yīngcùn [ying-tsun]

英寸

include bāokuò [bow-kwor]

包括

does that include meals? zhè bāokuò fàn qián ma? [jur-fahn chyen mah]

这包括饭钱吗？

is that included? nèige yě bāokuò zài nèi ma? [nay-gur yur]

那个也包括在内吗？

inconvenient bù fāngbiàn
[fahng-byen]
不方便

India Yìndù [yin-doo]
印度

Indian (adj) Yìndù
印度

indigestion xiāohuà bù liáng
[hsyow-hwah boo lyang]
消化不良

Indonesia Yìndùníxīyà
[yin-doo-nee-hshee-yah]
印度尼西亚

indoor pool shìnèi yóuyǒngchí
[shur-nay yoh-yoong-chur]
室内游泳池

indoors shìnèi [shur-nay]
室内

inexpensive piányi [pyen-yee]
便宜

infection gǎnrǎn [gahn-rahn]
感染

infectious chuánrǎn
[chwahn-rahn]
传染

inflammation fāyán [fah-
yen]
发炎

informal (clothes) suíbiàn
[sway-byen]
随便

(occasion) fēi zhèngshì [fay
jung-shur]
非正式

information xiāoxi

[hsyow-hshee]
消息

do you have any information
about ...? ní yǒu guānyú ...
de xiāoxi ma? [nee yoh
gwahn-yew dur – mah]
你有关于...的消息吗？

information desk wènxùnchù
[wun-hsyewn-choo]
问讯处

injection dǎzhēn [dah-jun]
打针

injured shòushāng
[shoh-shahng]
受伤

she's been injured tā
shòushāng le [tah – lur]
她受伤了

inner tube (for tyre) nèitāi [nay–]
内胎

innocent wúgū
无辜

insect kūnchóng [kun-choong]
昆虫

insect bite chóngzi yǎo de
[choong-dzur yow dur]
虫子咬的

do you have anything for
insect bites? yǒu yī chóng
yǎo de yào ma? [yoh yee
'choong yow dur yow mah]
有医虫咬的药吗？

insect repellent qūchóngjì
[chew-choong-jee]
驱虫剂

inside* zài ... lǐ [dzai ... lee]
在 ... 里
inside the hotel zài lǚguǎn lǐmiàn
在旅馆里面
let's sit inside wǒmen jìnqù zuò ba [wor-mun jin-chew dzwor bah]
我们进去坐吧
insist: I insist wǒ jiānchí [wor jyen-chur]
我坚持
instant coffee sùróng kāfēi [soo-roong kah-fay]
速溶咖啡
insulin yídǎosù [yee-dow-soo]
胰岛素
insurance báoxiǎn [bow-hsyen]
保险
intelligent cōngming [tsoong-ming]
聪明
interested: I'm interested in ... wǒ duì ... hén gǎn xìngqù [wor dway ... hun gahn hsing-chew]
我对...很感兴趣
interesting yǒu yìsi [yoh yee-sur]
有意思
that's very interesting hén yǒu yìsi [hun]
很有意思
international guójì [gwor-jee]
国际

interpreter fānyìzhě [fahn-yee-jur]
翻译者
intersection (US) shízì lùkǒu [shur-dzur loo-koh]
十字路口
interval (at theatre) mùjiān xiūxi [moo-jyen hsyoh-hshee]
幕间休息
into: I'm not into ... wǒ duì ... bù gǎn xìngqù [wor dway ... boo gahn hsing-chew]
我对...不感兴趣
introduce jièshào [jyeh-show]
介绍
may I introduce ...? wǒ lái jièshào yíxià, zhèi wèi shì ... [wor – yee-hsyah jay-way shur]
我来介绍一下这位是...
invitation yāoqǐng [yow-ching]
邀请
invite yāoqǐng
邀请
Ireland Ài'ěrlán [ai-er-lahn]
爱尔兰
Irish Ài'ěrlán [ai-er-lahn]
爱尔兰
I'm Irish wǒ shì Ài'ěrlán rén [wor shur ai-er-lahn run]
我是爱尔兰人
iron (for ironing) yùndǒu [yewn-doh]
熨斗

can you iron these for me?
qǐng nǐ bāng wǒ yùnyùn zhè
xié yīfu, hǎo ma? [ching nee
bahng wor yun-yun jur hsyeh
yee-foo how mah]
请你帮我熨熨这些衣
服好吗？

is* shì [shur]
是

island dǎo [dow]
岛

it tā [tah]
它

it is ..., it was ... shì ... [shur]
是...

is it ...? shì ... ma? [mah]
是...吗？

where is it? zài nǎr? [dzai]
在哪儿？

Italian (adj) Yìdàlì [yee-dah-lee]
意大利

Italy Yìdàlì
意大利

itch: it itches fāyǎng de (fa-yang
dur]
发痒的

J

jacket jiākè [jyah-kur]
茄克

jade yù [yew]
玉

jam guǒjiàng [gwor-jyang]
果酱

January yīyuè [yee-yew-eh]
一月

Japan Rìběn [ree-bun]
日本

jar guànzi [gwahn-dzur]
罐子

jasmine tea mòlìhuā chá
[mor-lee hwah chah]
茉莉花茶

jaw xiàba [hsyah-bah]
下巴

jazz juéshì yīnyuè [jyew-eh-shur
yin-yew-eh]
爵士音乐

jealous jìdù
忌妒

jeans niúzǎikù [nyoh-dzai-koo]
牛仔裤

jetty mǎtóu [mah-toh]
码头

jeweller's zhūbǎo (shāng)diàn
[joo-bow (shahng-)dyen]
珠宝(商)店

jewellery zhūbǎo
珠宝

Jewish Yóutàirén de
[yoh-tai-run dur]
犹太人的

job gōngzuò [goong-dzwor]
工作

jogging pǎobù [pow-boo]
跑步

to go jogging qù pǎobù
[chew]
去跑步

joke wánxiào [wahn-hsyow]

玩笑

journey lǚxíng [lyew-sing]

旅行

have a good journey! yílù shùnfēng! [shun-fung]

一路顺风

jug guàn [gwahn]

罐

a jug of water yí guànr shuǐ

一罐儿水

July qīyuè [chee-yew-eh]

七月

jumper tàoshān [tow-shahn]

套衫

junction (road) jiāochākǒu [jyow-chah-koh]

交叉口

June liùyuè [lyoh-yew-eh]

六月

just (only just) jínjǐn

尽尽

(with numbers) zhǐ [jur]

只

just two zhǐ yào liǎngge [yow]

只要两个

just for me jiù wǒ yào [jyoh wor]

就我要

just here jiù zài zhèr [dzai jer]

就在这儿

not just now xiànzài bùxíng [hsyen-dzai boo-hsing]

现在不行

we've just arrived wǒmen gāng dào [wor-mun gahng dow]

我们刚到

K

keep liú [lyoh]

留

keep the change búyòng zhǎo le [boo-yoong jow lur]

不用找了

can I keep it? wó kéyi liúzhe ma? [wor kur-yee lyoh-jur mah]

我可以留着吗？

please keep it qǐng liúzhe ba [ching – bah]

请留着吧

kettle shuǐhú [shway-hoo]

水壶

key yàoshi [yow-shur]

钥匙

the key for room 201, please qǐng géi wǒ èr líng yāo fáng de yàoshi [ching gay wor er ling yow fahng dur yow-shur]

请给我二零一房的钥匙

see hotel

keyring yàoshi quān [yow-shur choo-en]

钥匙圈

kidneys (in body) shènzàng [shun-dzahng]

肾脏

(food) yāozi [yow-dzur]

腰子

kill shā [shah]

杀

kilo gōngjīn [goong-jin]

公斤

kilometre gōnglǐ [goong-lee]

公里

how many kilometres is it to ...? qù ... yǒu daōshao gōnglǐ? [chew ... yoh dow-show]

去...有多少公里?

kind (type) zhǒng [joong]

种

that's very kind nǐ zhēn hǎo [nee jun how]

你真好

• • • • • DIALOGUE • • • • •

which kind do you want? nǐ yào nǎ yí zhǒng? [yow nah]

I want this/that kind wǒ yào zhèi/nèi yí zhǒng [wor yow jay/nay]

king guówáng [gwor-wahng]

国王

kiosk shòuhuòtíng [shoh-hwor-ting]

售货亭

kiss wěn [wun]

吻

kitchen chúfáng [choo-fahng]

厨房

Kleenex® zhǐjīn [jur-jin]

纸巾

knee xīgài [hshee-gai]

膝盖

knickers sānjiǎokù [sahn-jyow-koo]

三角裤

knife dāozi [dow-dzur]

刀子

knock (verb) qiāo [chyow]

敲

knock over (object) dǎ fān [dah fahn]

打翻

(pedestrian) zhuàng dǎo [jwahng dow]

撞倒

know (somebody) rènshi [run-shur]

认识

(something, a place) zhīdao [jur-dow]

知道

I don't know wǒ bù zhīdao

我不知道

I didn't know that nà wǒ bù zhīdao [nah]

那我不知道

do you know where I can buy ...? nǐ zhīdao wǒ zài nǎr néng mǎi dào ...? [wor dzai nar nung mai dow]

你知道我在哪儿能买到...?

Korean (adj) Cháoxiān [chow-hsyen]

朝鲜

L

lacquerware qīqì [chee-chee]
漆器

ladies' room, ladies' toilets nǚ
cèsuǒ [nyew tsur-swor]
女厕所

ladies' wear nǚzhuāng
[nyew-jwahng]
女装

lady nǚshì [nyew-shur]
女氏

lager píjiǔ [pee-jyoh]
啤酒
see **beer**

lake hú [hoo]
湖

lamb (meat) yángròu [yang-roh]
羊肉

lamp dēng [dung]
灯

lane (motorway) chēdào
[chur-dow]
车道
(small road) hútòng [hoo-toong]
胡同

language yǔyán [yew-yen]
语言

language course yǔyán kè
[kur]
语言课

Laos Lǎowō [low-wor]
老挝

large dà [dah]
大

last (final) zuìhòu [dzway-hoh]
最后

last week shàng xīngqī
[shahng hsing-chee]
上星期

last Friday shàng xīngqī wǔ
上星期五

last night zuótiān
wǎnshang [dzwor-tyen
wahn-shahng]
昨天晚上

**what time is the last train to
Beijing?** qù Běijīng de
zuìhòu yì bān huǒchē jí
diǎn kāi? [chew – dur
dzway-hoh yur bahn hwor-chur
jee dyen]
去北京的最后一班火
车几点开?

late (at night) wǎn [wahn]
晚
(delayed) chí [chur]
迟

sorry I'm late duìbuqǐ, wǒ lái
wǎnle [dway-boo-chee wor lai
wahn-lur]
对不起我来晚了

the train was late huǒchē lái
wǎnle [hwor-chur]
火车来晚了

we must go – we'll be late
wǒmen děi zǒule láibujíle
[wor-mun day dzoh-lur
lai-boo-jee-lur]
我们得走了来不极了

it's getting late bù zǎole
[dzow-lur]

不早了

later hòulái [hoh-lai]

后来

I'll come back later wǒ guò
yìhuǐr zài lái [wor gwor
yee-hwayr dzai]

我过一会儿再来

see you later huítóujiàn
[hway-toh-jyen]

回头见

later on hòulái

后来

latest zuìhòu [dzway-hoh]

最后

(most recent) zuìjìn [dzway-jin]

最近

by Wednesday at the latest
zuìhòu xīngqīsān

最后星期三

laugh (verb) xiào [hsyow]

笑

laundry (clothes) xǐyī [hshee-yee]

洗衣

(place) xǐyīdiàn [–dyen]

洗衣店

lavatory cèsuǒ [tsur-swor]

厕所

law fǎlǜ [fah-lyew]

法律

lawyer lǜshī [lyew-shur]

律师

laxative xièyào [hsyeh-hyow]

泄药

lazy lǎn [lahn]

懒

lead: where does this road
lead to? zhè tiáo lù tōng nǎr
qù? [jur tyow loo toong nar
chew]

这条路通哪儿去?

leak: the roof leaks wūdǐng
lòule [woo-ding loh-lur]

屋顶漏了

learn xuéxí [hsyew-eh-hshee]

学习

least: not in the least yīdiǎnr
dōu bù [yee-dyenr doh bu]

一点儿都不

at least zhìshǎo [jee-show]

至少

leather pígé [pee-gur]

皮革

leave (depart) zǒu [dzoh]

走

I am leaving tomorrow wǒ
míngtiān zǒu [wor ming-tyen]

我明天走

when does the bus for Beijing
leave? qù Běijīng de qìchē jí
diǎn kāi? [chew – dur chee-chur
jee dyen]

去北京的汽车几点开?

may I leave this here? wǒ
néng bǎ zhèige liú zài zhèr
ma? [wor nung bah jay-gur lyoh
dzai jer mah]

我能把这个留在这儿
吗?

he left yesterday tā shì zuótiān líkāi de [tah shur dzwor-tyen lee-kai dur]

他是昨天离开的

I left my coat in the bar wǒ ba wǒde dàyī liú zài jiǔbājiān [bah wor-dur dah-yee lyoh dzai jyoh-bah-jyen]

我把我的大衣留在酒吧间

there's none left shénme dōu wánle [shun-mur doh wahn-lur]

什么都完了

left zuǒ [dzwor]

左

on the left zài zuǒbiānr [dzai dzwor-byenr]

在左边儿

to the left wáng zuǒ [wahng]

往左

turn left wáng zuó guǎi [gwai]

往左拐

left-handed zuópiězi [dzwor-pyeh-dzur]

左撇子

left luggage (office) xíngli jìcúnchù [hsing-lee jee-tsun-choo]

行李寄存处

Most big hotels have reliable left luggage offices for those who have checked out and are awaiting an evening departure.

leg tuǐ [tway]

腿

lemon níngméng [ning-mung]

柠檬

lemonade níngméng qìshuǐr [chee-shwayr]

柠檬汽水儿

lemon tea níngméngchá [–chah]

柠檬茶

lend jiè [jyeh]

借

will you lend me your ...?
qǐng ba nǐde ... jiè géi wǒ [ching bah nee-dur ... jyeh gay wor]

请把你的...借给我?

lens (of camera) jìngtóu [jing-toh]

镜头

less shǎo [show]

少

less than ... bǐ ... shǎo

比...少

less expensive than ...
bǐ ... piányi [pyen-yee]

比...便宜

lesson kè [kur]

课

let: will you let me know? nǐ dào shíhou gàosu wǒ, hǎo ma? [dow shur-hoh gow-soo wor how mah]

你到时候告诉我好吗?

I'll let you know wǒ dào shíhou gàosu nǐ

我到时候告诉你

let's go for something to eat chīfàn, ba [chur-fahn bah]

吃饭吧

let off: will you let me off at ...? wǒ zài ... xià, xíng ma? [dzai ... hsyah hsing]

我在...下行吗？

letter xìn [hsin]

信

do you have any letters for me? yǒu xìn, ma? [yoh hsin mah]

有信吗？

letterbox xìnxiāng [hsin-hsyahng]

信箱

see **postal service**

library túshūguǎn [too-shoo-gwahn]

图书馆

lid gàir [gair]

盖儿

lie (tell untruth) shuōhuǎng [shwor-hwahng]

说谎

lie down tǎng [tahng]

躺

life shēnghuó [shung-hwor]

生活

lifebelt jiùshēngquān [jyoh-shung-choo-en]

救生圈

lifeguard jiùshēngyuán [jyoh-shung-yew-ahn]

救生员

life jacket jiùshēngyī [jyoh-shung-yee]

救生衣

lift (in building) diàntī [dyen-tee]

电梯

could you give me a lift? nǐ néng bù néng ràng wǒ dāge chē? [nung – rahng wor dah-gur chur]

你能不能让我搭个车？

light (noun) dēng [dung]

灯

(not heavy) qīng [ching]

轻

do you have a light? (for cigarette) nǐ yǒu huǒchái ma? [nur yoh hwor-chai mah]

你有火柴吗？

light bulb dēngpào [dung-pow]

灯泡

I need a new light bulb wǒ xūyào yíge dēngpào [wor hsyoo-yow yee-gur]

我须要一个灯泡

lighter (cigarette) dáhuǒjī [dah-hwor-jee]

打火机

lightning shǎndiàn [shahn-dyen]

闪电

like xǐhuan [hshee-hwahn]

喜欢

I like it wó xǐhuan [wor]

我喜欢

I don't like it wǒ bù xǐhuan

我不喜欢

I like you wó xǐhuan nǐ

我喜欢你

do you like ...? ní xǐhuan ...
ma? [mah]

你喜欢...吗？

I'd like a beer wó xiǎng hē
yìpíng píjiǔ [hsyahng hur
yee-ping]

我想喝一瓶啤酒

I'd like to go swimming wó
xiǎng yóuyǒng

我想游泳

would you like a drink? ní
xiǎng hē diǎnr shénme? [hur
dyenr shun-mur]

你想喝点儿什么？

would you like to go for a
walk? ní xiǎng bu xiǎng qù
zǒuyizǒu? [chew dzoh-yee-
dzoh]

你想不想去走一走？

what's it like? tā xiàng
shénme? [tah]

它象什么？

I want one like this wǒ yào
tónglèide [yow toong-lay-dur]

我要同类的

line xiàn [hsyen]

线

could you give me an outside
line? qíng gěi wǒ wàixiàn,

hǎo ma? [ching gay wor
wai-hsyen how mah]

请给我外线好吗？

lips chún

唇

lip salve chúngāo [chun-gow]

唇膏

lipstick kǒuhóng [koh-hoong]

口红

listen tīng

听

litre shēng [shung]

升

little xiǎo [hsyow]

小

just a little, thanks jiù yìdiǎnr,
xièxie [jyoh yee-dyenr
hsyeh-hsyeh]

就一点儿谢谢

a little milk yìdiǎnr níunǎi
[nyoh-nai]

一点儿牛奶

a little bit more duō yìdiǎnr
[dwor yee-dyenr]

多一点儿

live (verb) zhù [joo]

住

we live together wǒmen zhù
zài yìqǐ [wor-mun joo dzai
yee-chee]

我们住在一起

where do you live? nǐ zhù zài
nǎr? [joo dzai]

I live in London wǒ zhù zài
Lúndūn [wor]

lively (person) huópo [hwor-por]
活波

(town) rènao [rur-now]
热闹

liver (in body, food) gān [gahn]
肝

lobby (in hotel) qiántīng
[chyen-ting]
前厅

lobster lóngxiā [loong-hsyah]
龙虾

local dìfāngde [dee-fahng-dur]
地方的

lock suǒ [swor]
锁

it's locked suǒshang le [swor
shahng lur]
锁上了

lock out: I've locked myself out
wǒ guān zài ménwài le [wor
gwahn dzai mun-wai lur]
我关在门外了

locker (for luggage etc)
xiǎochúguì [hsyow-choo-gway]
小橱柜

London Lúndūn
伦敦

long cháng [chahng]
长

how long does it take? yào
duōchang shíjian? [yow
dwor-chahng shur-jyen]
要多长时间?

how long will it take to fix it?
ba zhèige dōngxi xiūlí hǎo
yào duōchang shíjian? [bah
jay-gur doong-hshee hsyoo-lee
hao]
把这个东西修理好要
多长时间?

a long time hěn cháng
shíjian [hun]
很长时间

one day/two days longer yí/
liǎng tiān duō [tyen dwor]
一/两天多

long-distance call chángtú
diànhuà [chahng-too
dyen-hwah]
长途电话

look: I'm just looking, thanks wǒ
zhǐshi kànyikàn, xièxie [wor
jur-shur kahn-yee-kahn
hsyeh-hsyeh]
我只是看一看谢谢

you don't look well kànqǐlái,
nǐ shēntǐ bù jiànkāng
[kahn-chee-lai nee shun-tee boo
jyen-kahng]
看起来你身体不健康

look out! xiǎoxīn! [hsyow-hsin]
小心

can I have a look? kéyi
kànkan ma? [kur-yee

ENGLISH ◆ CHINESE | **Lo**

kahn-kahn mah]

可以看看吗？

look after zhàokàn [jow-kahn]

照看

look at kàn [kahn]

看

look for zhǎo [jow]

找

I'm looking for ... wó zhǎo ...
[wor jow]

我找...

look forward to pànwàng
[pahn-wahng]

盼望

I'm looking forward to it wǒ
pànwàng [wor]

我盼望

loose (handle etc) sōng [soong]

松

lorry kǎchē [kah-chur]

卡车

lose diū [dyoh]

丢

I'm lost wǒ mílùle [wor
mee-loo-lur]

我迷路了

I've lost my bag wǒ ba dàizi
diūshīle [bah dai-dzur
dyoh-shur-lur]

我把带子丢失了

lost property (office) shīwù
zhāolǐng chù [shur-woo
jow-ling choo]

失物招领处

lot: a lot, lots hěnduō

[hun-dwor]

很多

not a lot bù duō

不多

a lot of people hěnduō rén
[run]

很多人

a lot bigger dà de duō [dah
dur]

大得多

I like it a lot wǒ hén xǐhuan
[wor hun hshee-hwahn]

我很喜欢

loud dàshēng de [dah-shung
dur]

大声的

lounge (in house) kètīng
[kur-ting]

客厅

(in hotel) xiūxishì
[hsyoh-hshee-shur]

休息室

love (noun) liàn'ài [lyen-ai]

恋爱

(verb) ài

爱

I love China wǒ ài Zhōngguó
[wor ai joong-gwor]

我爱中国

lovely (person) kěài [kur-ai]

可爱

(thing) hén hǎo [hun how]

很好

low (bridge) dī

低

(prices) **piányide** [pyen-yee-dur]

便宜的

luck yùnqi [yewn-chee]

运气

good luck! zhù nǐ shùnlì! [joo nee shun-lee]

祝你顺利

luggage xíngli [hsing-lee]

行李

luggage trolley xínglǐchē [–chur]

行李车

lunch wǔfàn [woo-fahn]

午饭

luxurious háohuá [how-hwah]

豪华

luxury (comfort etc) **gāojí** [gow-jee]

高级

(extravagance) **shēchǐ** [shur-chee]

奢侈

lychee lìzhī [lee-jur]

荔枝

M

machine jīqì [jee-chee]

机器

magazine zázhì [dzah-jur]

杂志

maid (in hotel) **nǚ fúwùyuán** [nyew foo-woo-yew-ahn]

女服务员

mail (noun) **yóujiàn** [yoh-jyen]

邮件

(verb) **jì**

寄

is there any mail for me? yóu wǒde xìn méiyou? [yoh wor-dur hsin may-yoh]

有我的信没有？

see **postal service**

mailbox xìnxiāng [hsin-hsyahng]

信箱

main zhǔyào de [joo-yow dur]

主要的

main course zhǔcài [joo-tsai]

主菜

main post office dà yóujú [dah yoh-joo]

大邮局

main road dàlù [dah-loo]

大路

make (brand name) **pái**

牌

(verb) **zhìzào** [jur-dzow]

制造

I make it 10 yuan, OK? wǒ suàn shí kuài qián, hǎo ma? [wor swahn shur kwai chyen how mah]

我算十块钱好吗？

what is it made of? zhè shì yòng shénme zào de? [jur shur yoong shun-mur dzow dur]

这是用什么造的？

make-up huàzhuāngpǐn
[hwah-jwahng-pin]
化妆品
Malaysia Mǎláixīyà
[mah-lai-hshee-yah]
马来西亚
man nánrén [nahn-run]
男人
manager jīnglǐ
经理
can I see the manager? kéyǐ
jiànjian jīnglǐ ma? [kur-yee
jyen-jyen – mah]
可以见见经理吗？
Mandarin Pǔtōnghuà
[poo-toong-hwah]
普通话
mandarin orange gānzi
[gahn-dzur]
柑子
many hěn duō [hun dwor]
很多
not many bù duō
不多
map dìtú
地图

Cheap city maps are widely
obtainable from hotel shops or
street kiosks, though nearly
always in Chinese only. Some of
the more visited cities do, however, sell different versions
of maps, including English-
language ones, marking local →

sights, hotels and restaurants
and also giving local train, bus
and flight timetables. For Tibet,
it is better and cheaper to bring
maps with you from outside.

March sānyuè [sahn-yew-eh]
三月
margarine rénzào
húangyóu [run-zow
hwahng-yoh]
人造黄油
market shìchǎng [shur-chahng]
市场
married: I'm married wǒ
jiéhūnle [wor jyeh-hun-lur]
我结婚了
are you married? nǐ jiéhūnle
ma? [nee jyeh-hun-lur mah]
你结婚了吗？
martial arts wǔshù
武术
mascara jiémáogāo
[jyeh-mow-gow]
睫毛膏
match (sport) bǐsài
比塞
football match zúqiú sài
[dzoo-chyoh]
组球塞
matches huǒchái [hwor-]
火柴
material (fabric) bù
布

matter: it doesn't matter méi
guānxi [may gwahn-hshee]

没关系

what's the matter? zěnmele?
[dzun-mur-lur]

怎么了？

mattress chuángdiàn
[chwahng-dyen]

床垫

May wǔyuè [woo-yew-eh]

五月

may: may I have another one?
qǐng zài lái yīge [ching dzai lai
yee-gur]

请再来一个

may I come in? wǒ néng
jìnlái ma? [wor nung jin-lai
mah]

我能进来吗？

may I see it? wǒ néng kàn
ma? [kahn]

我能看吗？

may I sit here? wǒ néng zuò
zhèr ma? [zwor jer]

我能坐这儿吗？

maybe kěnéng [kur-nung]

可能

me* wǒ [wor]

我

that's for me zhè shì wǒde
[jer shur wor-dur]

这是我的

send it to me qǐng sòng géi
wǒ [ching soong gay]

请送给我

me too wó yě [yur]

我也

meal fàn [fahn]

饭

• • • • • • DIALOGUE • • • • • •

did you enjoy your meal? chīle
hái hǎo ma? [chur-lur hai how
mah]

it was excellent, thank you hén
hǎo, xièxìe [hun how hsyeh-
hsyeh]

mean: what do you mean? nǐ
zhǐde shì shénme? [nee
jur-dur shur shun-mur]

你指得是什么？

• • • • • • DIALOGUE • • • • • •

what does this word mean?
zhèige cír shì shénme yìsi?
[jay-gur tsur – yee-sur]

it means ... in English yòng
yīngwen shì ... de yì yì [yoong
ying-wun – dur]

meat ròu [roh]

肉

medicine (Western) xīyào
[hshee-yow]

西药

(Chinese) zhōngyào
[joong-yow]

中药

medium (adj: size) zhōngděng
[joong-dung]

中等

medium-rare (steak)
bànshēngshú de
[bahn-shung-shoo dur]
半生熟的

medium-sized zhōnghào
[joong-how]
中号

meet pèngjiàn [pung-jyen]
碰见

nice to meet you jiàndào nǐ
hěn gāoxìng [jyen-dow nee hun
gow-hsing]
见到你很高兴

where shall I meet you?
wǒmen zài nǎr yào
pèngjiàn? [wor-mun dzai-nar
yow pung-jyen]
我们在哪儿要碰见？

meeting huì(yì) (hway-yee)
会（议）

melon guā [gwah]
瓜

men nánde [nahn-dur]
男的

mend (machine, bicycle) xiūlǐ
[hsyoh-lee]
修理

(clothes) féngbǔ [fung-boo]
缝补

could you mend this for me?
qíng géi wǒ xiūlǐ yíxià hǎo
ma? [ching gay wor – yee-hsyah
how mah]
请给我修理一下好吗？

men's room nán cèsuǒ [nahn
tsur-swor]
男厕所

menswear nánzhuāng
[nahn-jwahng]
男装

mention shuōdào [shwor-dow]
说到

don't mention it búyòng kèqi
[boo-yoong kur-chee]
不用客气

menu càidānr [tsai-dahnr]
菜单儿

may I see the menu, please?
qǐng lái càidānr, hǎo ma?
[ching lai tsai-dahnr – how mah]
请来菜单儿好吗？
see **menu reader** page 251

message xìnr [hsinr]
信儿

**are there any messages for
me?** yóu wǒde xìn
shénmede ma? [yoh wor-dur
hsin shun-mur-dur mah]
有我的信什么的吗？

**I want to leave a message
for ...** wó xiǎng gěi ... liúge
xìn [hsyahng gay ... lyoh-gur]
我想给...留个信

metal jīnshǔ [jin-shoo]
金属

metre mǐ
米

midday zhōngwǔ [joong-woo]
中午

at midday zhōngwǔ
中午
middle*: in the middle zài
zhōngjiān [dzai joong-jyen]
在中间
in the middle of the night yèli
[yur-lee]
夜里
the middle one zhōngde
[joong-dur]
中的
midnight bànyè [bahn-yur]
半夜
at midnight bànyè [bahn-yur]
半夜
might: I might ... yéxǔ ...
[yur-hsoo]
也许
I might not ... yéxǔ bù ...
也许不...
mild (taste) wèidàn [wei-dahn]
味淡
(weather) nuǎnhuo
[nwahn-hwor]
暖和
mile yīnglǐ
英里
milk niúnǎi [nyoh-nai]
牛奶
millimetre háomǐ [how-mee]
毫米
mind: never mind méi guānxi
[may gwahn-hshee]
没关系
I've changed my mind wó

gǎibiàn zhǔyì le [wor gai-byen
joo-yee lur]
我改变主意了

• • • • • • DIALOGUE • • • • • •

do you mind if I open the window?
wǒ kāi chuāng, xíngbùxíng?
[chwahng hsing-boo-hsing]
no, I don't mind xíng [hsing]

mine*: it's mine shì wǒde [shur
wor-dur]
是我的
mineral water kuàngquánshuǐr
[kwahng-choo-en-shwayr]
矿泉水儿
Ming Tombs shísānlíng
[shur-sahn-ling]
十三陵
minute fēn(zhōng)
[fun(-joong)]
分(钟)
in a minute yìhuǐr [yee-hwayr]
一会儿
just a minute jiù yìhuǐr [jyoh]
就一会儿
mirror jìngzi [jing-dzur]
镜子
Miss xiáojiě [hsyow-jyeh]
小姐
miss: I missed the bus méi
gǎnshàng chē [may
gahn-shahng chur]
没赶上车
missing: my ... is missing wǒde
... bèi diūle [wor-dur ... bay

dyoh-lur]

我的...被丢了

there's a suitcase missing

yíge yīxiāng bèi diūle [yee-gur

yee-hsyahng bay dyoh-lur]

一个衣箱被丢了

mist wù

雾

mistake cuò(wù) [tswor–]

错(误)

I think there's a mistake zhèr

yǒuge cuòr [jer yoh-gur]

这儿有个错儿

sorry, I've made a mistake

dùibúqǐ, wǒ nòngcuòle

[dway-boo-chee wor

noong-tswor-lur]

对不起我弄错了

misunderstanding wùhuì

[woo-hway]

误会

mobile phone shǒutí diànhuà

[shoh-tee dyen-hwah]

手提电话

modern xiàndài [hsyen-

dai]

现代

moisturizer cāliǎnyóu

[tsah-lyen-yoh]

擦脸油

moment: I won't be a moment

jiù yìfēn zhōng [jyoh yee-fun

joong]

就一分钟

monastery (Buddhist) sìyuàn

[sur-yew-ahn]

寺院

Monday xīngqiyī

[hsing-chee-yee]

星期一

money qián [chyen]

钱

Mongolia Ménggǔ [mung-goo]

蒙古

Mongolian (adj) Ménggǔ

蒙古

monk sēng [sung]

僧

month yuè [yew-eh]

月

monument jìniànbēi

[jin-yen-bay]

纪年碑

moon yuèliang [yew-eh-lyang]

月亮

more* duō yìdiǎnr [dwor

yee-dyenr]

多一点儿

can I have some more water,

please? qǐng zài lái shuǐ, hǎo

ma? [ching dzai lai shway how

mah]

请再来水好吗?

more expensive guì diǎnr

[gway dyenr]

贵点儿

more interesting than ... bǐ ...

yǒu xìngqù [yoh hsing-chew]

比...有兴趣

more than 50/100 wǔshí/

yībǎi duō

五十 / 一百多

more than that one bǐ nèige
duō [nay-gur]

比那个多

a lot more duōde duō
[dwor-dur]

多得多

•••••• DIALOGUE ••••••

would you like some more? nǐ hái
yào diǎnr shénme ma? [yow dyenr
shun-mur mah]

no, no more for me, thanks búyào,
xièxie [boo-yow hsyeh-hsyeh]

how about you? nǐne? [nee-nur]

I don't want any more, thanks wǒ
bú zàiyàole, xièxie [wor boo
dzai-yow-lur]

morning zǎoshang
[dzow-shahng]

早上

this morning jīntiān
zǎoshang [jin-tyen
dzow-shahng]

今天早上

in the morning zǎoshang
[dzow-shahng]

早上

mosquito wénzi [wun-dzur]

蚊子

Malaria and dengue fever are
not widespread in China: they
are only a problem in the south
→

of China in summer and all year
round in tropical areas such as
Hainan Island. Mosquitoes are
most active at dawn and dusk.
At these times wear long sleeves
and trousers, avoid dark colours
and use repellent on exposed
skin. Mosquito repellent is usually available in the shops in
areas where it is needed.

Most hotels and guesthouses in
affected areas provide mosquito
nets, but you may want to bring
your own if you intend going to
any rural areas. Air-conditioning
and fans help keep mosquitoes
at bay, as do mosquito coils and
insecticide sprays, both available in China.

If you're travelling in high-risk
areas, it's advisable to take
malaria tablets, which you need
to start taking a week before ex-
posure, and then continue with
them for four weeks after leaving a malarial region.

mosquito net wénzhàng
[wun-jahng]

蚊帐

mosquito repellent qūwénjì
[chew-wun-jee]

驱蚊剂

most*: I like this one most of all
wǒ zuì xǐhuān zhèige [wor

dzway hshee-hwahn jay-gur]

我最喜欢这个

most of the time dàbùfen
shíjiān [dah-boo-fun shur-jyen]

大部分时间

most tourists dà duōshù
lǚyóuzhe [dah dwor-shoo]

大多数旅游者

mostly dàgài [dah-gai]

大概

mother mǔqīn [moo-chin]

母亲

mother-in-law pópo [por-por]

婆婆

motorbike mótuōchē
[mor-twor-chur]

摩托车

motorboat qìtǐng [chee-ting]

汽艇

mountain shān [shahn]

山

in the mountains zài
shānzhōng [dzai shahn-
joong]

在山中

mountaineering dēngshān
[dung-shahn]

登山

mouse láoshǔ [low-shoo]

老鼠

moustache xiǎo húzi [hsyow
hoo-dzur]

小胡子

mouth zuǐ [dzway]

嘴

**move: he's moved to another
room** tā bāndào lìngwài yí
fángjiān qùle [tah bahn-dow
ling-wai yee fahng-jyen choo-lur]

他搬到另外一房间去
了

could you move it? qǐng nín
nuó yíxià, hǎo ma? [ching nin
nwor yee-hsyah how mah]

请您挪一下好吗？

could you move up a little?
qíng wǎng qián núo yíxià
[wahng chyen nwor yee-hsyah]

请往前挪一下

movie diànyǐng [dyen-ying]

电影

movie theater diànyǐng yuàn
[dyen-ying yew-ahn]

电影院

Mr xiānsheng [hsyen-shung]

先生

Mrs fūren [foo-run]

夫人

Ms nǚshì [nyew-shur]

女氏

much duō [dwor]

多

much better/worse hǎo/huài
de duō [dur]

好／坏得多

not (very) much bù duō

不多

I don't want very much wǒ
búyào tài dūo [wor boo-yow]

我不要太多

mug (for drinking) bēi [bay]

杯

I've been mugged wó gěi rén
qiǎngle [gay run chyang-lur]

我给人抢了

mum māma [mah-mah]

妈妈

museum bówùguǎn
[bor-woo-gwahn]

博物馆

see opening times

mushrooms mógu [mor-goo]

蘑菇

music yīnyuè [yin-yew-eh]

音乐

Muslim (adj) mùsīlín
[moo-sur-lin]

穆斯林

must*: I must wǒ bìxū [wor
bee-hsyew]

我比许

I mustn't drink alcohol wǒ
búhuì hē jiù [wor-boo-hway hur
jyoh]

我不回喝酒

my* wǒde [wor-dur]

我的

myself: I'll do it myself wǒ zìjǐ
lái [wor dzur-jee]

我自己来

by myself wǒ yīge rén
[yee-gur run]

我一个入

N

nail (finger) zhǐjiā [jur-jyah]

指甲

(metal) dīngzi [ding-dzur]

钉子

nail varnish zhǐjiā yóu [jur-jyah
yoh]

指甲油

name míngzi [ming-dzur]

名子

my name's John wǒde míngzi
jiào John [wor-dur – jyow]

我的名子叫John

what's your name? nǐ jiào
shénme míngzi? [nee –
shun-mur]

你叫什么名子？

what is the name of this
street? zhèi tiáo lù
jiào shénme? [jay
tyow]

这条路叫什么？

A Chinese name usually com-
prises three characters. The first
character is the family name,
inherited from the father. The
second two characters are the
first name, though strangers
find it embarrassing to address
each other by their first names
– instead a popular informal
convention is to add the epithets
xiǎo (young) or lǎo (old) to the
→

surnames. For example **lǎo Máo** ('Old Mao') would be a respectful but friendly way to address a person older than oneself. Young people of the same age would call each other **xiǎo Zhāng, xiǎo Lóng** etc. Women do not change their surnames when they marry.

Formal titles always come after names. The most commonly used are **xiānsheng** (Mr), **fūren** (Mrs), **xiáojie** (Miss) and **nǔshi** (Miss or Ms). For example, **Wáng xiānsheng** 'Mr Wang', and **Máo xiáojie** 'Miss Mao'.

napkin cānjīn [tsahn-jin]

餐巾

nappy niàobù [nyow-boo]

尿布

narrow (street) zhǎi [jai]

窄

nasty (person) ràng ren tǎoyàn [rahng run tow-yen]

让人讨厌

(weather, accident) zāotòu [dzow-toh]

糟透

national (state) guójiā [gwor-jyah]

国家

(nationwide) quánguó [choo-en-gwor]

全国

nationality guójí [gwor-jee]

国籍

(for Chinese minorities)

shǎoshù mínzú [show-shoo min-dzoo]

少数民族

natural zìrán [dzur-rahn]

自然

near jìn

近

near the ... lí ... hěnjìn [hun-jin]

离...很近

is it near the city centre?

lí shì zhōngxīn jìn ma? [shur joong-hsin jin mah]

离市中心近吗？

do you go near the Great Wall?

nǐ zài Chángchéng fùjìn tíngchē ma? [nee dzai chahng-chung foo-jin ting-chur mah]

你在长城附近停车吗？

where is the nearest ...? zuìjìn de ... zài nǎr? [dzway-jin dur ... dzai nar]

最近的...在哪儿？

nearby fùjìn [foo-jin]

附近

nearly chàbuduō [chah-boo-dwor]

差不多

necessary bìyào(de) [bee-yow(-dur)]

必要(的)

neck bózi [boh-dzur]
脖子

necklace xiàngliàn
[hsyahng-lyen]
项链

necktie lǐngdài
领带

need: I need ... wǒ xūyào ...
[wor hsyew-yow]
我需要

　do I need to pay? wǒ yīnggāi
　fùqián ma? [foo-chyen mah]
　我应该付钱吗？

needle zhēn [jun]
针

neither: neither (one) of them
liǎngge dōu bù [lyang-gur doh]
两个都不

Nepal Níbóěr [nee-bor-er]
尼泊尔

Nepali (adj) Níbóěr
尼泊尔

nephew zhízi [jur-dzur]
侄子

net (in sport) wǎng [wahng]
网

network map jiāotōngtú
[jyow-toong-too]
交通图

never (not ever) cónglái bù
[tsoong-lai]
从来不

　(not yet) hái méiyou [may-yoh]
　还没有

　have you ever been to Beijing? nǐ
　qùguo Běijīng méiyou?
　[chew-gwor – may-yoh]
　no, never, I've never been there
　cónglái méiqù [tsoong-lai
　may-chew]

new xīn [hsin]
新

news (radio, TV etc) xīnwén
[hsin-wun]
新闻

newspaper bào(zhǐ) [bow(-jur)]
报(纸)

New Year xīnnián [hsin-nyen]
新年

Chinese New Year chūnjié
[chun-jyeh]
春节

Happy New Year! xīnnián
hǎo! [how]
新年好

　(Chinese) gōnghè xīnxǐ!
　[goong-hur hsin-hshee]
　恭贺新禧

Chinese New Year, or Spring
Festival, is the biggest holiday
in the Chinese calendar, consisting of two weeks of festivities
marking the beginning of a
new year in the lunar calendar.
Each year it falls on a different
date in the Gregorian calendar,

between mid-January and mid-February. China is at its most colourful at this time, with shops and houses decorated with good luck messages and stalls and shops selling paper money, drums and costumes. During the festival itself, however, is not an ideal time to be travelling – everything closes for the holiday, and much of the population goes on the move, making travel impossible or extremely crowded.

The first day of the festival is marked by a family feast at which **jiǎozi** (dumplings), are eaten, sometimes with coins hidden inside, and followed by firecrackers which are supposed to frighten away demons. New Year in the cities is now a slightly more staid affair as fireworks are banned, though enterprising stall holders sell cassette tapes of explosions as a replacement. Outside the home, Spring Festival is publicly celebrated at temple fairs, which feature acrobats, drummers, and gusts of smoke as the Chinese light incense sticks to placate the gods. After two weeks, the celebrations end with the lantern →

festival, when the streets are filled with multicoloured paper lanterns, a tradition dating from the Han dynasty.

New Year's Eve: Chinese New Year's Eve chúxī [choo-hshee]
除夕
New Zealand Xīnxīlán
[hsin-see-lahn]
新西兰
New Zealander: I'm a New Zealander wǒ shì xīnxilánren
[–run]
我是新西兰人
next xià yíge [hsyah yee-gur]
下一个
　the next street on the left xià yíge zuǒbianr de lù
[dzwor-byenr dur]
下一个左边儿的路
　at the next stop xià yígezhàn
[hsyah yee-gur-jahn]
下一个站
　next week xià(ge) xīngqī
[hsyah(-gur) hsing-chee]
下(个)星期
next to ... zài ... pángbiān
[dzai ... pahng-byen]
在...旁边
nice (food) hǎochī [how-chur]
好吃
　(looks, view etc) hǎokàn
[how-kahn]
好看

(person) hǎo [how]
好

niece zhínǚ [jin-yew]
侄女

night yè [yur]
夜

at night yèli [yur-lee]
夜里

good night wǎn ān [wahn ahn]
晚安

• • • • • DIALOGUE • • • • •

do you have a single room for one
night? yǒu yítiān de dānrén jiān
ma? [yoh yee-tyen dur dahn-run jyen
mah]

yes, madam yǒu [yoh]

how much is it per night? yíwǎn
yào duōshaoqián? [yee-wahn yow
dwor-show-chyen]

it's 30 yuan for one night yíwǎn
yào sānshí kuài qián [sahn-shur –
chyen]

thank you, I'll take it xíng [hsing]

nightclub yèzǒnghuì
[yur-dzoong-hway]
夜总会

no* bù
不

I've no change wǒ méiyou
líng qián [wor may-yoh –
chyen]
我没有零钱

no way! bù xíng! [hsing]
不行

oh no! (upset) tiān na! [tyen
nah]
天哪

nobody méirén [may-run]
没人

there's nobody there méirén
zài [dzai]
没人在

noise zàoyīn [dzow-yin]
噪音

noisy: it's too noisy tài chǎole
[chow-lur]
太吵了

non-alcoholic bù hán
jiǔjīng de [hahn jyoh-jing dur]
不含酒精的

none shénme yě méiyǒu
[shun-mur yur may-yoh]
什么也没有

noon zhōngwǔ [joong-woo]
中午

at noon zhōngwǔ
中午

no-one méirén [may-run]
没人

nor: nor do I wó yě bù [wor yur]
我也不

normal zhèngcháng(de)
[jung-chahng(-dur)]
正常(的)

north běi [bay]
北

in the north běibian [bay-
byen]
北边

to the north wǎng běi [wahng]

往北

north of Luoma Luómǎ běi

罗马北

northeast dōngběi [doong-bay]

东北

northern běibù [bay-boo]

北部

Northern Ireland Běi Ài'ěrlán
[bay ai-er-lahn]

北爱尔兰

North Korea Běi Cháoxiān [bay
chow-hsyen]

北朝鲜

northwest xīběi [hshee-bay]

西北

Norway Nuówēi [nwor-way]

挪威

Norwegian (adj, language)
Nuówēiyǔ

挪威语

nose bízi [bee-dzur]

鼻子

not* bù

不

no, I'm not hungry wǒ búè
[wor bway]

我不饿

I don't want any, thank you
búyào, xièxie [boo-yow
hsyeh-hsyeh]

不要谢谢

it's not necessary búbì

不必

I didn't know that wǒ bù

zhīdao [wor boo jur-dow]

我不知道

not that one, this one búyào
nèige, yào zhèige [nay-gur yow
jay-gur]

不要那个要这个

note (banknote) chāopiào
[chow-pyow]

钞票

notebook bǐjìběn [bee-jee-bun]

笔记本

nothing méiyou shénme
[may-yoh shun-mur]

没有什么

nothing for me, thanks wǒ
shénme dōu bú yào, xièxie
[wor – doh boo yow hsyeh-hsyeh]

我什么都不要谢谢

nothing else, thanks qítade
búyào, xièxie [chee-tah-dur
boo-yow]

其他的不要谢谢

novel (noun) xiǎoshuō
[hsyow-shwor]

小说

November shíyīyuè
[shur-yee-yew-eh]

十一月

now xiànzài [hsyen-dzai]

现在

number hàomǎ [how-mah]

号码

(figure) shùzì [shoo-dzur]

数字

I've got the wrong number wó

dǎcuòle [wor dah-tswor-lur]

我打错了

what is your phone number?
nǐde diànhuà shì duōshao?
[nee-dur dyen-hwah shur
dwor-show]

你的电话是多少?

number plate chēpái [chur-pai]

车牌

nurse hùshi [hoo-shur]

护士

nut (for bolt) luósī [lwor-sur]

螺丝

nuts (chestnuts) lìzi [lee-dzur]

栗子

(hazelnuts) zhēnzi [jun-dzur]

榛子

(walnuts) hétao [hur-tow]

核桃

O

o'clock* diǎnzhōng [dyen-joong]

点钟

occupied (US) yǒurén [yoh-run]

有人

October shíyuè [shur-yew-eh]

十月

odd (strange) qíguài [chee-gwai]

奇怪

of* de [dur]

的

off (lights, machine) guān
shangle [gwahn shahng-lur]

关上了

it's just off ... (street etc) lí ...
bùyuǎn [boo-ywahn]

离...不远

we're off tomorrow wǒmen
míngtiān zǒu [wor-mun
ming-tyen dzoh]

我门明天走

office (place of work)
bàngōngshì [bahn-goong-
shur]

办公室

often jīngcháng [jing-chahng]

经常

not often bù jīngcháng [boo
jing-chahng]

不经常

how often are the buses? yíge
zhōngtóu duōshao qìchē?
[yee-gur joong-toh dwor-show
chee-chur]

一个钟头多少汽车?

oil (for car) yóu [yoh]

油

vegetable oil càiyóu [tsai-
yoh]

菜油

oily (food) yóunì [yoh-nee]

油腻

ointment yàogāo [yow-gow]

药膏

OK hǎo [how]

好

are you OK? hái hǎo ma?
[mah]

还好吗?

I feel OK hén hǎo [hun]

很好

is that OK with you? xíng bù xíng? [hsing]

行不行？

is it OK to …? wó kěyi …? [wor kur-yee]

我可以...？

that's OK, thanks xíngle xièxie [hsing-lur hsyeh-hsyeh]

行了谢谢

is this train OK for …? zhè liè huǒchē qù … ma? [jer lyeh hwor-chur chew … mah]

这列和车去...吗？

old (person) lǎo [low]

老

(thing) jiù [jyoh]

旧

• • • • • • DIALOGUE • • • • • •

how old are you? nín duō dà niánling? [dwor dah nyen-ling]

(to an old person) nín duō dà niánjì le? [dwor dah nyen-jee lur]

(to a child) ni jǐsuì le? [jee-sway lur]

I'm 25 wǒ èrshíwǔ suì [wor-sway]

and you? nǐ ne? [nur]

old-fashioned guòshí(de) [gwor-shur(-dur)]

过时(的)

(person) shǒujiù(de) [shoh-jyoh(-dur)]

守旧(的)

old town (old part of town) jiùchéng [jyoh-chung]

旧城

omelette chǎojīdàn [chow-jee-dahn]

炒鸡蛋

on*: on … (on top of) zài … shàngmian [dzai … shahng-myen]

在...上面

on the street zài lùshàng

在路上

on the beach zài hǎitān shàng

在海滩上

is it on this road? zài zhètíaolù ma? [jur-tyow-loo mah]

在这条路吗？

on the plane zài fēijī shàng

在飞机上

on Saturday xīngqī liù [lyoh]

星期六

on television zài diànshìshang

在电视上

I haven't got it on me wǒ shēnshang méiyǒu [wor shun-shahng may-yoh]

我身上没有

this one's on me (drink) wǒ

fùqián [wor foo-choo-en]

我付钱

the light wasn't on dēng méi kāi [dung may]

灯没开

what's on tonight? jīntiān wǎnshang yǒu shénme huódòng? [jin-tyen wahn-shahng you shun-mur hwor-dong]

今天晚上有什么活动?

once (one time) yícì [yee-tsur]

一次

at once (immediately) mǎshàng [mah-shahng]

马上

one* yī [yur]

一

the white one báisè de [bai-sur dur]

白色的

one-way ticket (dānchéng) piào [(dahn-chung) pyow]

(单程)票

onion yángcōng [yang-tsoong]

洋葱

only zhí yǒu [jur yoh]

只有

only one zhí yǒu yíge [yee-gur]

只有一个

it's only 6 o'clock cái liùdiǎn [tsai lyoh-dyen]

才六点

I've only just got here wǒ gāng dào le [wor gahng dow lur]

我刚到了

on/off switch kāiguān [kai-gwahn]

开关

open (adj) kāi(de) [kai(-dur)]

开(的)

(verb) kāi

开

when do you open? nǐmen shénme shíhou kāiménr? [nee-mun shun-mur shur-hoh kai-munr]

你们什么时候开门儿?

I can't get it open búhuì dǎkāi [boo-hway dah-kai]

不回打开

in the open air zài wàimian [dzai wai-myen]

在外面

opening times yíngyè shíjiān [ying-yur shur-jyen]

营业时间

ENGLISH ◆ CHINESE | Op

There is no equivalent to Sunday, the once-weekly day of rest, in China: all shops open every day, keeping long, late hours, especially in big cities. Banks and post offices close either on Sunday or for the whole weekend, though even this is not →

always the case. Museums sometimes close for one day a week, though most tourist sites or temples are open seven days a week.

opera gējù [gur-jyew]
歌剧

operation (medical) shǒushù [shoh-shoo]
手术

operator (telephone) zǒngjī [dzoong-jee]
总机

opposite: the opposite direction xiāngfǎn de fāngxiàng [hsyahng-fahn dur fahng-hsyahng]
相反的方向

the bar opposite zài duìmianr de jiǔbā [dzai dway-myenr dur]
在对面儿的酒吧

opposite my hotel zài wǒ fàndiàn duìmianr
在我饭店对面儿

optician yǎnjìngdiàn [yen-jing-dyen]
眼镜店

or (in statement) huòzhě [hwor-jur]
或着

(in question) háishi [hai-shur]
还是

orange (fruit) gānjú [gahn-joo]
柑橘

(colour) júhuángsè [jyew-sur]
橘黄色

orange juice (fresh) xiānjúzhī [hsyen-jyew-jur]
鲜橘汁

(fizzy) júzi qìshuǐ [jyew-dzur chee-shway]
橘子汽水

(diluted) júzishuǐr [jyew-dzur-shwayr]
橘子水儿

order: can we order now? (in restaurant) wǒmen kéyǐ diǎncài ma? [wor-mun kur-yee dyen-tsai mah]
我们可以点菜吗？

I've already ordered, thanks yǐjing diǎn le, xièxie [yee-jing dyen lur hsyeh-hsyeh]
已经点了谢谢

I didn't order this wǒ méiyǒu diǎn zhèige cài [wor may-yoh dyen jay-gur tsai]
我没有点这个菜

out of order huàile [hwai-lur]
坏了

ordinary pǔtōng [poo-toong]
普通

other qítā [chee-tah]
其他

the other one lìng yíge [yee-gur]
另一个

the other day zuìjìn

[dzway-jin]
最近

I'm waiting for the others wǒ
děngzhe qíyúde [wor dung-jer
chee-yoo-dur]
我等着其于的

do you have any others? (other
kinds) hái yǒu biéde ma? [yoh
byeh-dur mah]
还有别的吗？

otherwise yàobùrán
[yow-boor-ahn]
要不然

our/ours* wǒmende
[wor-mun-dur]
我们的

out: he's out tā chūqule [tah
choo-chew-lur]
他出去了

three kilometres out of town lí
shì sān gōnglǐ [shur –
goong-lee]
离市三公里

outdoors lùtiān [loo-tyen]
露天

outside* wàimian [wai-myen]
外面

can we sit outside? wǒmen
kéyi dào wàimian qù zuò
ma? [wor-mun kur-yee dow
wai-myen chew dzwor mah]
我们可以到外面去坐
吗？

oven kǎoxiāng [kow-syang]
烤箱

over: over here zài zhèr [dzai
jer]
在这儿

over there zài nàr
在那儿

over 500 wǔbǎi duō [dwor]
五百多

it's over wánle [wahn-lur]
完了

overcharge: you've overcharged
me nǐ duōshōule wǒde qián
[dwor-shoh-lur wor-dur chyen]
你多收了我的钱

overland mail lùshang yóudì
[loo-shahng yoh-dee]
路上邮递

overnight (travel) guòyè
[gwor-yur]
过夜

overtake chāoguò [chow-gwor]
超过

owe: how much do I owe you?
yígòng duōshao qián?
[yee-goong dwor-show chyen]
一共多少钱？

own: my own ... wǒ zìjǐde ...
[wor dzur-jur-dur]
我自己的...

are you on your own? jiù nǐ
yíge rén ma? [jyoh nee yee-gur
run mah]
就你一个人吗？

I'm on my own jiù wǒ yíge
rén [jyoh wor yee-gur run]
就我一个人

P

pack (verb) shōushi [shoh-shur]
收拾

package (parcel) bāoguǒ
[bow-gwor]
包裹

packed lunch héfàn [hur-fahn]
盒饭

packet: a packet of
cigarettes yìbāo yān [yee-bow
yen]
一包烟

paddy field dàotián [dow-tyen]
稻田

page (of book) yè [yur]
叶

could you page Mr …? nǐ
néng jiào yíxia …
xiānsheng ma? [nung jyow
yee-hsyah … hsyen-shung
mah]
你能叫一下…先生吗?

pagoda tǎ [tah]
塔

pain téng [tung]
疼

I have a pain here wǒ zhèr
téng [wor jer]
我这儿疼

painful téng
疼

painkillers zhǐténgyào
[jur-tung-yow]
止疼药

painting huà [hwah]
画

(oil) yóuhuà [yoh-hwah]
油画

(Chinese) guóhuà [gwor-hwah]
国画

pair: a pair of … yíduìr …
[yee-dwayr]
一对儿…

Pakistani (adj) Bājīsītǎn
[bah-jee-sur-tahn]
巴基斯坦

palace gōngdiàn [goong-dyen]
宫殿

pale cāngbái [tsahng-bai]
苍白

pale blue dàn lánsè [dahn
lahn-sur]
淡蓝色

panda xióngmāo [hsyoong-
mow]
熊猫

pants (underwear: men's) kùchǎ
[koo-chah]
裤衩

(women's) xiǎo sānjiǎokù
[hsyow sahn-jyow-koo]
小三角裤

(US: trousers) kùzi [koo-dzur]
裤子

pantyhose liánkùwà
[lyen-koo-wah]
连裤袜

paper zhǐ [jur]
纸

(newspaper) **bàozhǐ** [bow-jur]

报纸

a piece of paper yìzhāng zhǐ [yee-jahng jur]

一张纸

paper handkerchiefs zhǐjīn [jur-jin]

纸巾

parcel bāoguǒ [bow-gwor]

包裹

pardon (me)? (didn't understand/hear) nǐ shuō shénme? [shwor shun-mur]

你说什么?

parents fùmǔ

父母

park (noun) gōngyuán [goong-yew-ahn]

公园

(verb) tíngchē [ting-chur]

停车

can I park here? wǒ néng zài zhèr tíngchē ma? [wor nung dzai-jer ting-chur mah]

我能在这儿停车吗?

parking lot tíngchē chǎng [ting-chur chahng]

停车场

part (noun) bùfen

部分

partner (boyfriend, girlfriend etc) bànr [bahnr]

伴儿

party (group) tuántǐ [twahn-tee]

团体

(celebration) wǎnhuì [wahn-hway]

晚会

passenger chéngkè [chung-kur]

乘客

passport hùzhào [hoo-jow]

护照

past*: in the past guòqu [gwor-chew]

过去

just past the information office gāng jīngguò wènxùnchù [gahng jing-gwor wun-hsun-choo]

刚经过问讯处

path xiǎolù [hsyow-loo]

小路

pattern tú'àn [too-ahn]

图案

pavement rénxíng dào [run-hsing dow]

人行道

pavilion tíngzi [ting-dzur]

亭子

pay (verb) fù qián [foo(-chyen)]

付钱

can I pay, please? suànzhàng ba? [swahn-jahng bah]

算帐吧?

it's already paid for zhèige yǐjīng fùqián le [jay-gur yee-jing foo-chyen lur]

这个已经付钱了?

•••••• DIALOGUE ••••••

who's paying? shúi fùqián? [shway foo-chyen]

I'll pay wǒ fùqián [wor foo-chyen]

no, you paid last time, I'll pay bù, nǐ shì zuìhòu yícì fùde, wǒ fùqián [shur dzway-hoh yee-tsur foo-dur]

payphone jìfèi diànhuà [jee-fay dyen-hwah]
计费电话

peaceful ānjìng [ahn-jing]
安静

peach táozi [tow-dzur]
桃子

peanuts huāshēng [hwah-shung]
花生

pear lí
梨

peculiar (taste, custom) guài [gwai]
怪

pedestrian crossing rénxíng héngdào [run-hsing hung-dow]
人行横道

Peking Opera Jīngjù [jing-jew]
京剧

pen gāngbǐ [gahng-bee]
钢笔

pencil qiānbǐ [chyen-bee]
铅笔

penfriend bíyǒu [bee-yoh]
笔友

penicillin pánníxīlín [pahn-nee-see-lin]
盘尼西林

penknife qiānbǐdāo [chyen-bee-dow]
铅笔刀

pensioner lǐng yánglǎojīn de rén [yang-low-jin dur run]
领养老金的人

people rénmín [run-min]
人民

the other people in the hotel fàndiàn li de qítā kèrén [lee dur chee-tah ker-run]
饭店里的其他客人

too many people tài duō rén [dwor run]
太多人

People's Republic of China Zhōnghuá Rénmín Gònghéguó [joong-hwah run-min goong-hur-gwor]
中华人民共和国

pepper (spice) hújiāo [hoo-jyow]
胡椒

(vegetable, red) shìzijiāo [shur-dzur-jyow]
柿子椒

per: per night méi wǎnshang [may wahn-shahng]
每晚上

how much per day? yìtiān yào duōshao qián? [yee-tyen yow dwor-show chyen]
一天要多少钱?

... per cent **băifēn zhī** ...
[bai-fun jur]

百分之...

perfect wánmĕi [wahn-may]

完美

perfume xiāngshuĭr
[hsyahng-shwayr]

香水儿

perhaps kĕnéng [kur-nung]

可能

perhaps not kĕnéng bù

可能不

period (of time) **shíqī** [shur-chee]

时期

(menstruation) **yuèjīng**
[yew-eh-jing]

月经

permit (noun) **xúkĕ zhèng**
[hsyew-kur jung]

许可证

person rén [run]

人

personal stereo fàngyīnjī
[fahng-yin-jee]

放音机

petrol qìyóu [chee-yoh]

汽油

petrol can yóutŏng [yoh-toong]

油筒

petrol station jiāyóu zhàn
[jyah-yoh jahn]

加油站

pharmacy yàofáng [yow-fahng]

药房

Pharmacies can help with minor injuries or ailments and large ones sometimes have a separate counter offering diagnosis and advice, though you're unlikely to find any staff who can speak anything but Chinese. The selection of reliable Asian and Western products available has improved, and it's also possible to treat yourself with herbal medicines which are effective for minor complaints.

Philippines Fēiiùbīn [fay-lew-bin]

菲律宾

phone (noun) **diànhuà**
[dyen-hwah]

电话

(verb) **dă diànhuà** [dah]

打电话

China's phone system is expanding and both international and domestic calls can be made with little fuss. Local calls are free and long-distance calls within China are cheap. Most big hotels offer direct dialling abroad from your room, but will add a surcharge and a minimum charge of between one and three minutes will be levied even if the call goes unanswered.

→

International calls are best made from telecommunications offices, usually located next to or in the main post office and open 24 hours. You pay a deposit and are told to go to a particular booth. When you have finished, you pay at the desk. The minimum charge is for three minutes.

Card phones are now widely available in major cities. Cards can only be used in the province where you buy them. There's a big drawback with making an international call with one of these – as soon as the number of units left on the card drops below a certain level, you will be cut off, and left with a phonecard that can only be used to make calls within China. However, cards are the cheapest way to make long-distance calls.

phone book diànhuà hàomǎ bù [dyen-hwah how-mah]
电话号码簿

phone box diànhuàtíng
电话亭

phonecard diànhuàkǎ [dyen-hwah-kah]
电话卡

phone number diànhuà hàomǎ [how-mah]
电话号码

photo zhàopiàn [jow-pyen]
照片

could you take a photo of us, please? qǐng géi wǒ zhàoge xiàng [ching gay-wor jow-gur hsyahng]
请给我照个相

Common sense is required in the taking of photographs; do not photograph strategic buildings or structures such as airports and bridges. Good-quality film and fast, efficient processing are widely available.

phrasebook duìhuà shǒucè [dway-hwah shoh-tsur]
对画手册

piano gāngqín [gahng-chin]
钢琴

pickpocket páshǒu [pah-shoh]
扒手

pick up: will you be there to pick me up? nǐ lái jiē wó hǎo ma? [ni lai jyeh wor how mah]
你来接我好吗？

picnic (noun) yěcān [yur-tsahn]
野餐

picture (painting) huà [hwah]
画
(photo) zhàopiàn [jow-pyen]
照片

piece **kuàir** [kwair]
块儿
a piece of … yíkuàir …
[yee-kwair]
一块儿…

pig **zhū** [joo]
猪

pill **bìyùnyào** [bee-yewn-yow]
避孕药
I'm on the pill wǒ chī
bìyùnyào [wor chur
bee-yew-nyow]
我吃避孕药

pillow **zhèntou** [jun-toh]
枕头

pillow case **zhěntào** [jun-tow]
枕套

pin (noun) **biézhēn** [byeh-jun]
别针

pineapple **bōluó** [bor-lwor]
波罗

pineapple juice **bōluózhī**
[bor-lwor-jur]
波萝汁

pink **fěnhóng** [fun-hoong]
粉红

pipe (for smoking) **yāndǒu**
[yen-doh]
烟斗
(for water) **guǎnzi** [gwahn-
dzur]
管子

pity: **it's a pity** zhēn kěxī [jun
kur-hshee]
真可惜

place (noun) **dìfāng** [dee-
fahng]
地方
at your place nǐde jiā [nee-dur
jyah]
你的家

plain (not patterned) **biàn de**
[byen dur]
便的

plane **fēijī** [fay-jee]
飞机
by plane zuò fēijī [dzwor]
坐飞机

China has some fourteen regional airlines linking all major
cities and many important sites.
It's a luxury worth considering
for long distances, but you'll
have to offset comfort and time
saved against a poor safety
record, not to mention the cost
– foreigners currently have to
pay a hefty surcharge, making
flying slightly more expensive
than going soft berth on a train.
You can buy tickets from CAAC
(China Airlines) offices, hotel
desks, or tour agents.

plant **zhíwù** [jur-woo]
植物

plasters **xiàngpí gāo** [syang-pee
gow]
橡皮膏

plastic **sùliào** [soo-lyow]
塑料

plastic bag **sùliàodài**
塑料带

plate **pánzi** [pahn-dzur]
盘子

platform **zhàntái** [jahn-tai]
站台

which platform is it for
Beijing? **wǎng Běijīng de
huǒchē cóng něihào zhàntái
kāichū?** [wahng – dur
hwor-chur tsoong nay-how
jahn-tai kai-choo]
往北京的火车从哪号
站台开出？

play (verb) **wánr** [wahnr]
玩儿

(noun: in theatre) **huàjù**
[hwah-jew]
话剧

pleasant **lìngrén yúkuài**
[ling-run yew-kwai]
令人愉快

please **qǐng** [ching]
请

yes, please **hǎo, xièxie** [how
hsyeh-hsyeh]
好谢谢

could you please ...? **qǐng
nín ..., hǎo ma?** [mah]
请您...好吗？

please don't **qǐng nín bù**
请您不

pleased: pleased to meet you

hěn gāoxìng jiàndào nǐ [hun
gow hsing jyen dow]
很高兴见到你

pleasure: my pleasure **méi shìr**
[may shur]
没事儿

plenty: plenty of ... **xǔduō ...**
[hsyew-dwor]
许多

there's plenty of time **hǎo duō
shíjian** [how dwor shur-jyen]
好多时间

that's plenty, thanks **gòule,
xièxie** [goh-lur hsyeh-hsyeh]
够了谢谢

plug (electrical) **chātóu**
[chah-toh]
插头

(in sink) **sāizi** [sai-dzur]
塞子

plum **lǐzi** [lee-dzur]
李子

plumber **guǎnzigōng**
[gwahn-dzur-goong]
管子工

p.m. **xiàwǔ** [hsyah-woo]
下午

pocket **kǒudàir** [koh-dair]
口带儿

point: two point five **èr diǎn wǔ**
[dyen]
二点五

there's no point **bù zhíde**
[jur-dur]
不值得

poisonous yǒudúde
[yoh-doo-dur]
有毒的

police jǐngchá [jing-chah]
警查

  call the police! kuài jiào
  jǐngchá qu! [kwai jyow
  jing-chah chew]
  快叫警查去

China is basically a police state, with the State interfering with and controlling the lives of its subjects to a degree most Westerners would find hard to tolerate, as indeed many of the Chinese do. This should not affect foreigners much, however, as the State on the whole takes a hands-off approach to visitors. As a tourist you are an obvious target for thieves. Carry your passport and money in a concealed money belt. Be wary on buses, the favoured haunt of pickpockets, and trains, particularly in hard-seat class and on overnight journeys. Hotel rooms are on the whole secure, dormitories less so. At street level, try not to be too ostentatious. Avoid eye-catching jewellery and flash watches, and try to be discreet when taking out your cash. Not looking wealthy also helps if you →

want to avoid being ripped off by taxi drivers, as does telling them you are a student (**wǒ shì xuésheng**).

If you do have anything stolen, you'll need to get the police to write up a loss report in order to claim on your insurance. If possible take a Chinese speaker with you and be prepared to pay a small fee.

The emergency number for the police is 110.

policeman jǐngchá [jing-chah]
警查

police station pàichūsuǒ
[pai-choo-swor]
派出所

polish (for shoes) xiéyóu
[hsyeh-yoh]
鞋油

polite kèqi [kur-chee]
客气

polluted wūrǎnle de
[woo-rahn-lur dur]
污染了

pool (for swimming) yóuyǒngchí
[yoh-yoong-chur]
游泳池

poor (not rich) qióng [chyoong]
穷

  (quality) lièzhì [lyeh-jur]
  劣质

pop music liúxíng yīnyuè
[lyoh-hsing yin-yew-eh]
流行音乐

pop singer liúxíng gēshǒu
[gur-shoh]
流行哥手

pork zhūròu [joo-roh]
猪肉

port (for boats) gángkǒu
[gahng-koh]
港口

porter (in hotel) ménfáng
[mun-fahng]
门房

possible kěnéng [kur-nung]
可能

is it possible to ...?
kéyǐ...ma? [yoh]
可以...吗？

as ... as possible
yuè...yuèhǎo
越...越好

post (noun: mail) yóujiàn
[yoh-jyen]
邮件

(verb) jì

could you post this letter for
me? qǐng bāng wó bǎ
zhèifēng xìn jìzǒu, hǎo ma?
[ching bahng wor bah jay-fung
hsin jee-dzoh how mah]
请帮我把这封信寄走
好吗？

postal service

The Chinese postal service is, on the whole, reliable, with letters taking less than a day to reach destinations in the same city, two or more days to other destinations in China, and up to several weeks to destinations abroad. Express Mail Service operates to most countries and to most destinations within China; the service cuts down delivery times and the letter or parcel is automatically registered. Main post offices are open seven days a week from 8 a.m. to 6 p.m.; smaller offices may close for a lunch hour or be closed at weekends. As well as at post offices, you can also post letters in the green letterboxes, though these are few and far between except in the biggest cities, or at tourist hotels, which usually have a postbox at the front desk. Envelopes can be scarce; try the stationery sections of department stores.

Poste restante services are available in any city. A nominal fee has to be paid to pick up mail, which will be kept for several months, and you will sometimes need to present ID when

→

collecting it. Mail is often eccentrically filed – to cut down on misfiling, your name should be printed clearly at the top of the letter and the surname underlined, but it's still worth checking all the other pigeonholes just in case. Have letters addressed to you as follows: province, town or city, GPO, c/o Poste Restante.

postbox xìnxiāng [hsin-hsyahng]
信箱

postcard míngxìnpiàn
[ming-hsin-pyen]
名信片

poster zhāotiē [jow-tyeh]
招贴

poste restante dàilǐng yóujiàn
[yoh-jyen]
待领邮件

post office yóujú [yoh-jew]
邮局

potato tǔdòu [too-doh]
土豆

potato chips (US) zhá
tǔdòupiànr [jah too-doh-pyenr]
炸土豆片儿

pound (money) yīngbàng
[ying-bahng]
英镑
(weight) bàng [bahng]
磅

power cut tíngdiàn [ting-dyen]
停电

power point diànyuán chāzuò
[dyen-yew-ahn chah-dzwor]
电源插座

**practise: I want to practise my
Chinese** wǒ xiǎng liànxí
jiǎng Zhōngwén [wor hsyahng
lyen-hshee jyang joong-wun]
我想练习讲中文

prawn crackers xiābǐng
[hsyah-bing]
虾饼

prawns duìxiā [dway-hsyah]
对虾

prefer: I prefer … wǒ gèng
xǐhuan … [wor gung
see-hwahn]
我更喜欢…

pregnant huáiyùn [hwai-yewn]
怀孕

prescription (for medicine)
yàofāng [yow-fahng]
药方

present (gift) lǐwù
礼物

president (of country) zóngtǒng
[dzoong-toong]
总统

pretty piàoliang [pyow-lyang]
漂亮
it's pretty expensive tài guìle
[gway-lur]
太贵了

price jiàgé [jyah-gur]
价格

prime minister shǒuxiàng

[shoh-hsyahng]
首相

printed matter yìnshuāpǐn
[yin-shwah-pin]
印刷品

prison jiānyù [jyen-yew]
监狱

privacy

The Chinese have almost no concept of privacy. People will stare at each other at point-blank range and pluck letters or books out of their hands for a better look. Even toilets are built with partitions so low that you can chat with your neighbour while squatting. All activities, including visits to natural beauty spots or holy relics, are done in large, noisy groups. The desire of some Western tourists to be left alone is often interpreted as arrogance.

private sīrén(de)
[sur-run(-dur)]
私人(的)

private bathroom
sīrén(de)yùshì [–yoo-shur]
私人(的)浴室

probably dàgài [dah-gai]
大概

problem wèntí [wun-tee]
问题

no problem! méi wèntí! [may]
没问题

programme (theatre) jiémùdānr
[jyeh-moo-dahnr]
节目单儿

pronounce: how is this pronounced? zhèige zì zěnme fāyīn? [jay-gur dzur dzun-mur fah-yin]
这个字怎么发音?

Protestant jīdūjiàotú
[jee-doo-jyow-too]
基督教徒

public convenience gōnggòng cèsuǒ [goong-goong tsur-swor]
公共厕所

public holiday gōngjià
[goong-jyah]
公假

There are several different kinds of holidays in the Chinese calendar when various facilities will be closed. The biggest of all, Chinese New Year or Spring Festival, chūnjié, is the only traditional Chinese festival marked by a holiday. It sees nearly all shops and offices closing down for three days, and a large proportion of the population off work. Even after the third day, offices such as banks may operate on restricted hours until the official end of the →

holiday period, eleven days later. The other traditional Chinese festivals are not marked by official holidays, though you may notice a growing tendency for businesses to operate restricted hours at these times. There are also a number of secular public holidays which have been celebrated since 1949, the most important being 1 October (National Day). Offices close on these dates, though many shops will remain open. Finally, there are a few other dates, 8 March (Women's Day), 1 May (Labour Day), 1 June (Children's Day), 1 July (Chinese Communist Party Day) and 1 August (Army Day) which are celebrated by parades and festive activities by the groups concerned, but are not general holidays.

see **festival**

pull lā [lah]
拉

pullover tàoshān [mow-bay-hsin]
套衫

puncture (noun) pǎoqì
[pow-chee]
跑气

purple zǐ [dzur]
紫

purse (for money) qiánbāo

[chyen-bow]
钱包
(US: handbag) shǒutíbāo
[shoh-tee-bow]
手提包

push tuī [tway]
推

put fàng [fahng]
放

where can I put ...? wǒ bǎ ...
fàng zai nǎr? [wor bah –
dzai]
我把...放在哪儿?

**could you put us up for the
night?** wǒmen kéyi zai zhèr
guò yíyè ma? [wor-mun kur-yee
– jer gwor yee-yur mah]
我们可以在这儿过一
夜吗?

pyjamas shuìyī [shway-yee]
睡衣

Q

quality zhìliàng [jur-lyang]
质量

quarter sì fēn zhī yī [sur fun jur
yee]
四分之一

question wèntí [wun-tee]
问题

queue (noun) duì [dway]
队

quick kuài [kwai]
快

that was quick zhěn kuài
[jun]
真快

what's the quickest way there?
něitiáo lù zuì kuài? [nay-tyow
loo zway]
哪条路最快?

quickly hěn kuài di [hun kwai]
很快地

quiet (place, hotel) **ānjìng**
[ahn-jing]
安静

quite (fairly) **xiāngdāng**
[hsyahng-dahng]
相当

that's quite right zhēnduì
[jun-dway]
真对

quite a lot xiāngdāng duō
[hsyahng-dahng dwor]
相当多

R

rabbit (meat) **tùzi** [too-dzur]
兔子

race (for runners, cars) **bǐsài**
[bee-sai]
比塞

racket (tennis, squash) **qiúpāi**
[chyoh-pai]
球拍

radiator (in room) **nuǎnqì**
[nwahn-chee]
暖器

(of car) **sànrèqì** [sahn-rur-
chee]
散热器

radio shōuyīnjī [shoh-yin-
jee]
收音机

on the radio zài shōuyīnjī
[dzai]
在收音机

rail: by rail zuò huǒchē [dzor
hwor-chur]
坐火车

railway tiělù [tyeh-loo]
铁路

rain (noun) **yǔ** [yew]
雨

in the rain zài yǔli [dzai
yew-lee]
在雨里

it's raining xià yǔ le [hsyah
yew lur]
下雨了

raincoat yǔyī [yew-yee]
雨衣

rape (noun) **qiángjiān**
[chyang-jyen]
强奸

rare (uncommon) **xīyǒu**
[hshee-yoh]
稀有

(steak) **nèn diǎnr** [nun dyenr]
嫩点儿

rash (on skin) **pízhěn** [pee-jun]
皮疹

rat láoshǔ [low-shoo]
老鼠

rate (for changing money)
duìhuànlǜ [dway-hwahn-lyew]
对换率

rather: it's rather good búcuò
[boo-tswor]
不错

I'd rather ... wǒ háishi
xiǎng ... [wor hai-shur
hsyahng]
我还是想...

razor (wet) tìhúdāo
[tee-hoo-dow]
剃胡刀
(electric) diàntìdāo
[dyen-tee-dow]
电剃刀

razor blades tìhú
dāopiàn [tee-hoo dow-pyen]
剃胡刀片

read (book) kànshū [kahn-shoo]
看书
(newspaper) kànbào [kahn-bow]
看报

ready zhǔnbèi hǎole [jun-bay
how-lur]
准备好了
are you ready? zhǔnbèi
hǎole, ma? [mah]
准备好了吗?
I'm not ready yet wǒ hái méi
hǎo ne [wor hai may how nur]
我还没好呢

when will it be ready? (repair etc)
shénme shíhou xiūwánle?
[shun-mur shur-hoh hsyoh-wahn-lur]
it should be ready in a couple of
days liǎngtiān jiù hǎole
[lyang-tyen jyoh how-lur]

real (genuine) zhēn de [jun
dur]
真的

really zhēnde [jun-dur]
真的
I'm really sorry zhēn duìbuqǐ
[jun dway-boo-chee]
真对不起
that's really great bàngjíle
[bahng-jee-lur]
棒极了
really? (doubt) shì ma? [shur
mah]
是吗?
(polite interest) zhēnde ma?
[mah]
真的吗?

reasonable (prices etc) hélǐ
[hur-lee]
合理

receipt shōujù [shoh-jyew]
收据

recently zuìjìn [dzway-jin]
最近

reception (in hotel) fúwùtái
[foo-woo-tai]
服务台

(for guests) zhāodàihuì [jow-dai-hway]

招待会

reception desk zǒng fúwùtái [dzoong foo-woo-tai]

总服务台

receptionist fúwùyuán [foo-woo-yew-ahn]

服务员

recognize rènshi [run-shur]

认识

recommend: could you recommend ...? qǐng nín tuījiàn ..., hǎo ma? [ching nin tway-jyen ... how mah]

请您推荐...好吗？

red hóngsède [hoong-sur-dur]

红色的

red wine hóng pútaojiǔ [hoong poo-tow-jyoh]

红葡萄酒

refund (noun) tuìkuǎn [tway-kwahn]

退款

can I have a refund? qǐng nín ba qián huán géi wó hǎo ma? [ching nin bah chyen hwahn gay wor how mah]

请您把钱还给我好吗？

region dìqū [dee-chew]

地区

registered: by registered mail guàhàoxìn [gwah-how-hsin]

挂号心

registration number chēhào

[chur-how]

车号

religion zōngjiào [dzoong-jyow]

宗教

remember: I don't remember wǒ jìbude le [wor jee-boo-dur lur]

我记不得了

I remember wǒ jìzhe [wor jee-jur]

我记着

do you remember? nǐ jìde ma? [nee jee-dur mah]

你记得吗？

rent (noun: for apartment etc) fángzū [fahng-dzoo]

房租

(verb: car etc) chūzū [choo-dzoo]

出租

to rent chūzū

出租

I'd like to rent a bike wó xiǎng yào zū yīliàng zìxíng chē [wor hsyahng yow dzoo yee-lyang dzur-hsing chur]

我想要租一辆自行车

repair (verb) xiūlǐ [hsyoh-lee]

修理

can you repair it? ní kéyi xiūxiu ma? [kur-yee hsyoh-hsyoh mah]

你可以修修吗？

repeat chóngfù [choong-foo]

重复

could you repeat that? qǐng nǐ zài shuō yíbiān, hǎo ma? [ching nee dzai shwor yee-byen how mah]

请你再说一边好吗？

reservation yùdìng [yew-ding]

预定

I'd like to make a reservation for a train ticket wó xiǎng yùdìng huǒchēpiào [wor hsyahng yew-ding hwor-chur-pyow]

我想预定火车票

• • • • • DIALOGUE • • • • • •

I have a reservation wó yǐjing yùdìng le [yee-jing - lur]

yes sir, what name, please? hǎo, nín guì xìng ma? [how nin gway hsing mah]

reserve (verb) yùdìng [yew-ding]

预定

• • • • • DIALOGUE • • • • • •

can I reserve a table for tonight? wǒ kéyǐ dìng ge jīntiān wǎnshang de zuò ma? [kur-yee ding gur jin-tyen wah-shahng dur dzwor mah]

yes madam, for how many people? hǎo, yígòng jǐge rén? [how yee-goong jee-gur run]

for two liǎngge rén [lyang-gur run]

and for what time? jǐdiǎn zhōng? [jee-dyen joong]

for eight o'clock bā diǎn zhōng [bah dyen]

and could I have your name, please? hǎo, nín guì xìng ma? [how nin gway hsing mah]

rest: I need a rest wǒ xūyào xiūxi yíxià [wor hsyew-yow hsyoh-hshee yee-hsyah]

我需要休息一下

the rest of the group tāmen biéde rén [tah-mun byeh-dur]

他门别的人

restaurant cāntīng [tsahn-ting]

餐厅

(big) fàndiàn [fahn-dyen]

饭店

(small) fànguǎnr [fahn-gwahnr]

饭馆儿

(Western-style) xīcāntīng [hshee-tsahn-ting]

西餐厅

Small noodle shops and food-stalls around train and bus stations have flexible hours, but restaurant opening times, outside the big cities, tend to be early and short. By 6 a.m. breakfast is usually well under way, and by 9 a.m. the noodle soups, buns, dumplings and rice porridge will have run out. Get up late and you'll have to join the first sitting for lunch at →

11 a.m. or so, leaving you plenty of time to work up an appetite for the evening meal at 5 p.m. An hour later you'd be lucky to get a table in some places, and by 9 p.m. the staff will be sweeping the debris off the tables and from around your ankles.

Standard restaurants are often divided into two or three floors. The first will offer a limited choice, usually scrawled illegibly on strips of paper or a board hung on the wall. You buy chits from a cashier for what you want, which you exchange at the kitchen hatch for your food and sit down at large communal tables or benches. Upstairs will be pricier and have waitress service and a written menu, while further floors are generally reserved for banquet parties or foreign tour groups.

There is now a big selection of foreign cuisine in the major cities, especially in the best hotels. Western-style fast-food outlets such as McDonald's and Kentucky Fried Chicken are mushrooming throughout the big cities of China. There are also some Chinese fast-food restaurants. However, Chinese food is → by nature fast food so it is as well to go to proper restaurants. Getting fed is never difficult as everyone wants your custom.

Walk past anywhere that sells cooked food and you'll be hailed by cries of **chī fàn** – basically, 'come and eat!' Pointing is all that's required at street stalls and small restaurants. In bigger places you'll sometimes be escorted through to the kitchen to make your choice. Menus, where available, are often more of an indication of what's on offer than a definitive list.

When you enter a proper restaurant you'll be quickly escorted to a table – standing around dithering is impolite, so avoid it. In all but the cheapest places, tea, pickles and nuts immediately follow, to take the edge off your hunger while you order. The only tableware provided is a spoon, bowl, and a pair or chopsticks, and at this point the Chinese will ask for a flask of boiling water and a bowl to wash it all in – not usually necessary, but something of a ritual.

Dishes are generally all served at once, placed in the middle of the table for diners to share. →

Soup is generally fairly bland and is consumed last to wash the meal down, the liquid slurped from a spoon or the bowl once the noodles, vegetables or meat in it have been eaten. When you've finished your meal, rest your chopsticks together across the top of your bowl.

restaurant car cānchē
[tsahn-chur]
餐车

rest room cèsuǒ [tsur-swor]
厕所

retired: I'm retired wǒ tuìxiūle
[wor tway-hsyoh-lur]
我退休了

return: a return to ... dào ... de
láihui piào [dow ... dur
lai-hwuy pyow]
到...的来回票

return ticket láihui piào
来回票
see **ticket**

reverse charge call duìfāng
fùkuǎn [dway-fahng foo-kwahn]
对方付款

revolting ràng rén ěxīn [rahng
run ur-hsin]
让人恶心

rice (cooked) mǐfàn [mee-fahn]
米饭
(uncooked) dàmǐ [dah-mee]
大米

rice bowl fànwǎn [fahn-wahn]
饭碗

rice field dàotián [dow-tyen]
稻田

rice wine mǐjiǔ [mee-jyoh]
米酒

rich (person) yǒuqián [yoh-chyen]
有钱

ridiculous kěxiàode
[kur-hsyow-dur]
可笑的

right (correct) duì [dway]
对
(not left) yòu(biānr)
[yoh(-byenr)]
右(边儿)

you were right nǐ duìle [nee
dway-lur]
你对了

that's right duì le
对了

this can't be right zhè búduì
[jur boo-dway]
这不对

right! duì!
对

is this the right road for ...?
qù ..., zhème zǒu duì ma?
[chew ... jur-mur dzoh dway
mah]
去...这么走对吗?

on the right zài yòubiānr
[dzai]
在右边儿

turn right wǎng yòu guǎi

[wahng yoh gwai]

往右拐

ring (on finger) jièzhi [jyeh-jur]

戒指

I'll ring you wó géi ní dǎ diànhuà [wor gay nee dah dyen-hwah]

我给你打电话

ring back zài dǎ diànhuà [dzai]

再打电话

ripe (fruit) shú [shoo]

熟

rip-off: it's a rip-off zhè shi qiāozhúgàng [jur shur chyow-joo-gahng]

这是敲竹杠

rip-off prices qiāozhúgàng de jiàr [chyow-joo-gahng dur jyahr]

敲竹杠的价儿

risky màoxiǎn [mow-hsyen]

冒险

river hé [hur]

河

RMB rénmínbì [run-min-bee]

人民币

road lù [loo]

路

is this the road for ...? zhèi tiáo lù wǎng ... qù? [jay tyow loo wahng ... chew]

这条路往...去?

rob: I've been robbed wǒ ràng rén géi qiǎngle [wor rahng run gay chyang-lur]

我让人给抢了

rock yánshí [yen-shur]

岩石

(music) yáogǔn yīnyuè [yow-gun yin-yew-eh]

摇滚音乐

on the rocks (with ice) jiā bīngkuàir [jyah bing-kwair]

加冰块儿

roll (bread) miànbāo juǎnr [myen-bow jyew-ahnr]

面包卷儿

roof fángdǐng [fahng-ding]

房顶

room (hotel) fángjiān [fahng-jyen]

房间

(space) kōngjiān [koong-jyen]

空间

in my room zài wǒ fángjiānli [dzai]

在我房间里

• • • • • DIALOGUE • • • • •

do you have any rooms? yǒu fángjiān ma? [yoh – mah]

for how many people? jǐge rén? [jee-gur run]

for one/for two yí/liǎngge [yee/lyang-gur]

yes, we have rooms free yǒu fángjiān

for how many nights will it be? jǐtiān? [jee-tyen]

just for one night yìtiān [yee-tyen]

how much is it? duōshao qián? [dwor-show chyen]

... yuan with bathroom, and ... yuan without bathroom yǒu yùshì de fángjiān yào ... kuài, méiyou yùshì de yào ... kuài [yoh yoo-shee dur fahng-jyen yow ... kwai may-yoh yoo-shur]

can I see a room with bathroom? wó xiǎng kàn yíjian yǒu yùshìde fángjiān [wor hsyahng kahn yee-jyen yoh yoo-shur-dur]

OK, I'll take it hǎo, xíngle [how hsing-lur]

room service sòng fàn fúwù [soong fahn foo-woo]

送饭服务

rope shéngzi [shung-dzur]

绳子

roughly (approximately) dàyuē [dah-yew-eh]

大约

round: it's my round gāi wó mǎi le [gai wor mai lur]

该我买了

round trip ticket láihuí piào [lai-hway pyow]

来回票

route lùxiàn [loo-hsyen]

路线

what's the best route? něitiáo lùxiàn zuì hǎo? [nay-tyow loo-hsyen dzway how]

哪条路线最好？

rubber (material) xiàngjiāo [hsyahng-jyow]

橡胶

(eraser) xiàngpí [hsyahng-pee]

橡皮

rubbish (waste) lājī [lah-jee]

垃圾

(poor-quality goods) fèiwù [fay-woo]

废物

rubbish! (nonsense) fèihuà! [fay-hwah]

废话

rucksack bèibāo [bay-bow]

背包

rude bù lǐmào [lee-mow]

不礼貌

ruins fèixū [fay-hsyew]

废墟

rum lángmújiǔ [lahng-moo-jyoh]

朗姆酒

rum and Coke® kékoukělè jiā lángmújiǔ [kur-koh-kur-lur jyah lahng-moo-jyoh]

可口可了加朗姆酒

run (verb: person) pǎo [pow]

跑

how often do the buses run? gōnggòng qìchē duóchang shíjiān yítàng? [goong-goong chee-chur dwor-chahng shur-jyen yee-tahng]

公共汽车多长时间一趟？

Russia Éguó [ur-gwor]

俄国

Russian (adj) Éguó

俄国

S

saddle (for bike, horse) ānzi [ahn-dzur]
鞍子

safe (not in danger) píng'ān
平安
(not dangerous) ānquán [ahn-choo-en]
安全

safety pin biézhēn [byeh-jun]
别针

sail (noun) fān [fahn]
帆

salad shālà [shah-lah]
沙拉

salad dressing shālà yóu [yoh]
沙拉油

sale: for sale chūshòu [choo-shoh]
出售

salt yán [yahn]
盐

same: the same yíyàng [yee-yang]
一样
the same as this gēn zhèige yíyàng [gun jay-gur yee-yang]
跟这个一样
the same again, please qǐng zài lái yíge [ching dzai lai yee-gur]
请再来一个

it's all the same to me wǒ wú suǒwèi [wor woo swor-way]
我无所谓

sandals liángxié [lyang-hsyeh]
凉鞋

sandwich sānmíngzhì [sahn-ming-jur]
三明治

sanitary napkins/towels wèishēngjīn [way-shung-jin]
卫生巾

Saturday xīngqiliù [hsing-chee-lyoh]
星其六

say (verb) shuō [shwor]
说
how do you say ... in Chinese? yòng Zhōngwén zěnme shuō ...? [yoong joong-wun dzun-mur shwor]
用中文怎么说...?
what did he say? tā shuō shénme? [tah – shun-mur]
他说什么?
he said tā shuō [tah]
他说
could you say that again? qǐng zài shuō yíxià [ching dzai – yee-hsyah]
请再说一下

scarf (for neck) wéijīn [way-jin]
围巾
(for head) tóujīn [toh-jin]
头巾

scenery fēngjǐng [fung-jing]
风景

schedule (US: train) **lièchē shíkè biǎo** [lyeh-chur shur-kur byow]
列车时刻表

scheduled flight **bānjī** [bahn-jee]
班机

school **xuéxiào** [hsyew-eh-hsyow]
学校

scissors: a pair of scissors **yìbá jiǎnzi** [yee-bah jyen-dzur]
一把剪子

scotch **wēishìjì** [way-shur-jee]
威士忌

Scotch tape® **tòumíng jiāodài** [toh-ming jyow-dai]
透明胶带

Scotland **Sūgélán**
苏格兰

Scottish **Sūgélán** [soo-gur-lahn]
苏格兰

I'm Scottish **wǒ shi Sūgélánren** [wor shur – run]
我是苏格兰人

scrambled eggs **chǎo jīdàn** [chow jee-dahn]
炒鸡蛋

sea **hǎi**
海

by the sea **zaì hǎibiānr** [dzai hai-byenr]
在海边儿

seafood **hǎiwèi** [hai-way]
海味

seal (for printing name) **túzhāng** [too-jahng]
图章

seasick: I feel seasick **wǒ yūnchuánle** [wor yewn-chwahn-lur]
我晕船了

I get seasick **wǒ yūnchuán** [wor yewn-chwahn]
我晕船

seat **zuòwei** [dzwor-way]
座位

is this seat taken? **yǒu rén ma?** [yoh run mah]
有人吗？

second (adj) **di'èrge** [dee-er-gur]
第二个

(of time) **miǎo** [myow]
秒

just a second! **zhè jiù dé!** [jur jyoh dur]
这就得

second class (travel etc) **èr děng** [er dung]
二等

(hard sleeper) **yìngwò** [ying-wor]
硬卧

see **train**

second-hand **jiù(de)** [jyoh(-dur)]
旧（的）

see **kànjian** [kahn-jyen]
看见

can I see? **wó kéyi kànkan**

ma? [wor kur-yee kahn-kahn mah]

我可以看看吗？

have you seen ...? nǐ kànle ... ma? [kahn-lur mah]

你看了...吗？

I saw him this morning wǒ jīntian zǎoshang kànjian tā le [wor jin-tyen dzow-shahng kahn-jyen tah lur]

我今天早上看见他了

see you! zàijiàn! [dzai-jyen]

再见

I see (I understand) wǒ míngbai le [wor ming-bai lur]

我明白了

self-service zìzhù [dzur-joo]

自助

sell mài

卖

do you sell ...? nǐ mài bu mài ...?

你卖不卖...？

Sellotape® tòumíng jiāodài [toh-ming jyow-dai]

透明胶带

send sòng [soong]

送

(by post) jì

寄

I want to send this to England wó xiǎng ba zhèige jì gěi Yīngguó [wor syahng bah jay-gur jee dow ying-gwor]

我想把这个寄给英国

senior citizen lǎoniánren [low-nyen-run]

老年人

separate fēnkāi [fun-kai]

分开

separately (pay, travel) fēnkāi de

分开的

September jiǔyuè [jyoh-yew-eh]

九月

serious (problem, illness) yánzhòng(de) [yen-joong(-dur)]

严中(的)

service charge (in restaurant) xiǎofèi [hsyow-fay]

小费

serviette cānjīn [tsahn-jin]

餐巾

set menu fènrfàn [funr-fahn]

份儿饭

several jǐge [jee-gur]

几个

sew féng [fung]

缝

could you sew this ... back on? qíng nǐn bāng wó bǎ zhèige ... féngshangqu, hǎo ma? [ching nin bahng wor bah jay-gur ... fung-shahng-chew how mah]

请您帮我把这个...缝上去好吗？

sex (male/female) xìngbié [hsing-byeh]

性别

sexy xìnggǎn [hsing-gahn]
性感

shade: in the shade zài
yīnliáng chù [dzai yin-
lyang]
在阴凉处

shake: let's shake hands
wǒmen wòwo shǒu ba
[wor-mun wor-wor shoh bah]
我们握握手吧

shallow (water) qiǎn [chyen]
浅

shame: what a shame! zhēn
kěxī! [jun kur-hsee]
真可惜

shampoo (noun) xǐfàjì
[hshee-fah-jee]
洗发剂

share (verb: room, table etc)
héyòng [hur-yoong]
合用

sharp (knife) jiānruì [jyen-rway]
尖锐
(pain) ruì [rway]
锐

shaver diàndòng tìhú dāo
[dyen-doong tee-hoo dow]
电动剃胡刀

shaving foam guā hú pàomò
[gwah hoo pow-mor]
挂胡泡沫

shaving point diàntìdāo
chāxiāo [dyen-tee-dow
chah-hsyow]
电剃刀插销

she* tā [tah]
她
is she here? tā zài ma? [dzai
mah]
她在吗？

sheet (for bed) bèidān [bei-dahn]
被单

shelf jiàzi [jyah-dzur]
架子

shellfish bèilèi [bay-lay]
贝类

ship chuán [chwahn]
船
by ship zuò chuán
[dzwor]
坐船

shirt chènyī [chun-yee]
衬衣

**shock: I got an electric shock
from the ...** wǒ
pèngzhe... ér chùdiàn [wor
pung-jur – dyen]
我碰着...而触电

shocking jīngrénde
[jing-run-dur]
惊人的

shoe xié [hsyeh]
鞋
a pair of shoes yìshuāng xié
[yee-shwahng]
一双鞋

shoelaces xiédài [hsyeh-dai]
鞋带

shoe polish xiéyóu [hsyeh-yoh]
鞋油

shoe repairer xiūxiéjiàng
[hsyoh-hsyeh-jyang]
修鞋匠

shop shāngdiàn [shahng-dyen]
商店
see **opening times**

shopping: I'm going
shopping wǒ qù mǎi dōngxi
[wor chew mai doong-hshee]
我去买东西

shore (of sea, lake) àn [ahn]
岸

short (person) ǎi
矮
(time, journey) duǎn [dwahn]
短

shorts duǎnkù [dwahn-koo]
短

should: what should I do? wǒ
gāi zěnme bàn? [wor gai
dzun-mur bahn]
我该怎么办？

you should … nǐ
yīnggāi … [ying-gai]
你应该...

you shouldn't … nǐ bù
yīnggāi …
你不应该...

he should be back soon guò
yíhuìr, tā yīng zài huílai
[gwor yee-hwayr tah ying dzai
hway-lai]
过一回儿他应再回来

shoulder jiānbǎng [jyen-bahng]
肩膀

shout (verb) hǎn [hahn]
喊

show (in theatre) biáoyǎn
[byow-yahn]
表演

could you show me? nǐ néng
ràng wǒ kànkan ma? [nung
rahng wor kahn-kahn mah]
你能让我看看吗？

shower (of rain) zhènyǔ
[jun-yew]
阵雨
(in bathroom) línyù [lin-yew]
淋浴

with shower dài línyù
带淋浴

shrine shénkān [shun-kahn]
神龛

shut (verb) guān [gwahn]
关

when do you shut? nǐmen
jídiǎn guānménr? [nee-mun
jee-dyen gwahn-munr]
你们几点关门儿？

when does it shut? jídiǎn
guānménr? [jee-dyen]
几点关门儿？

they're shut guānménr le
[lur]
关门儿了

I've shut myself out wó bǎ
zìjǐ guān zài wàitou le [wor
bah dzur-jee gwahn dzai wai-toh
lur]
我把自己关在外头了

shut up! zhù zuǐ! [joo dzway]
住嘴

shy hàixiū [hai-hsyoh]
害羞

sick (ill) yǒubìng [yoh-bing]
有病

I'm going to be sick (vomit) wǒ
yào ǒutù [wor yow oh-too]
我要呕吐

side: the other side of the street
zài jiē de duìmian [dzai jyeh
dur dway-myen]
在街的对面

sidewalk rénxíng dào
[run-hsing dow]
人行道

sight: the sights of ... ... de
fēngjǐng [fung-jing]
...的风景

sightseeing: we're going
sightseeing wǒmen qù
yóulǎn [wor-mun chew
yoh-lahn]
我们去游览

silk sīchóu [sur-choh]
丝绸

Silk Road sīchóu zhī lù [jur]
丝绸之路

silly chǔn
蠢

silver (noun) yín(zi) [yin-dzur]
银 (子)

similar xiāngjìn de [hsyahng-jin
dur]
相近

simple (easy) jiǎndān
[jyen-dahn]
简单

since: since last week zìcóng
shànggge xīngqī yǐlái
[dzur-tsoong shahng-gur
hsing-chee yee-lai]
自从上个星其以来

since I got here zìcóng wǒ lái
yǐhòu [dzur-tsoong wor lai
yee-hoh]
自从我来以候

sing chànggē [chahng-gur]
唱歌

Singapore Xīnjiāpō
[hsin-jyah-por]
新加坡

singer gēchàngjiā
[gur-chahng-jyah]
歌唱家

single: a single to ... yìzhāng
qù ... de dānchéngpiào
[yee-jahng chew ... dur
dahn-chung-pyow]
一张去...的单程票

I'm single wǒ shì dúshēn [wor
shur dahn-shun]
我是独身

single bed dānrén chuáng
[dahn-run chwahng]
单人床

single room dānrén jiān
[jyen]
单人间

single ticket (dānchéng) piào

[pyow]

(单程)票

sink (in kitchen) shuǐchí

[shway-chur]

水池

sister (elder) jiějie [jyeh-jyeh]

姐姐

(younger) mèimei [may-may]

妹妹

sit: can I sit here? wǒ kéyi zuò

zhèr ma? [wor kur-yee dzwor jer

mah]

我可以坐这儿吗?

is anyone sitting here?

yǒu rén zài zhèr ma? [yoh

run]

有人在这儿吗?

sit down zuòxià [dzwor-hsyah]

坐下

sit down! qǐng zuòxià!

[chǐng]

请坐下

size chǐcùn [chur-tsun]

尺寸

skin (human) pífu

皮肤

(animal) pí

皮

skinny shòu [shoh]

瘦

skirt qúnzi [chewn-dzur]

裙子

sky tiān [tyen]

天

sleep (verb) shuìjiào

[shway-jyow]

睡觉

did you sleep well? nǐ shuì de

hǎo ma? [shway dur how mah]

你睡得好吗?

sleeper (on train) wòpù

[wor-poo]

卧铺

(soft) ruǎnwò [rwahn-wor]

软卧

(hard) yìngwò [ying-wor]

硬卧

sleeping bag shuìdài

[shway-dai]

睡带

sleeping car wòpù chēxiāng

[wor-poo chur-hsyahng]

卧铺车厢

sleeve xiùzi [hsyoh-dzur]

袖子

slide (photographic)

huàndēngpiānr

[hwahn-dung-pyenr]

幻灯片儿

slip (garment) chènqún

[chun-chewn]

衬裙

slow màn [mahn]

慢

slow down! màn diǎnr!

[dyenr]

慢点儿

slowly màn

慢

very slowly hěn màn

[hun]

很慢

small xiǎo [hsyow]

小

smell: it smells (bad) yǒu wèir le [yoh wayr lur]

有味儿了

smile (verb) xiào [hsyow]

笑

smoke (noun) yān [yahn]

烟

  do you mind if I smoke? wǒ kéyi zài zhèr chōu yān ma? [wor kur-yee dzai jer choh yahn mah]

我可以在这儿抽烟吗？

I don't smoke wǒ bú huì chōu yān [hway]

我不会抽烟

  do you smoke? nǐ chōu yān ma?

你抽烟吗？

  see **cigarette** XYZ

snack diǎnxīn [dyen-hsin]

点心

sneeze (noun) dǎ pēntì [da pun-tee]

打喷嚏

snow (noun) xuě [hsyew-eh]

雪

so: it's so good nàme [nah-mur]

那么好

  it's so expensive nàme guì

那么贵

  not so much méi nàme duō

[may – dwor]

没那么多

  not so bad méi nàme huài

没那么坏

  so-so búguò rúcǐ [boo-gwor roo-tsur]

不过如此

soap féizào [fay-dzow]

肥皂

soap powder xǐyīfěn [hshee-yee-fun]

洗衣粉

sock duǎnwà [dwahn-wah]

短袜

socket chāzuò [chah-dzwor]

插座

soda (water) sūdá [soo-dah]

苏打

sofa shāfā [shah-fah]

沙发

soft (material etc) ruǎn [rwahn]

软

soft drink qìshuǐr [chee-shwayr]

汽水儿

Canned drinks, usually sold unchilled, include various lemonades and colas, such as Coca-Cola, and the national sporting drink Jianlibao, an orange and honey confection which most foreigners find too sweet. Fruit juices can be unusual and refreshing, however, as →

they are often flavoured with chunks of lychee, lotus and water chestnuts.

Sweetened yoghurt drinks, available all over the country in little packs of six, are a popular treat for children.

soft seat ruǎnzuò [rwahn-dzwor]
软座
see **train**

sole (of shoe) xiédǐ [hsyeh-dee]
鞋底
(of foot) jiáodǐ [jyow-dee]
脚底

could you put new soles on these? qǐng nín huàn shuāng xīn xiédǐ, hǎo ma? [ching nin hwahn shwahng hsin – how mah]
请你换双新鞋底好吗？

some: can I have some water? qǐng lái yídiǎnr shuǐ, hǎo ma? [ching lai yee-dyenr – how mah]
请来一点儿水好吗？

can I have some apples? qǐng lái yíxiē píngguǒ, hǎo ma? [yee-hsyeh]
请来一些苹果好吗？

somebody, someone yǒurén [yoh-run]
有人

something mǒushì [moh-shur]
某事

I want something to eat wǒ xiǎng chī diǎn dōngxī [wor hsyahng chur dyen doong-hshee]
我想吃点东西

sometimes yǒushíhhou [yoh-shur-hoh]
有时候

somewhere mǒudì [moh-dee]
某地

I need somewhere to stay wǒ yào zhǎoge zhùchù [wor yow jow-gur]
我要找个住处

son érzi [er-dzur]
儿子

song gē [gur]
歌

son-in-law nǚxu [nyoo-hsoo]
女婿

soon (after a while) yìhuǐr [yee-hwayr]
一回儿
(quickly) kuài [kwai]
快

I'll be back soon wǒ yìhuǐr jiù huílai [wor yee-hwayr jyoh hway-lai]
我一回儿就回来

as soon as possible yuè kuài yuè hǎo [yew-eh – how]
越快越好

sore: it's sore téngde [tung-dur]
疼得

sore throat sǎngzīténg

[sahng-dzur-tung]

嗓子疼

sorry: (I'm) sorry duìbuqǐ
[dway-boo-chee]

对不起

sorry? (didn't understand) nǐ
shuō shenme? [shwor
shun-mur]

你说什么?

sort: what sort of ...? shénme
yàng de ...?
[dur]

什么样的...?

soup tāng [tahng]

汤

sour (taste) suān [swahn]

酸

south nán [nahn]

南

in the south nánfāng
[nahn-fahng]

南方

South Africa Nánfēi [nahn-fay]

南非

South African (adj) Nánfēi

南非

I'm South African wǒ shì
Nánfēirén [wor shur –run]

我是南非人

South China Sea Nánhǎi
[nahn-hai]

南海

southeast dōngnán
[doong-nahn]

东南

southern nánde [nahn-dur]

南的

South Korea nán Cháoxiān
[nahn chow-hsyen]

南朝鲜

southwest xīnán [hsin-ahn]

西南

souvenir jìniànpǐn [jin-yen-pin]

纪念品

soy sauce jiàngyóu [jyahn-gyoh]

酱油

Spain Xībānyá [hshee-bahn-yah]

西班牙

Spanish (adj) Xībānyáde
[hshee-bahn-yah-dur]

西班牙的

speak: do you speak English?
nín huì jiǎng Yīngyǔ ma?
[hway jyang ying-yew mah]

您回讲英语吗?

I don't speak ... wǒ búhuì
jiǎng ... [wor boo-hway]

我不回讲...

can I speak to ...? (in person)
máfan nín zhǎo yíxia ... hǎo
ma? [mah-fahn nin jow
yee-hsyah ... how]

麻烦您找一下...好
吗?

••••• DIALOGUE •••••

can I speak to Mr Wang? Wáng
xiānsheng zàibúzài?
[hsyahng-shung dzai-boo-dzai]

who's calling? nǐ shì shéi? [shur
shay]

it's Patricia wǒ shì Patricia [wor]
I'm sorry, he's not in, can I take a
message? duìbuqǐ, tā búzài,
yàobúyào liú gexìn?
[dway-boo-chee tah boo-dzai
-yow-boo-yow lyoh gur-hsin]
no thanks, I'll call back later
xièxie, guò yíhuìr wǒ zài dǎ
[hsyeh-hsyeh gwor yee-hwayr wor dzai
dah]
please tell him I called qǐng gàosu
tā wǒ dǎ le diànhuà [ching gow-soo
tah wor dah lur dyen-hwah]

spectacles yǎnjìng [yenjing]
眼镜
spend huāfèi [hwah-fay]
花费

---

spirits

In Chinese the word jiǔ, loosely
translated as 'wine', is used to
refer to all alcoholic drinks, including spirits, wine and beer.
The favourite drink is **báijiǔ**
('white alcohol') a clear vodka-
like spirit, made from rice or
millet, and nauseatingly strong
for the uninitiated. A lot of male
bonding takes place over glasses
of **báijiǔ**, normally drunk neat
during banquets from small
glasses, and in single gulps.
Local home-made varieties
can be quite good, but the
→

mainstream brands – especially
the nationally famous **Maotai** –
are pretty vile to the Western
palate. Imported spirits, particularly whiskies, are sold in
large department stores and in
tourist hotel bars, but are always
very expensive.
Wine is far less common, though
some very palatable wines are
produced locally and can be
found in tourist centres.

---

spitting

Spitting, as a means of clearing
the throat, is normal practice in
mainland China and takes place
not only in the street but also
inside trains, restaurants,
school classrooms and even
people's homes. There are now
government-led campaigns to
restrict the unhygienic habit,
but in the meantime it would
still not be considered disre-
spectful, for example, to spit
powerfully onto the floor during
conversation with guests or
strangers.

---

spoke (in wheel) fútiáo [foo-tyow]
辐条
spoon sháozi [show-dzur]
勺子

sport yùndòng [yewn-doong]
运动

sprain: I've sprained my ...
wǒde ... niǔ le [wor-dur ...
nyoh lur]
我的...扭了

spring (season) chūntian
[chun-tyen]
春天

in the spring chūntian
春天

square (in town) guángchǎng
[gwahng-chahng]
广场

stairs lóutī [loh-tee]
楼梯

stamp (noun) yóupiào
[yoh-pyow]
邮票

• • • • • DIALOGUE • • • • •

a stamp for England, please mǎi
yìzhāng dào Yīngguó de yóupiào
[mai yee-jahng dow ying-gwor dur
yoh-pyow]

what are you sending? nǐ jì
shénme? [shun-mur]

this postcard zhèizhāng
míngxìnpiàn [jay-jahng
ming-hsin-pyen]

star xīngxing [hsing-hsing]
星星

start kāishǐ [kai-shur]
开始

when does it start? jǐdiǎn
kāishǐ? [jee-dyen]
几点开始?

the car won't start chē
fādòngbùqǐlái [chur
fah-doong-boo-chee-lai]
车发动不起来

starter (food) lěngpánr
[lung-pahnr]
冷盘儿

station (train) huǒchē zhàn
[hwor-chur jahn]
火车站

(city bus) qìchē gòng zhàn
[chee-chur goong]
汽车共站

(long-distance bus) chángtú
chēzhàn [chahng-too chur-
jahn]
长途车站

(underground) dì tiě zhàn [tyeh
jahn]
地铁站

statue sùxiàng [soo-hsyahng]
塑像

stay: where are you staying?
nǐmen zhù zài nǎr? [nee-mun
joo dzai nar]
你们住在哪儿?

I'm staying at ... wǒ zhù
zài ... [wor joo dzai]
我住在...

I'd like to stay another two
nights wó xiǎng hái zhù
liǎng tiān [syahng hai joo]
我想还住两天

steak niúpái [nyoh-pai]

牛排

steal tōu [toh]

偷

my bag has been stolen wǒde
bāo bèi tōule [wor-dur bow bay
toh-lur]

我的包被偷了

steamed zhēng [jung]

蒸

steamed roll huājuǎnr
[hwah-jwahnr]

花卷儿

steep (hill) dǒu [doh]

陡

step: on the steps zài táijiē
shang [dzai tai-jyeh
shahng]

在台阶上

stereo lìtǐshēng [lee-tee-
shung]

立体声

Sterling yīngbàng [ying-bahng]

英镑

steward (on plane) fúwùyuán
[nahn foo-woo-yew-ahn]

服务员

stewardess fúwùyuán [nyew]

服务员

still: I'm still here wǒ hái zài
[wor hai dzai]

我还在

is he still there? tā hái zài
ma? [tah – mah]

他还在吗？

keep still! bié dòng! [byeh
doong]

别动

sting: I've been stung wó gěi
zhēle [wor gay jur-lur]

我给螫了

stockings chángtǒngwà
[chahng-toong-wah]

长统袜

stomach wèi [way]

胃

stomach ache wèiténg
[way-tung]

胃疼

stone (rock) shítou [shur-toh]

石头

stop (verb) tíng

停

please, stop here (to taxi driver
etc) qǐng tíng zài zhèr [ching
ting dzai jer]

请停在这儿

do you stop near ...?
zài ... fùjìn tíng ma? [mah]

在...附近停吗？

stop it! tíngzhǐ! [ting-jur]

停止

storm bàofēngyǔ [bow-fung-
yew]

暴风雨

straight (whisky etc) chún

纯

it's straight ahead yìzhí
cháoqián [yee-jur chow-chyen]

一直朝前

straightaway mǎshàng
[mah-shahng]

马上

strange (odd) qíguài de
[chee-gwai dur]

奇怪

stranger shēngrén [shun-
grun]

生人

strap dàir

带儿

strawberry cǎoméi [tsow-may]

草莓

stream xiǎoxī [hsyow-hshee]

小溪

street jiē(dào) [jyeh(-dow)]

街(道)

on the street zài jiēshang
[dzai jyeh-shahng]

在街上

streetmap jiāotōngtú
[jyow-toong-too]

交通图

string shéngzi [shung-dzur]

绳子

strong (person) qiángdàde
[chyang-dah-dur]

强大

(material) jiēshi [jyeh-shur]

结实

(drink, taste) nóng [noong]

浓

stuck: it's stuck kǎle [kah-lur]

卡了

student xuésheng

[hsyew-eh-shung]

学生

stupid bèn [bun]

笨

suburb jiāoqū [jyow-chew]

郊区

subway (US) dìtiě [dee-tyeh]

地铁

suddenly tūrán [too-rahn]

突然

sugar táng [tahng]

糖

suit (noun) tàozhuāng
[tow-jwahng]

套装

it doesn't suit me (jacket etc)
wǒ chuān bù héshì [wor
chwahn boo hur-shur]

我穿不合适

it suits you nǐ chuān héshì

你穿合适

suitcase shǒutíxiāng
[shoh-tee-hsyahng]

手提箱

summer xiàtian [hsyah-tyen]

夏天

in the summer xiàtian

夏天

sun tàiyáng

太阳

sunbathe shài tàiyáng

晒太阳

sunblock (cream) fángshàirǔ
[fahng-shai-roo]

防晒乳

sunburn rìzhì [rur-shur]

日炙

Sunday xīngqītiān
[hsing-chee-tyen]

星期天

sunglasses tàiyángjìng
[tai-yang-jing]

太阳镜

sunny: it's sunny yángguāng
chōngzú [yang-gwahng
choong-dzoo]

阳光充足

sunset rìluò [rur-lwor]

日落

sunshine yángguāng
[yang-gwahng]

阳光

sunstroke zhòngshǔ
[joong-shoo]

中暑

suntan lotion fángshài jì
[fahng-shai]

防晒剂

suntan oil fángshàiyóu [–yoh]

防晒油

super hǎojíle [how-jee-lur]

好极了

supermarket chāojí shìchǎng
[chow-jee shur-chahng]

超级市场

supper wǎnfàn [wahn-fahn]

晚饭

supplement (extra charge)
fùjiāfèi [foo-jyah-fay]

附加费

sure: are you sure? zhēnde ma?
[jun dur mah]

真的吗？

sure! dāngrán! [dahn-grahn]

当然

surname xìng [hsing]

姓

swearword zāngzìr
[dzahng-dzur]

脏字儿

sweater máoyī [mow-yee]

毛衣

sweatshirt (chángxiù)
hànshānr [chahng-hsyoh
hahn-shahnr]

(长袖)汗衫儿

Sweden Ruìdiǎn [rway-dyen]

瑞典

Swedish (adj) Ruìdiǎnyǔ

瑞典语

sweet (taste) tián [tyen]

甜

(noun: dessert) tiánshí
[tyen-shur]

甜食

sweets tángkuàir [tahng-kwair]

糖块儿

swim (verb) yóuyǒng
[yoh-yoong]

游泳

I'm going for a swim wǒ qù
yóuyǒng [wor chew yoh-
yoong]

我去游泳

let's go for a swim zánmen

qù yóuyǒng [zahn-mun]

咱们去游泳

swimming costume yóuyǒngyī
[yoh-yoong-yee]

游泳衣

swimming pool yóuyǒng chí
[chur]

游泳池

swimming trunks yóuyǒngkù
[yoh-yoong-koo]

游泳裤

switch (noun) kāiguān
[kai-gwahn]

开关

switch off guān [gwahn]

关

switch on kāi [kai]

开

swollen zhǒng [joong]

肿

T

table zhuōzi [jwor-dzur]

卓子

a table for two wéile liǎngge
rén de zhuōzi [way-lur
lyang-gur run dur]

为了两个人的卓子

tablecloth zhuōbù [jwor-boo]

卓布

table tennis pīngpāngqiú
[ping-pahng-chyoh]

乒乓球

tailor cáifeng [tsai-fung]

裁缝

Taiwan Táiwān [tai-wahn]

台湾

Taiwanese (adj) Táiwān(de)
[–dur]

台湾(的)

take ná [nah]

拿

(somebody somewhere) dàilǐng

带领

(something somewhere) dài

带

(accept) jiēshòu [jyeh-shoh]

接受

can you take me to the ...?
qǐng dài wǒ dào ...? [ching
dai wor dow]

请带我到...?

do you take credit cards? nǐ
jiēshòu xìnyòngkǎ ma?
[jyeh-shoh hsin-yoong-kah mah]

你接受信用卡吗?

fine, I'll take it hǎo, xíngle
[how hsing-lur]

好行了

can I take this? (leaflet etc)
kéyi ná ma? [kur-yee nah]

可以拿吗?

how long does it take? yào
duōcháng shíjiān? [yow
dwor-chahng shur-jyen]

要多长时间?

it takes three hours yào
sānge zhōngtóu [yow
sahng-gur joong-toh]

要三个钟头

is this seat taken? zhèr yǒu rén ma? [jer yoh run mah]

这儿有人吗？

talk (verb) shuōhuà [shwor-hwah]

说话

tall gāo [gow]

高

tampons miánsāi [myen-sai]

棉塞

tap shuǐlóng tóu [shway-loong toh]

水龙头

tape (cassette) cídài [tsur-dai]

磁带

taste (noun) wèir [wayr]

味儿

can I taste it? kéyi chángchang ma? [kur-yee chahng-chahng mah]

可以尝尝吗？

taxi chūzū qìchē [choo-dzoo chee-chur]

出租汽车

will you get me a taxi? qíng nǐn bāng wǒ jiào liàng chūzūchē, hǎo ma? [ching nin bahng wor jyow lyang choo-dzoo-chur how mah]

请您帮我叫辆出租车好吗？

where can I find a taxi? zài nǎr kéyi zhǎodao chūzū qìchē? [dzai nar kur-yee jow-dow]

在哪儿可以找到出租汽车？

• • • • • DIALOGUE • • • • •

to the airport/to the Xian Hotel, please qǐng dài wǒ dào fēijīchǎng/Xīān fàndiàn [dow – fay-jee-chahng]

how much will it be? duōshao qián? [dwor-show chyen]

30 yuan sānshí kuài qián [sahn-shur kwai]

that's fine right here, thanks jiù zài zhèr, xièxie [jyoh dzai jer hsyeh-hsyeh]

A taxi in China can be a car, a minivan, a motorbike or a three-wheeled rickshaw (sānlún chē) with pedals or a motor. For anything smaller than a car, you have to negotiate your fare in advance and at the very least foreigners will be expected to pay two or three times the local rate. By international standards, taxi cars are cheap: in major cities, taxis have meters and the rates (which increase in proportion to the size of the car) are displayed on the side window. To avoid being taken on unnecessary detours, sit in the front seat ostentatiously consulting a →

map. Late at night, meters will not be used, so, if at all possible, a price should be negotiated. You'll find taxis of all kinds outside just about every mainland bus and train station.

taxi driver chūzūchē sījī
[choo-dzoo-chur sur-jee]
出租车司机

taxi rank chūzūchē diǎnr
[dyenr]
出租车点儿

tea (drink) chá [chah]
茶

tea for one/two, please qǐng lái yí/liǎngge rén de chá
[ching – run dur]
请来一/两个人的茶

Chinese tea comes in black, red, green and flower-scented varieties. Some regional kinds, such as **pú'ěr** from Yunnan and oolong (**wūlóng**) from the east, are highly sought after. Though always drunk without milk and only very rarely with sugar, the method of serving tea varies from place to place: sometimes it comes in huge mugs with a lid, elsewhere in dainty cups served from a miniature pot. When drinking in company, it's polite →

to top up others' cups before your own, whenever they become empty; if somebody does this for you, lightly tap your first two fingers on the table to show your thanks. In a restaurant, take the lid off or turn it over if you want the pot refilled during the meal; if you've had enough, leave your cup full.

teach: could you teach me? nín kéyi jiāojiao wǒ ma? [kur-yee jyow-jyow wor mah]
您可以教教我吗？

teacher lǎoshī [low-shur]
老师

team duì [dway]
队

teaspoon cháchí [chah-chur]
茶匙

tea towel cāwǎnbù
[tsah-wahn-boo]
擦碗布

teenager qīngshàonián
[ching-show-nyen]
青少年

telegram diànbào [dyen-bow]
电报

telephone diànhuà [dyen-hwah]
电话
see **phone**

television diànshì [dyen-shur]
电视

tell: could you tell him ...? qíng nǐn gàosu tà ..., hǎo ma? [ching nin gow-soo tah ... how mah]

请您告诉他...好吗?

temperature (weather) qìwēn [chee-wun]

气温

(fever) fāshāo [fah-show]

发烧

temple (Buddhist) sì [sur]

寺

(Taoist) miào [myow]

庙

tennis wǎngqiú [wahng-chyoh]

网球

term (at university, school) xuéqī [hsyew-eh-chee]

学期

terminus (rail) zhōngdiǎnzhàn [joong-dyen-jahn]

中点站

terrible zāogāo [dzow-gow]

糟糕

that's terrible tài zāogāo le [lur]

太糟糕了

terrific bàngjíle [bahng-jee-lur]

棒极了

Thailand Tàiguó [tai-gwor]

泰国

than* bǐ

比

even more ... than ...
bǐ ... gèngduō

[gung ... dwor]

比...更多

smaller than bǐ ... xiǎo [hsyow]

比...小

thank: thank you xièxie [hsyeh-hsyeh]

谢谢

thank you very much duōxiè [dwor-hsyeh]

多谢

thanks for the lift xièxie nǐn ràng wǒ dāle chē [rahng wor dah-lur chur]

谢谢您让我搭了车

no, thanks xièxie, wǒ bú yào [boo yow]

谢谢我不要

• • • • • DIALOGUE • • • • •

thanks xièxie

that's OK, don't mention it bú kèqi [kur chee]

that* nèige [nay-gur]

那个

that one nèi yíge [yee-gur]

那一个

I hope that ... wǒ xīwàng ... [wor hshee-wahng]

我希望...

that's nice nà hǎo le [nah how lur]

那好了

is that ...? nà shì ... ma?

[shur ... mah]

那是...吗？

that's it (that's right) **duìle**
[dway-lur]

对了

the*

theatre jùyuàn [jyew-yew-ahn]

剧院

their/theirs* **tāmende**
[tah-mun-dur]

他们的

them* **tāmen** [tah-mun]

他们

then (at that time) **nèige shíhou**
[nay-gur shur-hoh]

那个时候

(after that) **ránhòu** [rahn-hoh]

然候

there nàr

那儿

over there zài nàr [dzai]

在那儿

up there zài shàngtou [dzai
shahng-toh]

在上头

is/are there ...? yǒu ... ma?
[yoh ... mah]

有...吗？

there is/are ... yǒu ...

有...

there you are (giving something)
géi nǐ [gay]

给你

Thermos® flask rèshuǐpíng

[rush-way-ping]

热水瓶

these* **zhèixie** [jay-hsyeh]

在这些

they* **tāmen** [tahmun]

他们

thick hòu [hoh]

厚

(stupid) **bèn** [bun]

笨

thief zéi [dzay]

贼

thigh dàtuǐ [dah-tway]

大腿

thin (person) **shòu** [shoh]

瘦

(object) **xì** [hshee]

细

thing (matter) **shìr** [shur]

事儿

(object) **dōngxi** [doong-hshee]

东西

my things wǒde dōngxi

我的东西

think xiǎng [hsyahng]

想

**I think so wǒ xiǎng shì
zhèiyang** [wor hsyahng shur
jay-yang]

我想是这样

**I don't think so wǒ bú
zhèiyang xiǎng** [jay-yang]

我不这样想

**I'll think about it wǒ
kǎolù yíxia** [kow-lyew

yee-hsyah]

我考虑一下

third class sānděng [sahn-dung]

三等

(hard seat) yìngzuò [ying-dzwor]

硬座

see train

thirsty: I'm thirsty wǒ kóukě
[wor koh-kur]

我口渴

this* zhèige [jay-gur]

这个

this one zhèige

这个

this is my wife zhè shì wǒ
qīzi [jur shur wor chee-dzur]

这是我妻子

is this ...? zhèige
shìbúshì ...? [shur-boo-shur]

这个是不是...？

those* nèixie [nay-hsyeh]

那些

thread (noun) xiàn [hsyen]

线

throat sǎngzi [sahng-dzur]

嗓子

throat lozenges rùnhóu piàn
[run-hoh pyen]

润吼片

through jīngguò [jing-gwor]

经过

does it go through ...? (train,
bus) jīngguò ... ma? [mah]

经过...吗？

throw/throw away rēng [rung]

扔

thumb dàmúzhǐ [dah-moo-jur]

大拇指

thunderstorm léiyǔ [lay-yew]

雷雨

Thursday xīngqīsì
[hsing-chee-sur]

星期四

Tibet Xīzàng [hshee-dzahng]

西藏

Tibetan (adj) Xīzàngde
[hshee-dzahng]

西藏的

ticket piào [pyow]

票

• • • • • • DIALOGUE • • • • • •

a return to Xian wǎng Xīān de
huílái piào [wahng – dur hway-lai]

coming back when? nǐ shì nèitiān
yào huílái? [shur nay-tyen yow]

today/next Tuesday jīntian/xiàge
xīngqīèr

that will be 30 yuan sānshí kuài
qián [chyen]

ticket office (bus, rail)
shòupiàochù [shoh-pyow-choo]

售票处

tie (necktie) lǐngdài

领带

tight (clothes etc) xiǎo [hsyow]

小

it's too tight tài xiǎo le [lur]

太小了

tights **liánkùwà** [lyen-koo-wah]
连裤袜

time* **shíjiān** [shur-jyen]
时间

　what's the time? jídiǎn le?
　[jee-dyen lur]
　几点了?

　this time zhèicì [jay-tsur]
　这次

　last time shàng yícì [shahng
　yee-tsur]
　上一次

　next time xià yícì [hsyah]
　下一次

　three times sāncì
　三次

timetable (train) **lièchē shíkè
biǎo** [lyeh-chur shur-kur byow]
裂车时刻表

tin (can) **guàntou** [gwahn-toh]
罐头

tinfoil **xīzhǐ** [hshee-jur]
锡纸

tin-opener **guàntou qǐzi**
[gwahn-toh chee-dzur]
罐头起子

tiny **yìdiánrdiǎnr** [yee-dyenr-
dyenr]
一点儿点儿

tip (to waiter etc) **xiǎo fèi** [hsyow
fay]
小费

tire (US) **lúntāi** [lun-tai]
轮胎

tired **lèi** [lay]
累

　I'm tired wǒ lèi le [wor lay lur]
　我累了

tissues **báozhǐ** [bow-jur]
薄纸

to*: **to Shanghai/London dào
Shànghǎi/Lúndūn** [dow]
到上海/伦敦

　**to China/England qù
Zhōngguó/Yīnggélán** [chew]
去中国/英格兰

　to the post office dào yóujú
　到邮局

toast (bread) **kǎo miànbāo** [kow
myen-bow]
烤面包

today **jīntian** [jin-tyen]
今天

toe **jiáozhǐtou** [jyow-jur-toh]
脚指头

together **yìqǐ** [yee-chee]
一起

　we're together (in shop etc)
　wǒmen shì yíkuàir de
　[wor-mun shur yee-kwair
　dur]
　我们是一块儿的

toilet cèsuǒ [tsur-swor]

厕所

where is the toilet? cèsuǒ zai nǎr? [dzai]

厕所在哪儿？

I have to go to the toilet wǒ děi qù fāngbian fāngbian [wor day chew fahng-byen]

我得去方便方便

There are public toilets everywhere in China. In the more remote towns and villages they can be fairly stomach-churning. Public toilets are always of the squatting variety and consist of a hole in the ground. You should bring your own toilet paper. The contents of public toilets are collected for fertilizer, known as 'night soil'.

toilet paper wèishēngzhǐ [way-shung-jee]

卫生纸

tomato xīhóngshì [hshee-hoong-shur]

西红柿

tomato juice fānqié zhī [fahn-chyeh jur]

番茄汁

tomorrow míngtian [ming-tyen]

明天

tomorrow morning míngtian zǎoshang [dzow-shahng]

明天早上

the day after tomorrow hòutian [hoh-tyen]

后天

tongue shétou [shur-toh]

舌头

tonic (water) kuàngquánshuǐ [kwahng-choo-en-shway]

矿泉水

tonight jīntian wǎnshang [jin-tyen wahn-shahng]

今天晚上

too (also) yě [yur]

也

(excessively) tài

太

too hot tài rè [rur]

太热

too much tài duō [dwor]

太多

me too wǒ yě [wor]

我也

tooth yá [yah]

牙

toothache yáténg [yah-tung]

牙疼

toothbrush yáshuā [yah-shwah]

牙刷

toothpaste yágāo [yah-gow]

牙膏

top: on top of ... zài ... shàngtou [dzai ... shahng-toh]

在...上头

at the top zài dǐngshang [ding-shahng]

在顶上

torch shǒudiàntǒng
[shoh-dyen-toong]
手电筒

total (noun) zǒnggòng
[dzoong-goong]
总共

tour (noun) lǚxíng [lyew-hsing]
旅行

is there a tour of ...? yǒu
méiyou wǎng ... de lǚxíng?
[yoh may-yoh wahng ... dur]
有没有往...的旅行？

tour guide dǎoyóu [dow-yoh]
导游

tourist lǚyóu zhě [lyew-yoh jur]
旅游者

---

tourist information office
Inside the People's Republic,
there is no such thing as a tourist information office. CITS, the
state tour operator with a special responsibility for foreigners,
is just one of a large number of
operators who have no function
other than selling tours and tickets, and renting cars. However,
it may still be worthwhile drop-
ping in on the local branch of
CITS, or an affiliated organiza-
tion, especially in out-of-the-
way places, as sometimes it is
here that you will find the only
person in town who can speak
English. As for handouts, in the
→

---

form of leaflets, brochures or
maps, these are never free in
China. Other sources of information are your hotel staff (in
upmarket places) and, in certain tourist centres, restaurant
proprietors who give advice in
exchange for custom.

---

tour operator lǚxíng shè
[lyew-hsing shur]
旅行社

towards cháozhe [chow-jur]
朝着

towel máojīn [mow-jin]
毛巾

town chéngzhèn [chung-jun]
城镇

in town (zai) chénglǐ [(dzai)
chung-lee]
（在）城里

out of town (zài) chéngwài
[chung-wai]
（在）城外

town centre zhōngxīnqū
[joong-hsing-chew]
中心区

town hall shì zhèngfǔ dàlóu
[shur-jung-foo]
市政府大楼

toy wánjù [wahn-jyew]
玩具

track (US) zhàntái [jahn-tai]
站台

184

tracksuit yùndòngfú
[yewn-doong-foo]
运动服

traditional chuántǒng
[chwahn-toong]
传统

train huǒchē [hwor-chur]
火车

by train zuò huǒchē [dzwor hwor-chur]
坐火车

China's rail network is vast, efficient, and definitely the safest, most reliable way to travel through the country, even though getting hold of a seat can be difficult. There is an incredible demand for train tickets and you'll need to buy one well in advance. Theoretically, tickets are sold up to three days in advance, and stations in most big cities have foreigners' ticket offices which makes buying what's available fairly straightforward.

There are four train classes. The best is **ruǎnwò** (soft berth), roughly the same price as flying, and generally patronized by foreigners, party officials, and successful entrepreneurs. It's a pleasant experience; there's a plush waiting room at the

station, and on the train itself, you get a wood-panelled four-berth compartment with a soft mattress, fan, optional radio, and a choice of Western or Chinese-style toilets. There's an attendant on hand, too, and meals – though good in all classes – are more varied and taken separately from the other passengers. If you've a long way to travel and can afford it, soft berth is well worth the money.

Yìngwò (hard berth) is about half the price of ruǎnwò, is favoured by China's emerging middle class and money-conscious foreigners, and hence is the most difficult to book in advance. Unreserved hard travel can be hellishly crowded; reserved hard travel, however, is perfectly comfortable if you book a sleeper: clean sheets and blankets are supplied, and constant supplies of hot water are available. Carriages are divided into twenty rows of three bunks each. To every six bunks is allocated a Thermos flask of boiled water (topped up from the huge urn at the end of each carriage), and you bring your own mugs and beverage. Polystyrene boxes of rice and stir-fries are wheeled around from time to time, or you can use the restaurant car. Every carriage also has a toilet and washbasin.

For the really impecunious there's **yìngzuò** (hard seat), sometimes the only advance ticket available. Much rarer is the more upmarket **ruǎnzuò** (soft seat), only found on short-haul trains. Hard-seat train travel is cheaper and faster than bus travel, though on long journeys the discomfort can be excruciating, especially as the air is thick with cigarette smoke and every available inch of floor space is crammed with travellers who were unable to book a seat.

There are three types of train in China, and not all have the three main classes. Express trains do – they're identified by a number between 1 and 90, and you pay a small supplement to the standard fare. Trains numbered 100–350 or so are marginally cheaper, but make more stops, and have fewer berths. Anything marked 400 or above will stop whenever possible and have seats only, →

and should be avoided if possible.

Chinese train travellers nearly all bring slippers, a facecloth, a jam jar with a lid (to drink from) and tea leaves, as well as large quantities of food. Music and news is played incessantly over loudspeakers up and down the train.

•••••• DIALOGUE ••••••

is this the train for Shanghai?
zhèliè huǒchē qù Shànghǎi ma?
[jur-lyeh hwor-chur chew – mah]
sure qù [chew]
no, you want that platform there
búqù, nǐ yào dào nèige zhàntái
qù [boo-chew nee yow dow nay-gur jahn-tai]

trainers (shoes) **lǚyóuxié**
[lyew-yoh-hsyeh]
旅游鞋
train station huǒchēzhàn
[hwor-chur-jahn]
火车站
tram yóuguǐ diànchē [yoh-gway dyen-chur]
有轨电车
translate fānyì [fahn-yee]
翻译
could you translate that? qǐng nín fānyì yíxia, hǎo ma?
[chìng nin fahn-yee yee-hsyah

how mah]

请您翻译一下好吗？

translator fānyìzhě [fahn-yee-jur]
翻译者

trash lājī [lah-jee]
垃圾

travel lǚxíng [lyew-hsing]
旅行

we're travelling around
wǒmen zài lǚxíng [wor-mun
dzai]
我们在旅行

travel agent's lǚxíngshè
[lyew-hsing-shur]
旅行社

traveller's cheque lǚxíng
zhīpiào [lyew-hsing jur-
pyow]
旅行支票

Traveller's cheques, available
through banks and travel agents,
are the best way to carry your
funds around; their exchange
rate in China is fixed and better
than for cash. However, in mainland China they can only be
cashed at major branches of the
Bank of China and tourist hotels
and the process always involves
lengthy paperwork. Stick to
well-known names such as
Thomas Cook or American Express. Charges for transactions
are variable. →

In case you find yourself in dif-
ficulties, it's also worth taking
along a small supply of foreign
currency such as US dollars or
British sterling, which are more
widely exchangeable. There's a
low-key black market in China
for foreign currency, but the
small profits you'll make and the
risks of getting ripped off or
attracting police attention don't
make it worthwhile.

tray chápán [chah-pahn]
茶盘

tree shù [shoo]
树

trim: just a trim, please (to
hairdresser) qǐng zhǐ xiūxiu
diǎnr [ching jur hsyoh-hsyoh
byenr]
请只修修点儿

trip: I'd like to go on a trip to ...
wó xiǎng dào ... qù [wor
hsyahng dow ... chew]
我想到...去

trouble (noun) máfan [mah-fahn]
麻烦

I'm having trouble with ...
wǒ ... yùdàole diǎnr máfan
[wor ... yew-dow-lur dyenr]
我...遇到了点儿麻烦

trousers kùzi [koo-dzur]
裤子

true zhēnde [jun-dur]
真的
that's not true bú duì [dway]
不对

trunk (US: of car)
xínglǐxiāng [hsing-lee-hsyahng]
行李箱

trunks (swimming) yóuyǒngkù
[yoh-yoong-koo]
游泳裤

try (verb) shì [shur]
试
can I try it? kéyi shìyishì ma?
[kur-yee shur-yee-shur mah]
可以试一试吗？

try on: can I try it on? kéyi
shìyishì ma?
可以试一试吗？

T-shirt T xùshān [tee hsoo
shahn]
T恤衫

Tuesday xīngqièr
[hsing-chee-er]
星期二

tunnel suídào [sway-dow]
隧道

turn: turn left wǎng zuó [wahng
dzwor]
往左
turn right yòu guǎi [yoh gwai]
右拐

turn off: where do I turn off? wó
déi zài nǎr guǎiwān? [wor day
dzai nar gwai-wahn]
我得在哪儿拐弯？

can you turn the heating off?
qǐng ba nuǎnqì guānshang
[ching bah
nwahn-chee-gwahn-shahng]
请把暖器关上？

turn on: can you turn the heating
on? qǐng ba nuǎnqì dǎkāi
yíxià [dah-kai yee-hsyah]
请把暖器打开一下？

turning (in road) zhuǎnwānr
[jwahn-wahnr]
转弯儿

TV diànshì [dyen-shur]
电视

twice liǎngcì [lyang-tsur]
两次
twice as much duō yíbèi
[dwor yee-bay]
多一倍

twin beds liǎngge
dānrenchuáng [lyang-gur
dahn-run-chwahng]
两个单人床

twin room shuāngrén fángjiān
[shwahng-run fahng-jyen]
双人房间

twist: I've twisted my ankle
wǒde jiǎobózi niùle [wor-dur
jyow-bor-dzur nyoh-lur]
我的脚脖子扭了

type (noun) zhǒng [joong]
种
another type of ... lìng
yìzhǒng ... [ling yee-joong]
另一种...

typical **diǎnxíng** [dyen-hsing]
典型

tyre **lúntāi**
轮胎

U

ugly **nánkàn** [nahn-kahn]
难看

UK **Yīngguó** [ying-gwor]
英国

umbrella **yúsǎn** [yew-sahn]
雨伞

uncle (father's elder brother) **bófù**
伯父

(father's younger brother) **shūshu**
[shoo-shoo]
叔叔

(mother's brother) **jiùjiu**
[jyoh-jyoh]
舅舅

under ... (in position)
zài ... xià [dzai ...
hsyah]
在...下

(less than)
shǎoyú ... [show-yew]
...少于

underdone (meat) **bàn shēng
bù shú** [bahn shung boo shoo]
半生不熟

underground (railway) **dìtiě**
[dee-tyeh]
地铁
see bus

underpants **kùchǎ** [koo-chah]
裤衩

understand: I understand **wó
dǒng le** [wor doong lur]
我懂了

I don't understand **wǒ bù
dǒng**
我不懂

do you understand? **ní
dǒngle, ma?**
你懂了吗？

unemployed **shīyè** [shur-
yur]
失业

unfashionable **bù shímáo** [boo
shur-mow]
不时髦

United States **Měiguó**
[may-gwor]
美国

university **dàxué**
[dah-hsyew-eh]
大学

unlock **kāi**
开

unpack **dǎkāi** [dah-kai]
打开

until ... **dào ... wéizhǐ**
[dow ... way-jur]
到...为止

unusual **bù chángjiàn(de)**
[chahng-jyen(-dur)]
不常见(的)

up **shàng** [shahng]
上

up there zài nàr [dzai]
在那儿
he's not up yet tā hái méi
qǐlai [tah hai may chee-lai]
他还没起来
what's up? zěnme huí shìr?
[dzun-mur hway shur]
怎么回事儿?
upmarket gāojí [gow-jee]
高级
upset stomach wèi bù shūfu
[way boo shoo-foo]
胃不舒服
upside down dàoguolai
[dow-gwor-lai]
倒过来
upstairs lóushàng [loh-shahng]
楼上
urgent jǐnjí(de) [jin-jee(-dur)]
紧急(的)
us* wǒmen [wor-mun]
我们
with us gēn wǒmen yìqǐ [gun
– yee-chee]
跟我们一起
for us wéi wǒmen [wei]
为我们
use (verb) yòng [yoong]
用
may I use ...? wǒ kéyi yòng
... yíxia ma? [wor kur-yee
yoong ... yee-hsyah mah]
我可以用...一下吗?
useful yǒuyòng [yoh-yoong]
有用

usual (normal) píngcháng
[ping-chahng]
平常
(habitual) yuánlái de
[yew-ahn-lai dur]
原来的

V

**vacancy: do you have any
vacancies?** (hotel) zhèr yǒu
kòng fángjiān ma? [jer yoh
koong fahng-jyen mah]
这儿有空房间吗?
see **room**
vacation (holiday) jiàqī
[jyah-chee]
假期
on vacation xiūjià [hsyoh-
jyah]
休假
vacuum cleaner xīchénqì
[hshee-chun-chee]
吸尘器
valid (ticket etc) yǒuxiào
[yoh-hsyow]
有效
how long is it valid for? duō
cháng shíjiǎnnei yǒuxiào?
[dwor chahng shur-jyen nay
yoh-hsyow]
多长时间内有效?
valley shāngǔ [shahn-goo]
山谷
valuable (adj) bǎoguì(de)

[bow-gway(-dur)]

宝贵(的)

can I leave my valuables here?

wǒ kéyi bǎ guìzhòng de
dōngxi fàng zai zhèr ma?

[wor kur-yee bah gway-joong dur
doong-hshee fahng dzai jer mah]

我可以把贵重的东西
放在这儿吗？

van huòchē [hwor-chur]

货车

vary: it varies jīngcháng biàn
[jing-chahng byen]

经常变

vase huāpíng [hwah-ping]

花瓶

vegetables shūcài [shoo-tsai]

蔬菜

vegetarian (noun) chīsùde
[chur-soo-dur]

吃素的

Vegetarianism has been prac-
tised for almost two thousand
years in China for both religious
and philosophical reasons. Vegetarian cooking takes at least
three recognized forms: plain
vegetable dishes, commonly
served at home or in ordinary
restaurants; imitation meat
dishes, derived from Qing court
cuisine, which use gluten,
beancurd, and potato to mimic
meat, fowl and fish; and
→

Buddhist cooking, which avoids
onions, ginger, garlic and other
spices considered stimulating.
Having said all this, strict veg-
etarians visiting China will find
their options limited. Vegetables might be considered intrin-
sically healthy, but the Chinese
also believe that they lack any
fortifying properties, and vegetarian diets are unusual except
for religious reasons. There's
also a stigma of poverty attached to not eating meat. Although you can get vegetable
dishes everywhere, be aware
that cooking fat and stocks in
the average dining room are of
animal origins.

very fēicháng [fay-chahng]

非常

very little for me hén xiǎo
[hun hsyow]

很小

I like it very much wǒ hén
xǐhuan [wor hun hshee-hwahn]

我很喜欢

via jīngguò [jing-gwor]

经过

Vietnam Yuènán [yew-eh-nahn]

越南

view jǐng

景

village cūnzi [tsun-dzur]
村子

vinegar cù [tsoo]
醋

visa qiānzhèng [chyen-jung]
签证

All foreign nationals require a visa to enter China. Single entry tourist visas must be used within three months of date of issue: they are usually valid for thirty days from your date of entry into China, but regulations vary to control tourist traffic. Visas are available worldwide from Chinese embassies and consulates and through specialist tour operators and visa agents; if you are planning to enter China through Hong Kong, you'll find this is probably the best place to buy your visa.

Visa extensions are handled by the Foreign Affairs section of the Public Security Bureau (PSB), so you can apply for one in any reasonably-sized town. The amount of money you'll pay for this, and the amount of hassle you'll have, will vary greatly depending where you are. A first extension, valid for a month, is not usually difficult to obtain. A second extension is much →

---

harder to get, though not impossible. If the PSB refuse to grant an extension they may be able to point you in the direction of a private office which can.

---

visit (verb: person) qù kàn [chew kahn]
去看

(place) cānguān [tsahn-gwahn]
参观

I'd like to visit ... wó xiǎng cānguān ... [wor hsyahng]
我想参观...

voice shēngyīn [shung-yin]
声音

voltage diànyā [dyen-yah]
电压

Voltage is 220V, 50Hz AC. Sockets are generally two-pin so bring an adaptor with you. Certain parts of China have frequent power cuts.

---

vomit ǒutù [oh-too]
呕吐

W

waist yāo [yow]
腰

wait děng [dung]
等

wait for me děngdeng wǒ

[wor]

等等我

don't wait for me **búyòng déng wǒ** [boo-yoong dung wor]

不用等我

can I wait until my wife gets here? **wǒ néng děngdào wǒ qīzi lái de shíhou ma?** [nung dung-dow wor chee-dzur lai dur shur-hoh mah]

我能等到我妻子来的时候吗?

can you do it while I wait? **shìbúshì lìděng kéqǔ?** [shur-boo-shur lee-dung kur-chew]

是不是立等可取?

could you wait here for me? **qǐng děng zài zhèr hǎo ma?** [ching dung dzai jer how mah]

请等在这儿好吗?

waiter/waitress **fúwùyuán** [foo-woo-yew-ahn]

服务员

waiter!/waitress! **fúwùyuán!**

服务员

wake: can you wake me up at 5.30? **qǐng zài wǔdiǎnbàn jiàoxǐng wǒ, hǎo ma?** [ching dzai – jyow-hsing wor]

请在五点半叫醒我好吗?

Wales **Wēiěrshì** [way-er-shur]

威尔士

walk: is it a long walk? **yào zǒu hén yuǎn ma?** [yow dzoh hun yew-ahn mah]

要走很远吗?

it's only a short walk **zhǐ shì liūdaliūda** [jur shur lyoh-dah–]

只是溜达溜达

I'll walk **wǒ zǒuzhe qù** [wor dzoh-jur chew]

我走着去

I'm going for a walk **wǒ chūqu sànsan bù** [choo-chew sahn-sahn]

我出去散散步

wall **qiáng** [chyang]

墙

the Great Wall of China **Chángchéng** [chahng-chung]

长城

wallet **qiánbāo** [chyen-bow]

钱包

want: I want a ... **wǒ yào yíge ...** [wor yow yee-gur]

我要一个

I don't want any ... **wǒ bú yào ...**

我不要

I want to go home **wǒ yào huíjiā** [hway-jyah]

我要回家

I don't want to **wǒ bú yào**

我不要

he wants to ... **tā xiǎng ...** [tah hsyahng]

他想...

what do you want? **nǐ yào**

shénme? [shun-mur]
你要什么?

ward (in hospital) bìngfáng
[bing-fahng]
病房

warm nuǎnhuo [nwahn-hwor]
暖和

was*: he/she was tā shì [tah
shur]
他/她是
it was shì
是

wash (verb) xǐ [hshee]
洗
can you wash these? qíng
xǐxi zhèixie, hǎo ma? [ching
hshee-hshee jay-hsyeh how mah]
请洗洗这些好吗?

washhand basin liǎnpén
[lyen-pun]
脸盆

washing (dirty clothes) dài xǐ de
yīfu [yow hshee dur yee-foo]
待洗的衣服
(clean clothes) yíxǐ de yīfu
[yee-hshee-how]
已洗的衣服

washing machine xǐyījī
[hshee-yee-jee]
洗衣机

washing powder xǐyīfěn
[–fun]
洗衣粉

wasp huángfēng [hwahng-fung]
黄蜂

watch (wristwatch) shóubiǎo
[shoh-byow]
手表

water shuǐ [shway]
水
may I have some water? qǐng
lái diǎnr shuǐ, hǎo ma? [ching
lai dyenr shway how mah]
请来点儿水好吗?

> It's best not to drink what
> comes out of the tap; however
> tap water should be OK for
> brushing your teeth if you don't
> swallow it. Hotels provide a
> Thermos of drinkable water that
> can be refilled any time by the
> floor attendant. On trains, hot
> water is provided by an urn
> in each carriage. Boiled water
> is available just about every-
> where; bottled spring water is
> widely available.

water melon xīguā [hshee-gwah]
西瓜

waterproof (adj) fángshuǐ
[fahng-shway]
防水

way: it's this way shì zhèitiáo
lù [shur jay-tyow]
是这条路
it's that way shì nèitiáo lù
[nay-tyow]
是那条路

is it a long way to …?
dào … yuǎn ma?
[dow … chew yew-ahn mah]
到...远吗？

no way! bù kěnéng!
[kur-nung]
不可能

• • • • • DIALOGUE • • • • •

could you tell me the way to …?
qǐng nín gàosu wǒ,
dào … zěnme zǒu, hǎo ma?
[ching nin gow-soo wor
dow … dzun-mur dzoh how mah]

**go straight on until you reach the
traffic lights** yìzhí zǒu
hónglǜdēng [yee-jur dzoh
hoong-loo-dung]

turn left wǎng zuǒ guǎi [wahng
dzwor gwai]

take the first on the right yào
yòubiānr dì yìzhuǎn [yow
yoh-byenr dee yee-jwahn]

see where XYZ

we* wǒmen [wor-mun]
我们

weak (person) ruò [rwor]
弱
(drink) dàn [dahn]
淡

weather tiānqì [tyen-chee]
天气

wedding hūnlǐ [hun-lee]
婚礼

wedding ring jiéhūn jièzhi

[jyeh-hun jyeh-jur]
结婚戒指

Wednesday xīngqīsān
[hsing-chee-sahn]
星期三

week xīngqī [hsing-chee]
星期

a week (from) today xiàge
xīngqī de jīntian [hsyah-gur –
dur jin-tyen]
下个星期的今天

a week (from) tomorrow xiàge
xīngqī de míngtian
[ming-tyen]
下个星期的明天

weekend zhōumò [joh-mor]
周末

at the weekend zhōumò
周末

weight zhòngliàng [joong-
lyang]
重量

welcome: welcome to …
huānyíng dào … [hwahn-ying
dow]
欢迎到...

you're welcome (don't mention
it) búyòng xiè [boo-yoong
hsyeh]
不用谢

well: I don't feel well wǒ juéde
bù shūfu [wor jyew-eh-dur boo
shoo-foo]
我觉得不舒服

she's not well tā bù shūfu

[tah]
她不舒服

you speak English very well nǐ
Yīngyǔ jiǎngde hén hǎo
[ying-yew jyang-dur hun how]
你英语讲得很好

well done! tài hǎole! [how-lur]
太好了

I would like this one as well
wǒ hái yào zhèige [wor hai
yow jay-gur]
我还要这个

well well! āiyā! [ai-yah]
哎呀

• • • • • • DIALOGUE • • • • • •

how are you? nǐn hǎo ma? [how
mah]

very well, thanks, and you? hén
hǎo xièxie, nǐne? [hun how
hsyeh-hsyeh nee-neh]

well-done (meat) zhǔdetòu
[low-yee-dahnr]
煮得透

Welsh Wēi'ěrshì [way-er-shur]
威尔士

I'm Welsh wǒ shì
Wēi'ěrshìrén [wor shur – run]
我是威尔士人

were*: we were wǒmen shì
[wor-mun shur]
我们是

you were nǐmen shì
[nee-mun]
你们是

west xī [hshee]
西

in the west xībiānr
[hshee-byenr]
西边儿

West (European etc) Xīfāng
[hshee-fahng]
西方

in the West Xīfāng
西方

West Indian (adj) Xī Yìndù
qúndǎo rén [hshee yin-doo
chun-dow run]
西印度群岛人

western (adj) xī [hshee]
西

Western (adj: European etc)
xīfāng de [hshee-fahng dur]
西方的

Western-style xīshì [hshee-shur]
西式

Western-style food xīcān
[hshee-tsahn]
西餐

wet shī [shur]
湿

what? shénme? [shun-mur]
什么?

what's that? nà shì shénme?
[nah shur]
那是什么?

what should I do? wǒ yīnggāi
zuò shénme? [wor ying-gai
dzwor]
我应该作什么?

what a view! kàn zhè jǐngr!
[kahn jur]

看这景儿

what bus do I take? wǒ gāi
zuò nèihào chē? [wor gai
dzwor nay-how chur]

我该坐哪号车?

wheel lúnzi [lun-dzur]

轮子

wheelchair lúnyǐ [lun-yee]

轮椅

when? shénme shíhou?
[shun-mur shur-hoh]

什么时侯?

when we get back wǒmen
huílai de shíhou [wor-mun
hway-lai dur]

我们回来的时侯

when's the train/ferry?
huǒchē/dùchuán jídiǎn kāi?
[hwor-chur/doo-chwahn jee-dyen]

火车／渡船几点开?

where? nǎr?

哪儿?

I don't know where it is wǒ
bù zhīdao zài nàr [wor boo
jur-dow dzai nar]

我不知道在那儿

• • • • • • DIALOGUE • • • • • •

where is the Dragon temple? lóng
miào zài nǎr? [dzai]

it's over there jiù zài nàr [jyoh]

**could you show me where it is on
the map?** qǐng zài dìtúshang

zhǐshì gěi wǒ ba [ching –
dee-too-shahng jur-shur gay wor bah]

it's just here jiù zài zhèr [jyoh –
jer]

see **way**

which: which bus? něilù chē?
[nay-loo chur]

哪路车?

• • • • • • DIALOGUE • • • • • •

which one? nǎ yíge? [nah yee-gur]

that one nèige [nay-gur]

this one? zhèige? [jay-gur]

no, that one búshì, nèige
[boo-shur]

while: while I'm here wǒ zài
zhèr de shíhou [wor dzai jer
dur shur-hoh]

我在这儿的时侯

whisky wēishìjì [way-shur-jee]

威士忌

white bái

白

white wine bái pútaojiǔ
[poo-tow-jyoh]

白葡萄酒

who? shéi? [shay]

谁

who is it? shéi? [shway]

谁

the man who ... ... de
nèige ren [dur nay-gur run]

...的那个人

whole: the whole week
zhěngzheng yíge xīngqī

[jung-jung yee-gur hsing-chee]

整整一个星期

the whole lot quánbù

[choo-en-boo]

全部

whose: whose is this? zhèi shì shéide? [jay shur shay-dur]

这是谁的？

why? wèishénme?

[way-shun-mur]

为什么？

why not? wèishénme bù?

为什么不？

wide kuān de [kwahn dur]

宽的

wife qīzi [chee-dzur]

妻子

will*: will you do it for me? qíng géi wǒ zuò yíxià [ching gay wor dzwor yee-hsyah]

请给我作一下

wind (noun) fēng [fung]

风

window chuānghu

[chwahng-hoo]

窗户

near the window kào chuānghu [kow]

靠窗户

in the window (of shop) zài chúchuāngli [dzai choo-chwahng-lee]

在橱窗里

window seat kào chuāng de zuòwei [kow chwahng dur dzwor-way]

靠窗的座位

windy: it's windy guāfēng

[gwah-fung]

挂风

wine pútaojiǔ [poo-tow-jyoh]

葡萄酒

can we have some more wine?

qǐng zài lái diǎnr pútaojiǔ, hǎo ma? [ching dzai lai dyenr – how mah]

请再来点儿葡萄酒好吗？

see spirits

wine list jiǔdān [jyoh-dahn]

酒单

winter dōngtian [doong-tyen]

冬天

in the winter dōngtian

冬天

with* hé ... yìqǐ

[hur ... yee-chee]

和...一起

I'm staying with ... wǒ gēn ... zhù zài yìqǐ [wor gun ... joo dzai yee-chee]

我跟...住在一起

without méiyǒu [may-yoh]

没有

witness zhèngren [jung-run]

证人

wok guō [gwor]

锅

woman fùnǚ [foo-nyew]

妇女

women

Women travellers usually find incidences of sexual harassment much less of a problem than in other Asian countries. You may get some hassles, however, in Dongbei, where Chinese men may take you for a Russian prostitute (much embarrassment ensues when they realize their mistake) and in Muslim Xinjiang. As ever, it pays to be aware of how local women are dressing and follow their lead.

wonderful hǎojíle [how-jee-lur]
好极了

won't*: it won't start bù dáhuǒ
[dah-hwor]
不打火

wood (material) mùtou
[moo-toh]
木头
(forest) shùlín [shoo-lin]
树林

wool yángmáo [yang-mow]
羊毛

word cí [tsur]
词

work (noun) gōngzuò
[goong-dzwor]
工作
it's not working huàile [lur]
坏了

world shìjiè [shur-jyeh]
世界

worry: I'm worried wǒ bù ān
[wor bwahn]
我不安

worse: it's worse huàile
[hway-lur]
坏了

worst zuì huài [dzway hwai]
最坏

**would: would you give this
to ...?** qǐng nín bǎ zhèige
gěi ..., hǎo ma? [ching nin
bah jay gay ... how mah]
请您把这个给...好吗？

wrap: could you wrap it up?
qǐng nín bāng wǒ bāo yíxia,
hǎo ma? [ching nin bahng wor
bow yee-hsyah how mah]
请您帮我包一下好吗？

wrapping paper bāozhuāngzhǐ
[bow-jwahng-jur]
包装纸

wrist shǒuwànr [shoh-wahnr]
手腕儿

write xiě [hsyeh]
写

writing paper xìnzhǐ [hsin-jur]
信纸

wrong: this is the wrong train
wǒmen chéngcuòle huǒchē
[wor-mun chung-tswor-lur
hwor-chur]
我们乘错了火车
the bill's wrong zhàngdānr

cuòle [jahng-dahnr tswor-lur]

帐单儿错了

sorry, wrong number duìbuqǐ,
dǎcuòle [dway-boo-chee dah–]

对不起打错了

sorry, wrong room duìbuqǐ,
zhè búshì wǒde fángjiān [jer
wor-dur fahng-jyen]

对不起这不是我的房间

there's something wrong
with ... ... yǒu máobìng
[yoh mow-bing]

...有毛病

what's wrong? zěnmele?
[dzun-mur-lur]

怎么了？

Y

yacht fānchuán [fahn-chwahn]

帆船

Yangtze Gorge Chángjiāng
sānxiá [chahng-jyang sahn-syah]

长江三峡

Yangtze River Chángjiāng

长江

year nián [nyen]

年

yellow huángsè [hwahng-sur]

黄色

Yellow River Huáng Hé [hwahng
hur]

黄河

Yellow Sea Huánghǎi

黄海

yes* shìde [shur-dur]

是的

yesterday zuótian [dzwor-tyen]

昨天

yesterday morning zuótian
zǎoshang [dzow-shahng]

昨天早上

the day before yesterday
qiántian [chyen-tyen]

前天

yet hái

还

•••••• DIALOGUE ••••••

is it here yet? hái láile méiyou?
[lai-lur may-yoh]

no, not yet hái méilái [may-lai]

you'll have to wait a little longer yet
nǐ hái yào děng yídiǎnr [yow dung
yee-dyenr]

yoghurt suānnǎi [swahn-nai]

酸奶

you* (sing) nǐ

你

(sing, pol) nín

您

(pl) nǐmen [nee-mun]

你们

(pl, pol) nínmen [nin-mun]

您们

this is for you zhèi shì
géi nǐ de [jay shur gay nee
dur]

这是给你的

with you gēn nǐ yìqǐ [gun nee

yee-chee]

跟你一起

young niánqīng [nyen-ching]

年轻

your/yours* (sing) nǐde [nee-dur]

你的

(sing, pol) nínde [nin-dur]

您的

(pl) nǐmende [nee-mun-dur]

你们的

(pl, pol) nínmende

[nin-mun-dur]

您们的

Z

zero líng

零

zip lāliàn [lah-lyen]

拉链

could you put a new zip on?

qíng nín bāng wǒ huànge

xīn lāliànr, hǎo ma? [ching

nin bahng wor hwahn-gur hsin –

how mah]

请您帮我换个新拉链好

吗？

zoo dòngwùyuán

[doong-woo-yew-ahn]

动物园

Chinese-English

COLLOQUIALISMS

You might well hear the following expressions, but on no account should you use any of the stronger ones – they will cause great offence if used by a foreigner.

bèndàn! [bun-dahn] idiot!

chǔnhuò! [chun-hwor] idiot!

dàbízi! [dah-bee-dzur] big nose!

dà tuánjié [dah twahn-jyeh] ten-yuán note

fèihuà! [fay-hwah] rubbish!

gàile màorle [gai-lur mow-lur] absolutely the best

gǔn! [goon] go away!, get lost!

gǔnchūqù! [goon-choo-chyew] get out!

húndàn! [hoon-dahn] bastard!

juéle [jweh-lur] wonderful, unique

lǎowài! [low-wai] foreigner!

liǎobude [lyow-boo-dur] terrific, extraordinary

méizhìle [may-jur-lur] excellent

nǎli, nǎli [nah-lee] oh, it was nothing, you're welcome

suànle [swahn-lur] forget it

suíbiàn [sway-byen] as you wish

tāmāde! [tah-mah-dur] hell!, damn!

tài bàngle [bahng-lur] that's great

tài zāogāole [dzow-gow-lur] that's terrible

tài zāotòule [dzow-toh-lur] that's awful

xīpíshì [hshee-pee-shur] hippy

yángguǐzi! [yang-gway-dzur] foreign devil!

yāpíshì [yah-pee-shur] yuppie

yílù píng'ān [yee-loo ping-ahn] safe journey, bon voyage

yuánmù qiúyú [yew-ahn-moo choh-yoo] a waste of time (literally: climbing a tree to catch fish)

zāole! [dzow-lur] damn!, shit!

zhù zuǐ! [joo dzway] shut up!

zǒu kāi! [dzoh] go away!

A

ǎi short
Àiěrlán [ai-ur-lahn] Ireland;
Irish
àizībìng [ai-dzur-bing] AIDS
àn [ahn] dark; shore
ānjìng [ahn-jing] quiet
ānquán [ahn-choo-en] safe
ānzuò [ahn-dzwor] saddle
Àodàlìyà [or-dah-lee-yah]
Australia; Australian (adj)

B

ba [bah] particle at the end of
a sentence to indicate a
suggestion, piece of advice
etc
bā eight
bǎ measure word* used for
chairs, knives, teapots, tools
or implements with handles,
stems and bunches of
flowers
bàba [bah-bah] father
bābǎi eight hundred
bái white
bǎidù ferry
báisè [bai-sur] white
bái tiān [tyen] day, daytime
bǎiwàn [bai-wahn] one million
bàn [bahn] half
bàndá [bahn-dah] half a dozen
bàngjíle [bahng-jee-lur] terrific
bàngōngshì [bahn-goong-shur]
office
bāngzhù [bahng-joo] help
bànr [bahnr] partner,

boyfriend; girlfriend
bànyè [bahn-yur] midnight; at
midnight
báo [bow] thin
bàofēngyǔ [bow-fung-yew]
storm
bàozhǐ [bow-jur] newspaper
bāoguǒ [bow-gwor] package,
parcel
bāokuò [bow-kwor] include
bǎole [bow-lur] full
bǎozhèng [bow-jung] promise;
guarantee
báozhǐ [bow-jur] tissues,
Kleenex®
bāshí [bah-shur] eighty
bāyuè [bah-yew-eh] August
bēi [bay] cup, glass
běi north
Běi Ài'ěrlán [ai-er-lahn]
Northern Ireland
bēizi [bay-dzur] cup
bèn [bun] stupid
běn measure word* used for
books, magazines etc
bēngdài [bung-dai] bandage
bǐ [bee] than
    bǐ ... gèng [gung] even more
    than ...
    bǐ nèi duō diǎnr [nay dwor
    dyenr] more than that
biānjiè [byen-jyeh] border
biānjìng [byen-jing] border
biānr [byenr] side
biǎo [byow] form
biǎodì [byow-dee] cousin (male,
younger than speaker)
biǎogē [byow-gur] cousin (male,
older than speaker)

biáojiě [byow-jyeh] cousin
(female, older than speaker)

biǎomèi [byow-may] cousin
(female, younger than speaker)

biéde dìfang [byeh-dur dee-fahng]
somewhere else

biéde dōngxi [byeh-dur
doong-hshee] something else

bīng ice

bīngdòngde [–doong-dur]
frozen

bìngfáng [–fahng] ward

bīnguǎn [–wahn] hotel

bīngxiāng [–hsyang] fridge

bǐsài game; match; race

bìxū [bee-hsyew] must

bìyào(de) [bee-yow(-dur)]
necessary

bǐyǒu [bee-yoh] penfriend

bízi [bee-dzur] nose

bōhào [bor-how] dial

bōli [bor-lee] glass (material)

bōli bēi [bay] glass (for drinking)

bówùguǎn [bor-woo-gwahn]
museum

bózi [boh-dzur] neck

bù [boo] no; not; material,
fabric

bù duō [dwor] not much

bù chángjiàn(de)
[chahng-jyen(-dur)] unusual

bú kèqi [kur-chee] not at all

bùfen [boo-fun] part

bùhǎo [boo-how] bad

bù jiǔ [jyoh] soon

bù kěnéng [kur-nung]
impossible

bùliào [boo-lyow] cloth, fabric

bù lǐmào [lee-mow] rude

búshì [boo-shur] no, it is not
the case

búshì ... jiùshì ... [jyoh-shur]
either ... or ...

bùtóng [boo-toong] different;
difference

bùxíng [boo-sing] on foot

búyào! [boo-yow] don't!

búyàole [–lur] that's all;
nothing else

búyòng kèqi [boo-yoong kur-chee]
you're welcome, don't
mention it

búyòng xiè [hsyeh] you're
welcome, don't mention it

C

cài [tsai] dish; meal

cái only

cānchē [tsahn-chur] buffet car

cánfèi [tsahn-fay] disabled

cáng [tsahng] hide

cāngbái [–bai] pale

cānguān [–wahn] visit

cāngying fly (noun)

cānjin [tsahn-jin] napkin

cāntīng restaurant; dining
room

cǎo [tsow] grass

cǎoyào [tsow-yow] herbs
(medicinal)

céng [tsung] floor (in hotel etc)

cèsuǒ [tsur-swor] toilet, rest
room

chá [chah] tea (drink)

chà to (the hour)

chàbuduō [chah-boo-dwor]
almost, nearly

cháchí [chah-chur] teaspoon

cháhàotái [chah-how-tai]
  directory enquiries

chán [chahn] greedy

cháng [chahng] long

chànggē [–gur] sing

chàngpiàn [–pyen] record
  (music)

chángshāfā [–shah-fah] couch,
  sofa

chángtú chēzhàn [–too
  chur-jahn] long-distance bus
  station

chángtú diànhuà [dyen-hwah]
  long-distance call

chángtú qìchē [chee-chur]
  long-distance bus

chángtú qūhào [chew-how]
  dialling code

chāojí shìchǎng [chow-jee
  shur-chahng] supermarket

chǎole [chow-lur] noisy

chāopiào [chow-pyow]
  banknote, (US) bill

cháoshī [chow-shur] damp;
  humid

cháozhe [chow-jur] towards

chápán [chah-pahn] tray

chāzi [chah-dzur] fork

chē [chur] city bus

chēfèi [chur-fay] fare

chēlún [chur-lun] wheel

chéngbǎo [chung-bow] castle

chéngjiā [–jyah] married

chéngkè [–kur] passenger

chénglǐ [–lee] in town, in the
  city

chéngshì [–shur] city, town

chéngshí honest

chéngzhèn [–jun] town

chènyī [chun-yee] shirt

chētāi [chur-tai] tyre

chēzhàn [chur-jahn] bus
  station; bus stop

chī [chur] eat

chí late

chǐcùn [chur-tsun] size

chīde [chur-dur] food

chīle ... yǐhòu [chur-lur ...
  yee-hoh] after ...

chīsùde [chur-soo-dur]
  vegetarian

chóngfù [choong-foo] repeat

chuán [chwahn] ship, boat

chuáncāng [–tsahng] cabin

chuáng [chwahng] bed

chuángdān [–dahn] sheet

chuángdiàn [–dyen] mattress

chuānghu [–hoo] window

chuānkǒng [chwahn-koong]
  puncture

chuánrǎn [–rahn] infectious

chuántǒng [–toong] traditional

chuánzhēn [–jun] fax

chúfáng [choo-fahng] kitchen

chūkǒu [choo-koh] exit

chúle ... yǐwài [choo-lur ...
  yee-wai] except ..., apart
  from ...

chǔn silly

chūnjié [chun-jyeh] Chinese
  New Year

chūntiān [chun-tyen] spring; in
  the spring

chúxī [choo-hshee] New Year's
  Eve

chǔxù [choo-hsyew] deposit

chūzū [choo-dzoo] hire, rent

chūzūchē diǎnr [–chur dyenr]
taxi rank

chūzū qìchē [chee-chur] taxi

cí [tsur] word

cídài [tsur-dai] tape, cassette

cóng [tsoong] from

cōngcong hurriedly

cónglái bù never (referring to the
past or present)

cōngming clever, intelligent

cūnzhuāng [tsun-jwahng]
village

cuò(wù) [tswor(-woo)] mistake,
error; fault

D

dà [dah] big, large

dǎ hit

dàbó [dah-bor] brother-in-law
(husband' s elder brother)

dà bùfen shíjiān [dah boo-fun
shur-jyen] most of the time

dǎcuòle [dah-tswor-lur] wrong
number

dǎ diànhuà [dyen-hwah] phone,
call

dàgài probably

dàhuì [dah-hway] conference

dáhuǒjī [dah-hwor-jee]
cigarette lighter

dài take (something somewhere)

dàilái bring

dàilǐng take (someone somewhere)

dàilǐng yóujiàn [yoh-jyen] poste
restante

dàitì instead

dàjíle [dah-jee-lur] enormous

dàlù main road

dàmǐ uncooked rice

dàn [dahn] weak; pale

dānchéngpiào
[dahn-chung-pyow] single
ticket, one-way ticket

dāndú alone

dāngrán [dahn-grahn] of
course, certainly

dànián sānshí [dah-nyen
sahn-shur] Chinese New
Year's Eve

dānrén jiān [dahn-run jyen]
single room

dānshēn [dahn-shun] single,
unmarried

dànshì [dahn-shur] but

dānyuán [dahn-yew-ahn] flat,
apartment

dǎo [dow] island

dāo knife

dào to; arrive

dào ... wéizhǐ [way-jur] until ...

dàodá [dow-dah] arrive

dàodá shíjiān [shur-jyen]
arrival

dàotián [dow-tyen] paddy field,
rice field

dǎoyóu [dow-yoh] tour guide

dāozi [dow-dzur] knife

dàrén [dah-run] adult

dàshēng de [dah-shung dur]
loud

dàshǐguǎn [dah-shur-gwahn]
embassy

dàxué [dah-hsyew-eh]
university

dàyī [dah-yee] coat, overcoat

dàyuē [dah-yew-eh] roughly,
approximately

dǎzhàng [dah-jahng] fight

de [dur] of (particle inserted between adjective and noun to denote possession)

dé get, obtain

de duō: ... de duō [dwor] much more ...

Déguó [dur-gwor] Germany; German (adj)

dēng [dung] light; lamp

děng wait

dēngjì [dung-jee] check-in

dēngjìkǒu [–koh] gate (at airport)

dēngjī pái boarding pass

dēngpào [dung-pow] lightbulb

dì [dee] floor

dì èr tiān [tyen] the day after

dī low

diàn [dyen] electric; electricity

-diǎn hour; o'clock

diànchí [dyen-chur] battery

diànchuīfēng [dyen-chway-fung] hairdryer

diàndòng tìhú dāo [dyen-doong tee-hoo dow] shaver

diàngōng [dyen-goong] electrician

diànhuà [dyen-hwah] phone

diànhuà hàomǎ bù [how-mah] phone book

diànhuàtíng phone box

diànnǎo [dyen-now] computer

diǎnr [dyenr] a little bit

... diǎnr more ...

diànshì [dyen-shur] television

diàntī lift, elevator

diàntìdāo [dyen-tee-dow] electric shaver

diànxiàn [dyen-hsyen] wire; lead

diànxíng [dyen-hsing] typical

diànyā [dyen-yah] voltage

diànyǐng [dyen-ying] film, movie

diànyǐng yuàn [yew-ahn] cinema, movie theater

diànyuán chāzuò [dyen-yew-ahn chah-dzwor] power point

diànzi [dyen-dzur] cushion

diàochuáng [dyow-chwahng] cot

dìbā [dee-bah] eighth

dìdi younger brother

dì'èr(ge) [–gur] second

diézi [dyeh-dzur] dish, bowl; saucer

dìfāng [dee-fahng] place

dìjiǔ [dee-jyoh] ninth

dìliǎng [dee-lyang] second

dìliù [dee-lyoh] sixth

dìnghūnle [–hun-lur] engaged (to be married)

dǐngshang: zài dǐngshang [dzai ding-shahng] at the top

dìngzuò [–dzwor] reserve

dìqī [dee-chee] seventh

dìqū [dee-chew] region

dǐr [deer] bottom

dìsān [dee-sahn] third

dìshang [dee-shahng] on the ground

dìshí [dee-shur] tenth

dìsì [dee-sur] fourth

dísīkē [–kur] disco

dìtǎn [dee-tahn] carpet

dìtiě [dee-tyeh] underground, (US) subway

dìtiě zhàn [jahn] underground station, subway station

dìtú [dee-too] map

diū [dyoh] lose

dìwǔ [dee-woo] fifth

dìyī first

dìzhǐ [dee-jur] address

dǒng: ní dǒngle? [doong-lur] do you understand?

wǒ bù dǒng [wor] I don't understand

dōng [doong] east

dòng hole; puncture

dōngběi [–bay] northeast

dōngfāng [–fahng] in the east

dōngnán [–nahn] southeast

dǒngshì [–shur] director

dōngtian [–tyen] winter; in the winter

dòngwù [–woo] animal

dòngwùyuán [–yew-ahn] zoo

dōngxi [–hshee] thing (object)

dōu [doh] both, all

dǒu steep

dú [doo] read

duǎn [dwahn] short

duǎnkù shorts

duànle [–lur] broken

duǎnwà [–wah] sock

duì [dway] right, correct; towards; with regard to; queue; side

duìbuqǐ [dway-boo-chee] sorry, excuse me

duìfāng fùkuǎn [–fahng foo-kwahn] collect call

duìhuàn [dway-hwahn] change (verb: money)

duìhuànlù [–lyew] exchange rate

duìjile! [–jee-lur] exactly!

duìle yes, that's it, that's right

duō [dwor] much; more than

duōde duō [–dur] a lot more

duōle: ... duōle [–lur] far more ...

duōshao? [dwor-show] how much?, how many? (if answer is likely to be more than ten)

duōxiè [–hsyeh] thank you very much

duō yíbèi [yee-bay] twice as much

duō yidiǎnr [yee-dyenr] a bit more

duōyòng chātóu [–yoong chah-toh] adapter

dúpǐn [doo-pin] drugs, narcotics

dǔzhùle [doo-joo-lur] blocked

E

è [ur] hungry

Éguó [ur-gwor] Russia; Russian (adj)

èr [ur] two

èrbǎi two hundred

èr děng [dung] second class

ěrduo [er-dwor] ear

ěrhuán [er-hwahn] earrings

ěr lóng [loong] deaf

èrlóu [er-loh] first floor, (US) second floor

èrshí [er-shur] twenty

értóng [er-toong] children

èrwàn [er-wahn] twenty
thousand
érxí [er-hshee] daughter-in-law
èryuè [er-yew-eh] February
érzi [er-dzur] son
ĕxīn [ur-hsin] disgusting;
nausea

F

Fǎguó [fah-gwor] France;
French (adj)
fán [fahn] bored
fàn meal
fàndiàn [fahn-dyen] large
restaurant; luxury hotel
fǎng [fahng] imitation
fàng put
fāngbiàn [–byen] convenient
fángdǐng roof; ceiling
fángfǔjì [–foo-jee] antiseptic
fángjiān [–jyen] room
fànguǎnr [fahn-gwahnr] small
restaurant
fāngxiàng [–hsyang] direction
fángzi [–dzur] building; house
fángzū [–dzoo] rent (noun)
fànwǎn [fahn-wahn] rice bowl
fānyì translate; translation;
translator
fāshēng [fah-shung] happen
fēi [fay] fly (verb)
fēicháng [fay-chahng] very,
extremely
fēijī [fay-jee] plane
zuò fēijī [dzwor] by air
fēijīchǎng [–chahng] airport
fèixū [fay-hsyew] ruins
féizào [fay-dzow] soap

fēi zhèngshì [jung-shur]
informal
fēn [fun] minute
fēng [fung] mad, insane; wind
fèng measure word* used for
letters
fēngjǐng [fung-jing] scenery;
sights
fēngshàn [fung-shahn] fan
(electrical)
fēngsú [fung-soo] custom
fěnhóng [fun-hoong] pink
fēnjī [fun-jee] extension
fēnkāi separate
fēnzhōng [fun-joong] minute
Fó [for] Buddha
Fójiào [for-jyow] Buddhism;
Buddhist
fù(qián) [foo(-chyen)] pay
fūfù couple (two people)
fùjiāfèi [foo-jyah-fay]
supplement, extra charge
fùjìn [foo-jin] nearby; near
fùmǔ parents
fùnǚ [foo-nyew] woman
fùqin [foo-chin] father
fūren [foo-run] Mrs
fúshǒu [foo-shoh] handle
fúwùtái reception
fúwùyuán [–yew-ahn]
receptionist
fùzá [foo-zah] complicated

G

gàir [gai-r] lid
gālí [gah-lee] curry
gān [gahn] dry; liver
gǎn catch up

gānbēi! [gahn-bay] cheers!

gāngbǐ [gahng-bee] pen

gángkǒu [-koh] port,
harbour

gānjìng [gahn-jing] clean

gǎnjué [gahn-jyew-eh] feel

gǎnmào [gahn-mow] cold
(illness)

gǎnrǎn [gahn-rahn] infection

gāo [gow] high; tall

gāodiǎndiàn [-dyen] cake
shop

gāomíng [gow-ming] brilliant

gāoxìng [gow-hsing] pleased,
glad

hěn gāoxìng jiàndào nǐ [hun-
jyen dow] pleased to meet
you

ge [gur] general all-purpose
measure word*

gē song

gēbo [gur-bor] arm

gēbozhǒu [-joh] elbow

gēchàngjiā [gur-chahng-jyah]
singer

gēge [gur-gur] elder brother

gěi [gay] give; for

gējù [gur-jyew] opera

gēn [gun] with

gèng: ... gèng [gung] even
more ...

gèng hǎo [how] better; even
better

Gòngchándǎng
[goong-chahn-dahng]
Communist Party

Gòngchándǎngyuán [-yew-ahn]
Communist Party member

gōngchǎng [-chahng] factory

gòngchánzhǔyì [-chahn-joo-yee]
communism

gōngchǐ [-chur] metre

gōngdiàn [-dyen] palace

gōnggòng cèsuǒ [tsur-swor]
public convenience

gōnggong pópo [por-por]
wife's parents-in-law

gōnggòng qìchē [chee-chur]
city bus

gōnggòng qìchē zhàn [jahn]
bus stop

gōnggòng qìchē zǒngzhàn
[dzoong-jahn] bus station

gōngjià [-jyah] public holiday

gōngjīn [-jin] kilogram

gōnglǐ kilometre

gōnglù motorway, (US)
highway, (US) freeway

gōngsī [-sur] company,
business, firm

gōngxǐ! gōngxǐ! [-hshee]
congratulations!

gōngyuán [-yew-ahn] park

gōngzuò [-dzwor] job;
work

gǒu [goh] dog

gòu(le) [-lur] enough

guài [gwai] peculiar

guān [gwahn] close, shut

guàn jug

guǎngchǎng [gwahng-chahng]
square

Guǎngdōng [-doong]
Cantonese (adj)

Guǎngdōnghuà [-hwah]
Cantonese (language)

Guǎngdōng rén [run]
Cantonese (person)

guānkǒu [gwahn-koh] pass (in mountains)

guānle [–lur] closed

guānménle [–mun-lur] closed

guānshang le [shahng] off, switched off

guàntou [–toh] can, tin

guānyú [–yew] about, concerning

gúdǒng [goo-doong] antique

gūgu aunt (father's sister)

gui(le) [gway(-lur)] expensive

guìzi [gway-dzur] cupboard

-guo [gwor] verb suffix indicating a past experience

guóhuà [–hwah] Chinese painting

guójí [–jee] nationality

guóji [–jee] international

guójiā [–jyah] country, nation; national, state

guòle [–lur] beyond

guòmǐn allergic

guòqu [–chew] in the past

guòshí(de) [–shur(-dur)] old-fashioned

guówài abroad

guòyè [–yur] overnight

gútou [goo-toh] bone

gùyì deliberately

gǔzhé [gyew-jur] fracture

H

hǎi sea

hái still

　hái hǎo ma? [how mah] are you OK?

hǎibiānr [hai-byenr] sea; seaside

hǎibīn coast

hǎiguān [hai-gwahn] Customs

háishi [hai-shur] or

hǎitān [hai-tahn] beach

hǎiwān [hai-wahn] bay

háizi [hai-dzur] child

hǎn [hahn] shout

hángbān [hahng-bahn] flight

hángbān hào [how] flight number

hángkōng [–koong] by airmail

hángkōng xìnfēng [hsin-fung] airmail envelope

Hànyǔ [hahn-yew] Chinese (spoken language)

hǎo [how] good; nice; all right, OK

hǎo, xièxie [hsyeh-hsyeh] yes, please

hǎochī [how-chur] delicious

háohuá [how-hwah] luxurious; posh

hǎojíle [how-jee-lur] great, wonderful, excellent

hǎokàn [how-kahn] attractive

hàomǎ [how-mah] number

hǎo yìdiǎnr [yee-dyenr] better

hé [hur] and; river

　hé ... yìqǐ [yee-chee] together with ...

　... hé ... dōu bù ... [doh boo] neither ...nor ...

hē drink (verb)

hēi [hay] black

hēi àn [ahn] dark

hélǐ [hur-lee] reasonable

hěn [hun] very

hěnduō [hun-dwor] a lot, lots; many

hěnkuài di [kwai] quickly

hézi [hur-dzur] box

hēzuìle [hur-dzway-lur] drunk

hóngsède [hoong-sur-dur] red

hóngshuǐ [–shway] flood

hòu [hoh] thick

hòulái later; later on

hóulóng [hoh-loong] throat

hòumian [hoh-myen] behind
zài hòumian [dzai] at the back
zài ... hòumian behind ...

hòutiān [hoh-tyen] the day after tomorrow

hú lake

huā [hwah] flower

huà picture, painting

huāfèi [hwah-fay] spend

huài [hwai] bad

huàile [hwai-lur] broken

huáiyùn [hwai-yewn] pregnant

huáji [hwah-jee] funny

huàjù [hwah-jew] play (in theatre)

huáng [hwahng] yellow

huángdì emperor

huángfēng [–fung] wasp

huángjīn gold

huángsè [–sur] yellow

huānyíng dào ... [hwahn-ying dow] welcome to ...

huāpíng [hwah-ping] vase

huàr [hwar] painting, picture

huàxiàng [hwah-hsyang] portrait

huāyuán [hwah-yew-ahn] garden

huì [hway] meeting, conference

huílai come back

huīsède [hway-sur-dur] grey

huítóujiàn [hway-toh-jyen] see you later

huìyì [hway-yee] meeting, conference

hūnlǐ [hun-lee] wedding

huǒ [hwor] fire

huǒchái [hwor-chai] matches

huǒchē [hwor-chur] van

huǒchē train
zuò huǒchē [dzwor] by train

huǒchēzhàn [–jahn] railway station

huǒzāi [hwor-dzai] fire

huòzhe ... huòzhe ... [hwor-jur] either ...or ...

huòzhě or

hùshi [hoo-shur] nurse

hútòng [hoo-toong] lane; side street

hùzhào [hoo-jow] passport

húzi [hoo-dzur] beard

J

jì [jee] post, mail (verb)

jǐ few

jiā [jyah] home
zài jiā [dzai] at home

jiàgé [jyah-gur] price

jiǎn [jyen] cut

jiàn measure word* used for things, affairs etc

Jiānádà [jyah-nah-dah] Canada; Canadian (adj)

jiānbǎng [jyen-bahng] shoulder

jiǎndān [jyen-dahn] simple,
  easy
jiāng [jyang] river
jiǎng speak
jiānglái future; in future
jiànkāng [jyen-kahng] healthy
jiànzhù [jyen-joo] building
jiǎnzi [jyen-dzur] scissors
jiǎo [jyow] foot (of person)
jiào call, greet
jiāochākǒu [jyow-chah-koh]
  junction
jiáodǐ sole (of foot)
jiǎo hòugēn [hoh-gun] heel (of
  foot)
jiāojuǎnr [jyow-jew-ahnr] film
  (for camera)
jiāoqū [jyow-chew] suburb
jiāoqūchē [–chur] bus (in
  suburbs)
jiàotáng [jyow-tahng] church
jiāotōng tú [jyow-toong]
  streetmap
jiāoyì huì [jyow-yee hway]
  exhibition, trade fair
jiáozhǐtou [jyow-jur-toh] toe
jiàqī [jyah-chee] holiday,
  vacation
jiàqián [jyah-chyen] cost (noun)
jiātíng family
jiǎyá [jyah-yah] dentures
jiāyóu zhàn [jyah-yoh jahn]
  petrol station, gas station
jiàzhí [jyah-jur] value
jiàzi [jyah-dzur] shelf
jíbìng illness, disease
jīchǎng bānchē [jee-chahng
  bahn-chur] airport bus
jiē(dào) [jyeh(-dow)] avenue;

street
jiè [jyeh] borrow
jiěfū [jyeh-foo] brother-in-law
  (elder sister's husband)
jiéhūn [jyeh-hun] married
  nǐ jiéhūnle ma? [jyeh-hun-lur
  mah] are you married?
jiějie [jyeh-jyeh] elder sister
jiémùdānr [jyeh-moo-dahnr]
  programme
jiérì [jyeh-rur] festival; holiday
jiēshi [jyeh-shur] strong
jièzhi [jyeh-jur] ring (on finger)
jǐfèi diànhuà [jee-fay dyen-hwah]
  payphone
jǐge [jee-gur] several
  jǐge? how much?, how
  many? (if answer is likely to be ten
  or fewer)
jíjiù [jee-jyoh] first aid
jíjiùxiāng [–hsyang] first-aid kit
jìn near
jǐngchá [jing-chah] police;
  policeman
jīngcháng [jing-chahng] often,
  frequent
jīngguò [jing-gwor] through;
  via
jīnglǐ manager
jǐngr view
jīngrén de [jing-run dur]
  astonishing
jìngzi [jing-dzur] mirror
jīnhuángsè [jin-hwahng-sur]
  blond
jìniànbēi [jee-nyen-bay]
  monument
jìniànpǐn [jee-nyen-pin]
  souvenir

jīnjí(de) [−dur] urgent

jǐnjin just, only

jīnshǔ metal

jīntiān [jin-tyen] today
 jīntiān wǎnshang
 [wahn-shahng] tonight

jìntóu [jin-toh] end (of street etc)

jīnwǎn [jin-wahn] tonight

jīnzi [jin-dzur] gold

jīqi [jee-chee] machine

jìshì ... yě [jee-shur ... yur] even
 if ...

jìsuànjī [jee-swahn-jee]
 computer

jiǔ [jyoh] nine; alcohol;
 alcoholic drink

jiù just; then; secondhand
 jiù yìdiǎnr [yee-dyenr] just a
 little
 jiù yìhuǐr [yee-hwayr] just a
 minute

jiúbǎi nine hundred

jiǔbājiān [jyoh-bah-jyen] bar

jiùde [jyoh-dur] secondhand

jiùhùchē [jyoh-hoo-chur]
 ambulance

jiùjiu uncle (mother's brother)

jiǔshí [jyoh-shur] ninety

jiǔyuè [jyoh-yew-eh]
 September

juǎnqūde [jwahn-chew-dur]
 curly

jué búhuì [jew-eh boo-hway]
 never (referring to the future)

juéde [−dur] feel

juédìng decide; decision

juéduì bàng [−dway bahng]
 perfect

juéduìde! [−dur] absolutely!

júhuángsè [jyew-hwahng-sur]
 orange (colour)

jùlí [joo-lee] distance

jùyuàn [jyew-yew-ahn] theatre

K

kǎchē [kah-chur] lorry

kāfēi diàn [kah-fay dyen] café

kāfēiguǎnr [−gwahnr] café

kāi open (adj)

kāichē [kai-chur] drive

kāide [kai-dur] open (adj)

kāile [kai-lur] open (adj)

kāishǐ [kai-shur] begin; start;
 beginning
 yì kāishǐ at the beginning

kāishuǐ [kai-shway] boiled
 water

kànbào [kahn-bow] read
 (newspaper)

kàngjūnsù [kahng-jyewn-soo]
 antibiotics

kànjian [kahn-jyen] see

kànshū [kahn-shoo] read (book)

kànyikàn [kahn-yee-kahn] have
 a look

kào [kow] near

kǎoshì [kow-shur] exam

kǎoxiāng [kow-hsyang] oven

kè [kur] lesson; gram(me)

kē measure word* used for
 trees, flowers etc

kěài lovely

kěnéng [kur-nung] maybe,
 perhaps; possible

kěpà [kur-pah] horrible

kèqi [kur-chee] polite

kèrén [kur-run] guest

kěshì [kur-shur] but
késou [kur-soh] cough
kètīng lounge
kéyi [kur-yee] be able
  kéyi qǐng [ching] yes please
  nín kéyi ... ma? [mah] could
  you ...?
kōng [koong] empty
kōngjiān [−jyen] room, space
kōngqì [−chee] air
kōngtiáo [−tyow]
  air-conditioning
kóukě [koh-kur] thirsty
kǔ [koo] bitter
kū cry
kuài [kwai] quick, fast; sharp;
  soon; measure word* used
  for lumps or pieces
kuài chē [chur] express (train)
kuàidì express (mail)
kuài diǎnr! [dyenr] hurry up!
kuàilè [kwai-lur] happy
kuàir [kwai-r] piece
kuàizi [kwai-dzur] chopsticks
kuān de [kwahn dur] wide
kuāng [kwahng] basket
kuánghuānjié [−hwahn-jyeh]
  carnival
kùchǎ [koo-chah] underpants,
  men's underwear
kūnchóng [kun-choong] insect
kùnle [kun-lur] sleepy
kùnnan [kun-nahn] difficult;
  difficulty
kùzi [koo-dzur] trousers, (US)
  pants

L

là [lah] hot, spicy
lā pull
lái come, arrive
láide: nǐ shì cóng nǎr láide?
  [shur tsoong nar lai-dur] where
  do you come from?
láihuí piào [lai-hway pyow]
  return/round-trip ticket
lājī [lah-jee] rubbish, trash
lājīxiāng [−hsyang] dustbin,
  trashcan
lán [lahn] blue
lǎn lazy
lánzi [lahn-dzur] basket
lǎo [low] old
lǎolao grandmother (maternal)
lǎoniánren [low-nyen-run]
  senior citizen
lǎoshī [low-shur] teacher
lǎoshǔ [low-shoo] rat; mouse
Lǎowō [low-wor] Laos
lǎoye [low-yeh] grandfather
  (maternal)
làzhú [lah-joo] candle
le [lur] sentence particle
  indicating something in the
  past which is still relevant to
  the present or a change of
  circumstances in the
  present or future
-le [-lur] verb suffix indicating completion of action
lèi [lay] tired
léiyǔ [lay-yew] thunderstorm
lěng [lung] cold
li: zài ... li [dzai ... lee]
  inside ...

lí [lee] from; to; pear

-lǐ inside

liǎn [lyen] face

liǎng [lyang] two

liàng measure word* used for vehicles

liǎngcì [–tsur] twice

liǎngge dānrénchuáng [–gur dahn-run-chwahng] twin beds

liǎngge dōu [dow] both

liǎngge dōu bù [doh] neither (one) of them

liǎngge xīngqī [hsing-chee] fortnight

liángkuai [–kwai] cool

liángxié [–hsyeh] sandals

liánkùwà [lyen-koo-wah] tights, pantyhose

liánxi [lyen-hshee] contact

liányīqún [lyen-yee-chewn] dress

liányùn [lyen-yewn] connection

liǎobuqǐ [lyow-boo-chee] incredible, amazing

lièchē shíkè biǎo [lyeh-chur shur-kur byow] timetable, (US) schedule

lièzhì [lyeh-jur] poor

lǐfà [lee-fah] haircut

lǐfàdiàn [–dyen] hairdresser's; barber's

lǐfàshī [–shur] hairdresser's

líhūn [lee-hun] divorced

límǐ centimetre

límíng dawn

líng zero

língdài [ling-dye] tie, necktie

língqián [ling-chyen] change (noun: money)

língrén yúkuài [ling-run yew-kwai] pleasant

língshìguǎn [ling-shur-gwahn] consulate

língwài another, different

líng yánglǎojīn de rén [–low-jin dur run] pensioner

lìng yíge [yee-gur] another, different; the other one

línyù [lin-yew] shower

dài línyù with shower

lìrú for example

liù [lyoh] six

liùbǎi six hundred

liúgǎn [lyoh-gahn] flu

liúlì fluent

liùshí [lyoh-shur] sixty

liúxíng [lyoh-hsing] popular, fashionable

liúxíngxìng gǎnmào [gahn-mow] flu

liúxíng yīnyuè [yin-yew-eh] pop music

liùyuè [lyoh-yew-eh] June

lǐwù [lee-woo] present, gift

lìzi [lee-dzur] example; chestnut

lóng [loong] dragon

lóu [loh] floor, storey; building (with more than one storey)

lóushàng [loh-shahng] upstairs

lóutī [loh-tee] stairs

lóuxià [loh-hsyah] downstairs

lǚxíng [lyew-hsing] travel; tour; journey

lǚxíngshè [–shur] travel agent's

lǔxíngzhě [–jur] tourist

lǔxíng zhīpiào [jur-pyow]
travellers' cheque

lǔyóuchē [lyew-yoh-chur]
tourist bus, coach

lǔyóuzhě [lyew-joh-jur] tourist

lǔguǎn [lyew-gwahn] small
hotel

lǜsède [lyew-sur-dur] green

lù road; way

lúntāi tyre

lúnzi [lun-dzur] wheel

lùtiān [loo-tyen] outdoors

lùxiàn [loo-hsyen] route

lùxiàngdài [loo-hsyang-dai]
video tape

lúzào [loo-dzow] cooker

M

ma? [mah] question particle

mā mother

mǎ horse

mà scold

máfan [mah-fahn] trouble

máfan nín excuse me

mǎi buy

mài sell

mǎimài business deal

mǎn [mahn] full

màn slow; slowly

hěn màn [hun] very slowly

màn diǎnr! [dyenr] slow
down!

mángmang [mahng–] busy

māo [mow] cat

máobèixīn [mow-bay-hsin]
pullover

máojīn towel

màopáirhuò [mow-pai-r-hwor]
fake

máotǎn [mow-tahn] blanket

máoyī sweater

màozi [mow-dzur] hat, cap

mǎshàng [mah-shahng] at
once, immediately

mǎtóu [mah-toh] jetty

Máo zhǔxí [mow jyew-hshee]
Chairman Mao

měi [may] each, every;
beautiful

méi not; does not; no; have
not

mèifū [may-foo] brother-in-law
(younger sister's husband)

méi ...-guò [-gwor] has never;
have never

měige [may-gur] every

měige dìfāng [dee-fahng]
everywhere

měige rén [run] everyone

méi guānxi [gwahn-hshee]
never mind, it doesn't
matter

Měiguó [may-gwor] America;
American (adj)

měijiàn shìqíng [may-jyen
shur-ching] everything

měijiàn shìr [shur] everything

méi jìnr boring

měilì beautiful

mèimei younger sister

méiqì [may-chee] gas

měirén [may-run] everybody

méishìr le [may-shur lur] safe

měishùguǎn [may-shoo-gwahn]
art gallery

měitiān [may-tyen] every day

méi wǎnshang [wahn-shahng]
per night

méi wèntí! [wun-tee] no
problem!

méixiǎngdào [may-hsyang-dow]
amazing, surprising

měiyíge [may-yee-gur] each,
every

měiyíge rén [run] everyone

méiyǒu [may-yoh] did not; has
not, have not; without

méi ...-zhe [-zhur] was
not ...-ing; is not ...-ing

-men suffix indicating the
plural

mén [mun] door

Ménggǔ [mung-goo] Mongolia;
Mongolian (adj)

mǐ metre; uncooked rice

Miǎndiàn [myen-dyen] Burma;
Burmese (adj)

miǎn fèi [fay] free (no charge)

miánhuā [myen-hwah] cotton

miǎnshuì [myen-shway]
duty-free goods

miǎo [myow] second (of time)

miào Taoist temple

míngbai: wǒ míngba le [wor –
lur] I see, I understand

míngpiàn [ming-pyen] card

míngtian [ming-tyen] tomorrow

míngtian zǎoshang
[dzow-shahng] tomorrow
morning

míngxìnpiàn [ming-hsin-pyen]
postcard

míngzi [ming-dzur] name; first
name

mòduān [mor-dwahn] end

mótuōchē [mor-twor-chur]
motorbike

mǒudì [moh-dee]
somewhere

mùdì cemetery

mùdìdì destination

mùjiān xiūxi [moo-jyen
hsyoh-hshee] interval

mǔqīn [moo-chin] mother

mùtou [moo-toh] wood

N

ná [nah] carry; take

nà that; that one; the

nǎinai grandmother
(paternal)

nǎiniú [nai-nyoh] cow

nǎli? [nah-lee] where?

nán [nahn] south; hard,
difficult; man

nán cèsuǒ [tsur-swor] gents'
toilet, men's room

nánfāng [nahn-fahng] in the
south

Nánfēi [nahn-fay] South Africa;
South African (adj)

nán fúwùyuán [foo-woo-yew-ahn]
waiter; steward

nánguò [nahn-gwor] sad

nánhái boy

nánkàn [nahn-kahn] ugly

nán péngyou [pung-yoh]
boyfriend

nánrén [nahn-run] man

nǎr? where?

zài nǎr? [dzai] where is it?

nǐ qù nǎr? [chew] where are
you going?

nàr there

nà shí [nah shur] then, at that
time

nà shì ... ma? [mah] is
that ...?

nà shì shénme? [shun-mur]
what's that?

názhe [nah-jur] keep

ne [nur] sentence particle
which adds emphasis or
conveys the idea ' and what
about ...?'

nèi [nay] that; that one
nèi? [nay] which?

nèidì brother-in-law (wife's
younger brother)

nèige [nay-gur] that; that one

nèige shíhou [shur-hoh] then,
at that time

nèixiōng [nay-hsyoong] brother-
in-law (wife's elder brother)

nèi yíge [yee-gur] that one

néng: nǐ néng ... ma? [nung ...
mah] can you ...?

wǒ bù néng ... [wor] I
can't ...

nǐ you (sing)

niàn [nyen] read (aloud)

nián year

niánjì [nyen-jee] age
nín duō dà niánjì le? [dwor dah
nyen-jee lur] how old are
you?

niánlíng: nín duō dà niánlíng?
[nyen-ling] how old are you?

niánqīng [nyen-ching] young

niǎo [nyow] bird

niàobù [nyow-boo] nappy,
diaper

Níbóěr [nee-bor-er] Nepal;
Nepali (adj)

nǐde [nee-dur] your; yours
(sing)

nǐ hǎo [nee how] hello; hi; how
do you do?

nǐ hǎo ma? [mah] how are
you?

nǐmen [nee-mun] you (pl)

nǐmende [–dur] your; yours
(pl)

nín you (sing, pol)

nínde [nin-dur] your; yours
(sing, pol)

nínmen [nin-mun] you (pl, pol)

nínmende [–dur] your; yours
(pl, pol)

niúzǎikù [nyoh-dzai-koo] jeans

nóng [noong] strong

nóngchǎng [–chahng] farm

nóngcūn [–tsun] countryside

nǚ'ér [nyew-er] daughter

nǚ cèsuǒ [tsur-swor] ladies'
room, ladies' toilets

nǚ chènshān [nyew-chun-shahn]
blouse

nǚ fúwùyuán [foo-woo-yew-ahn]
waitress; maid; stewardess

nǚ háir [hai-r] girl

nǚpéngyou [nyew-pung-yoh]
girlfriend

nǚshì [nyew-shur] Ms, lady

nǚzhāodài [nyew-jow-dai]
waitress

nuǎnhuo [nwahn-hwor] warm;
mild

nuǎnqì [nwahn-chee] heating;
central heating; radiator

O

Ōuzhōu [oh-joh] Europe;
European (adj)

P

pàichūsuǒ [pai-choo-swor]
police station
pán [pahn] measure word*
used for round objects
pàng [pahng] fat
páng side
pángbiān: zài ... pángbiān
[dzai ... pahng-byen] beside
the ..., next to ...
pánzi [pahn-dzur] plate
pǎo [pow] run
péngchē [pung-chur] van
pèngtóu dìdiǎn [pung-toh
dee-dyen] meeting place
péngyou [pung-yoh] friend
pēnquán [pun-choo-en]
fountain
piányi [pyen-yee] be
inexpensive; inexpensive
piào [pyow] ticket; single
ticket, one-way ticket
piàoliang [pyow-lyang]
beautiful; pretty
pífu skin
pígé [pee-gur] leather
píng' ān [ping-ahn] safe
píngcháng [ping-chahng] usual,
normal
pīngpāngqiú [ping-pahng-chyoh]
table tennis
píngtǎn [ping-tahn] flat (adj)
píngzi [ping-dzur] bottle

pǔtōng [poo-toong] ordinary
Pǔtōnghuà [–hwah] Mandarin

Q

qī [chee] seven
qián [chyen] money
qiánbāo [–bow] wallet; purse
qiānbǐ pencil
qiánbianr: zài qiánbianr [dzai
chyen-byenr] in front; at the
front
qiáng [chyang] wall
qiángjiān [–jyen] rape
qiǎngle [–lur] robbed
qiánmiàn [chyen-myen] front
qiántiān [–tyen] the day
before yesterday
qiántíng lobby
qiānwàn [–wahn] ten million
qiánxiōng [–hsyoong] breast;
bust; chest
qián yì tiān [tyen] the day
before
qiánzhèng [–jung] visa
qiānzì [–dzur] signature
qiáo [chyow] bridge
qiǎokèlì [–kur-lee] chocolate
qiáozhúgàng [–joo-gahng]
rip-off
qībǎi [chee-bai] seven hundred
qìchē [chee-chur] car
zuò qìchē [dzwor] by car
qìchē chūzū [choo-dzoo] car
rental
qìchē gōngzhàn [goong-jahn]
bus station (for city buses)
qìchē xiūlíchǎng [hsyoh-
lur-chahng] garage (for repairs)

qǐchuáng [chee-chwahng] get
up (in the morning)

qiè [chyeh] cut

qǐfēi shíjiān [chee-fay shee-jyen]
departure

qíguài(de) [chee-gwai(-dur)]
weird, strange, odd

qí mǎ [chee mah] horse riding

qīng [ching] light (not heavy)

qǐng please; ask, request

qīngdàn [–dahn] mild

qǐng jìn come in

qīngshàonián [–show-nyen]
teenager

qīngxīn [–hsin] fresh

qióng [chyoong] poor

qīshí [chee-shur] seventy

qítā [chee-tah] other

qǐtǐng [chee-ting] motorboat

qiú [chyoh] ball

qiúmí sports fan

qiúpāi racket (tennis, squash)

qiūtian [chyoh-tyen] autumn,
(US) fall; in the autumn/fall

qìxiè [chee-hsyeh] equipment

qìyóu [chee-yoh] petrol, (US)
gas

qīyuè [chee-yew-eh] July

qīzi [chee-dzur] wife

qí zìxíngchē de rén [chee
dzur-sing-chur dur run] cyclist

qù [chew] go; to

qǔ get, fetch

quánbù [choo-en-boo] all; all of
it, the whole lot

quánguó [–gwor] national,
nationwide

qùnián [chew-nyen] last year

qúnzi [chewn-dzur] skirt

R

ránhòu [rahn-hoh] then, after
that

rè [rur] hot; heat

rèdù [rur-doo] temperature;
fever

rèle [rur-lur] hot

rén [run] person
wǒ shì ... rén [wor shur] I
come from ...

rènao [rur-now] busy,
lively

rēng [rung] throw

rènhé [run-hur] any

rènhé rén anybody

rènhé shénme [shun-mur]
anything

rénkǒu [run-koh] population

rénmín people

rénqún [run-chewn] crowd

rènshi [run-shur] know;
recognize

rénxíng dào [run-hsing dow]
pavement, sidewalk

rénxíng héngdào [hung-dow]
pedestrian crossing

rèshuǐpíng [rur-shway-ping]
Thermos® flask

Rìběn [ree-bun] Japan

rìjì [rur-jee] diary

róngyì [roong-yee] easy

ròu [roh] meat

ruǎn [rwahn] soft

ruǎnpán [–pahn] disk

ruǎnwò [–wor] soft sleeper,
first class sleeper

ruǎnzuò [–dzwor] soft seat,
first class seat

rúguǒ [roo-gwor] if

Ruidiǎn [rway-dyen] Sweden

rùkǒu [roo-koh] entrance

ruò [rwor] weak

S

sāi cheek

sāizi [sai-dzur] plug (in sink)

sān [sahn] three

sānbǎi three hundred

sānděng [sahn-dung] third class

sānkè [sahn-kur] quarter to

sǎngzi [sahng-dzur] Thursday

sānjiǎokù [sahn-jyow-koo] pants, panties

sānshí [sahn-shur] thirty

sānyuè [sahn-yew-eh] March

sēnlín [sun-lin] forest

shā [shah] sand; kill

shāfā [shah-fah] sofa

shǎguā [shah-gwah] idiot

shàiyīshéng [shai-yee-shung] clothes line

shān [shahn] mountain, hill

shāndòng [–doong] cave

shàng [shahng] up; above
zài ...-shàng [dzai] above ...

shàngdì God

shāngdiàn [–dyen] shop

shàngmian: zài ... shàngmian [dzai –myen] on ...

shàngtou: zài ... shàngtou [–toh] on top of ...

shāngǔ [shahn-goo] valley

shǎnguāngdēng [shahng-wahng-dung] flash (for camera)

shàngwǔ a.m. (from 9 a.m. to noon)

shāngxīn [–hsin] sad

shàng xīngqī [hsing-chee] last week

shàngyī jacket

shàng yícì [yee-tsur] last time

shànzi [shahn-dzur] fan (hand-held)

shǎo [show] less

shāoshāng [show-shahng] burn (noun)

shǎoshù mínzú [show-shoo mind-zoo] nationality (for Chinese minorities)

shǎoyú [show-yew] under, less than

sháozi [show-dzur] spoon

shēchǐ [shur-chur] luxury

shéi? [shay] who?

shéide? [shay-dur] whose?

shēn [shun] deep

shēng [shung] be born; litre

shēng bìngle [shung bing-lur] ill

shèngdàn jié [–dahn jyeh] Christmas

shēngqì [–chee] angry

shēngrén [–run] stranger

shēngrì [–rur] birthday

shēngyì business

shēngyīn voice

shéngzi [–dzur] string; rope

shénjingbìng [shun-jing-bing] crazy

shénkān [shun-kahn] shrine

shénme [shun-mur] anything; something

shénme? what?

shénme shíhòu? [shur-hoh] when?

shénme yàng de ...? [dur] what sort of ...?

nǐ shuō shénme? [shwor] sorry?, pardon (me)?

shénme yě méiyǒu [yur may-yoh] none

shēntǐ [shun-tee] body

shèshì [shur-shur] centigrade

shì [shur] to be; is; are; was; were; will be; it is; it was; yes, it is the case

shì ... ma? [mah] is it ...?

shí ten

shī wet

shíbā [shur-bah] eighteen

shìchǎng [shur-chahng] market

shìde [shur-dur] yes, it is the case

shíèr [shur-er] twelve

shíèr yuè [yew-eh] December

shìgù [shur-goo] accident

shíhou: zài ... de shíhou [dzai ... dur shur-hoh] during ...

shíjiān [shur-jyen] time

shíjiānbiǎo [–byow] timetable, (US) schedule

shìjiè [shur-jyeh] world

shíjiǔ [shur-jyoh] nineteen

shíliù [shur-lyoh] sixteen

shímáo [shur-mow] fashionable

shìnèi [shur-nay] indoors; indoor

shípǐn diàn [shur-pin dyen] food store

shíqī [shur-chee] seventeen; period (of time)

shìqūchē [shur-chew-chur] city bus

shìr [shur] thing, matter

shísān [shur-sahn] thirteen

shísì [shur-sur] fourteen

shíwàn [shur-wahn] hundred thousand

shíwù [shur-woo] food

shíwǔ fifteen

shíwù zhòngdú [joong-doo] food poisoning

shíyī [shur-yee] eleven

shíyīyuè [shur-yee-yew-eh] November

shíyuè [shur-yew-eh] October

shìzhèngfǔ dàlóu [shur-jung-foo dah-loh] town hall

shì zhōngxīn [shur joong-sin] city centre

shízì lùkǒu [shur-dzur loo-koh] crossroads, intersection

shǒu [shoh] hand

shòu thin

shòu huānyíng [hwahn-ying] popular

shòuhuòtíng [shoh-hwor-ting] kiosk

shōujù [shoh-jyew] receipt

shǒujuànr [shoh-jwahnr] handkerchief

shòupiàochù [shoh-pyow-choo] ticket office; box office

shòushāng [shoh-shahng] injured

shǒushì [shoh-shur] jewellery

shǒushù operation

shǒutào [shoh-tow] gloves

shǒutíbāo [shoh-tee-bow] handbag, (US) purse

shŏutíxiāng [shoh-tee-hsyang] suitcase

shŏutí xíngli [shoh-tee hsing-lee] hand luggage

shŏuwànr [shoh-wahnr] wrist

shŏuxiān [shoh-hsyen] at first

shŏuyīnjī [shoh-yin-jee] radio

shŏuzhĭ [shoh-jur] toilet paper; finger

shŏu zhítou [jur-toh] finger

shŏuzhuó [shoh-jwor] bracelet

shū [shoo] book

shú ripe

shù tree

shuāng [shwahng] double

shuāngrén chuáng [–run chwahng] double bed

shuāngrén fángjiān [fahng-jyen] double room

shūdiàn [shoo-dyen] bookshop, bookstore

shūfu well; comfortable

shuĭ [shway] water

shuĭchí [–chur] sink; swimming pool

shuĭguănr [–gwahnr] pipe

shuĭguŏ [–gwor] fruit

shuìjiào [–jyow] sleep; asleep

shuĭlóng tóu [–loong toh] tap, faucet

shuìqún [–chewn] nightdress

shuìyī pyjamas

shùlín woods, forest

shuō [shwor] say

shuōhuà [–hwah] talk

shuōmíngshū leaflet; brochure

shūshu uncle (father's younger brother)

shùzì [shoo-dzur] number

sĭ [sur] die; dead

sì four; Buddhist temple

sìbăi four hundred

sīchóu [sur-choh] silk

sì fēn zhī yī [fun jur] quarter

sījī [sur-jee] driver

sĭle [sur-lur] dead

sīrén(de) [sur-run(-dur)] private

sìshí [sur-shur] forty

sĭwáng [sur-wahng] death

sìyuàn [sur-yew-ahn] Buddhist monastery

sìyuè [sur-yew-eh] April

sòng [soong] deliver; send

sòng fàn fúwù [fahn foo-woo] room service

sòngxìn delivery (of mail)

suān [swahn] be sour; sour

suānténg [–tung] ache

Sūgélán [soo-gur-lahn] Scotland; Scottish

suíbiàn [sway-byen] informal

suídào [sway-dow] tunnel

suīrán [sway-rahn] although

sùliào [soo-lyow] plastic

sùliàodài plastic bag

sūnnŭr [sun-nyewr] granddaughter (son's daughter)

sūnzi [sun-dzur] grandson (son's son)

suŏ [swor] lock; locked; measure word* used for buildings

suóyŏu de dōngxi [swor-yoh dur doong-hshee] everything

sùshăir de [soo-shai-r dur] plain, not patterned

sùxiàng [soo-hsyang] statue

T

tā [tah] he; she; it; him; her

tǎ pagoda

tāde [tah-dur] his; her; hers; its

tài too (excessively)
  tài duō [dwor] too much

Tàiguó [tai-gwor] Thailand

tàihǎole [tai-how-lur] fantastic; well done

tài shòu [tai shoh] skinny

tàiyáng sun

tàiyángjìng sunglasses

tāmen [tah-mun] they; them
  tāmen quánbù [choo-en-boo] all of them

tāmende [tah-mun-dur] their; theirs

tān [tahn] greedy

tángdì [tahng-dee] cousin (son of father's brother)

tángjiě [–jyeh] cousin (daughter of father's brother)

tángkuàir [–kwai-r] sweets, candies

tángmèi [–may] cousin (daughter of father's brother)

tángniàobìng [–nyow-bing] diabetic

tángxiōng [–hsyoong] cousin (son of father's brother)

tǎnzi [tahn-dzur] blanket

táoqì [tow-chee] pottery

tàoshān [tow-shahn] jumper

tàozhuāng [tow-jwahng] suit

tèbié [tur-byeh] especially

téng [tung] pain, ache; painful

tiān [tyen] day; sky

tián sweet (taste)

tiándì field

tiānqi [tyen-chee] weather

tiáo [tyow] measure word* used for fish and long narrow objects

tiàowǔ [tyow-woo] dance

tiàozǎo [tyow-dzow] flea

tiělù [tyeh-loo] railway

tìhúdāo [tee-hoo-dow] razor

tíng stop

tíngchē [–chur] park

tíngchēchǎng [–chahng] car park, parking lot; garage

tíngdiàn [–dyen] power cut

tíngzi [–dzur] pavilion

tíqián [tee-chyen] in advance

tǐyùguǎn [tee-yoo-gwahn] gym

tǒng [toong] bucket

tóngyì agree

tóu [toh] head

tōu steal

tóufa [toh-fah] hair

tóujīn headscarf

tòumíng jiāodài [jyow-dai] Sellotape®, Scotch tape®

tóuténg [toh-tung] headache

tóuyūn [toh-yewn] dizzy, faint

tú'àn [too-ahn] pattern

tuán [twahn] group

tuántǐ [twahn-tee] party, group

tuì [tway] cancel

tuǐ leg

tuī push

tuìkuǎn [tway-kwahn] refund

túpiàn [too-pyen] picture

tūrán [too-rahn] suddenly

W

-wài outside

wàigōng [wai-goong]
grandfather (maternal)

wàiguó [wai-gwor] foreign

wàiguó rén [run] foreigner

wàimian [wai-myen] outside

wàipó [wai-por] grandmother
(maternal)

wàisūn [wai-sun] grandson
(daughter's son)

wàisūnnǔr [–nyewr]
granddaughter (daughter's
daughter)

wài sūnzi [sun-dzur] grandson
(daughter's son)

wàitào [wai-tow] jacket

wàiyī jacket; coat

wǎn'ān [wahn-ahn] good night

wǎn [wahn] late (at night)

wàn ten thousand

wǎncān [wahn-tsahn] dinner

wǎndiǎn [wahn-dyen] delay

wǎnfàn [wahn-fahn] evening
meal; supper

wàng [wahng] forget

wǎng towards; net (in sport)

wǎnhuì [wahn-hway] party
(celebration)

wánjù [wahn-jyew] toy

wánquándi [wahn-choo-en-dee]
completely

wánr [wahnr] play (verb)

wǎnshang [wahn-shahng]
evening; in the evening
jīntiān wǎnshang [jin-tyen]
this evening

wánxiào [wahn-hsyow] joke

Wēi'ěrshì [way-er-shur] Welsh

wéi [way] hello

wèi because of; stomach;
measure word* used
politely to refer to ladies,
gentlemen, guests etc

wèidao [way-dow] flavour

Wēiěrshì [way-er-shur] Wales

wèihūnfū fiancé

wèihūnqī [–chee] fiancée

wéijīn [way-jin] scarf

wèir [wayr] taste; smell

wèishēngjīn [way-shung-jin]
sanitary napkins/towels

wèishēngzhǐ [way-shung-jur]
toilet paper

wèishénme? [way-shun-mur]
why?

wèishénme bù? why not?

wēixiǎn [way-hsyen] dangerous

wèn [wun] ask (a question)

wénhuà dà gémìng [wun-hwah
dah gur-ming] Cultural
Revolution

wénjiàn [wun-jyen] document

wèntí [wun-tee] problem,
question

wènxùnchù [wun-hsyewn-choo]
information desk

wénzhàng [wun-jahng]
mosquito net

wénzi [wun-dzur] mosquito

wǒ [wor] I; me

wǒde [wor-dur] my; mine

wǒmen [wor-mun] we; us

wǒmende [–dur] our; ours

wòpù [wor-poo] couchette;
sleeper; berth

wòpù chēxiāng [chur-hsyang]

sleeping car
wòshì [wor-shur] bedroom
wǔ [woo] five
wù mist; fog
wúbǎi five hundred
wǔfàn [woo-fahn] lunch
wùhuì [woo-hway]
  misunderstanding
wūjiǎor [woo-jyowr] in the
  corner of a room
wǔshí [woo-shur] fifty
wǔshù [woo-shoo] martial arts
wǔyuè [woo-yew-eh] May

X

xǐ [hshee] wash
xī west
xiā [hsyah] blind
xià down; below
· xià yícì [yee-tsur] next time
  xià yígè [yee-gur] next
  xià xīngqī [hsing-chee] next
    week
  zài …-xià [dzai] under …
xiàba [–bah] jaw, chin
xià chē [–chur] get out
xiàge [–gur] next
xiàmian: zài … xiàmian [dzai –
  myen] below …
xiàn [hsyen] line; thread
xiān: nǐ xiān qǐng [ching] after
  you
xiàndài modern
xiǎng want; think
xiāngdāng [–dahng] quite,
  fairly
  xiāngdāng duō [dwor] quite a
    lot

xiàngdǎo [–dow] guide
Xiānggǎng [–gahng] Hong
  Kong
xiàngjiāo [–jyow] rubber
xiāngjìn de [dur] similar
xiàngliàn [–lyen] necklace
xiàngpí rubber, eraser
xiàngqí [–chee] chess
xiāngshuǐr [–shwayr] perfume
xiāngxìn [–hsin] believe
xiāngyān [–yahn] cigarette
xiànqián [hsyen-chyen] cash
xiānsheng [hsyen-shung] Mr
xiānyàn [–yen] bright
xiànzài [–dzai] now
xiào [hsyow] laugh; smile
xiǎo little, small; tight
xiǎofángduì [–fahng-dway] fire
  brigade
xiǎofèi [–fay] service charge;
  tip
xiǎo húzi [hoo-dzur]
  moustache
xiǎojiě [–jyeh] Miss
xiǎolù path
xiǎo qìchē [chee-chur] car
xiǎo sānjiǎokù [sahn-jyow-koo]
  pants, panties
xiǎoshān [–shahn] hill
xiǎosháor [–showr] spoon
xiǎoshí [–shur] hour
xiǎoshū brother-in-law
  (husband's younger brother)
xiāoxi [–hshee] information
xiǎoxī stream
xiǎoxīn! [–hsin] look out!
xiáozǔ [–dzyew] group
xiàshuǐdào [hsyah-shway-dow]
  drain

xiàtian [–tyen] summer; in the summer

xiàwǔ afternoon; in the afternoon; p.m.

jīntian xiàwǔ [jin-tyen] this afternoon

xià yíge [yee-gur] next

Xībānyá [hshee-bahn-yah] Spain; Spanish (adj)

xīběi [hshee-bay] northwest

xībiānr [–byenr] in the west

xīcān [–tsahn] Western-style food

xīcāntīng [–tsahn-ting] Western-style restaurant

xiě [hsyeh] blood; write

xié shoe

xiē a little bit

... xiē a bit more ...

xiédǐ [–dee] sole (of shoe)

xié hòugēn [hoh-gun] heel (of shoe)

xièxie [hsyeh-hsyeh] thank you

xièxie, wǒ bú yào [wor boo yow] no thanks

Xīfāng [hshee-fahng] West; in the West; Western

Xīfāng de [dur] Western (adj)

xīgài knee

xǐhǎo de yīfu [–how dur yee-foo] washing (clean)

xǐhuan [–hwahn] like

xìn [hsin] letter, message

xīn new

xī'nán [hshee-ahn] southwest

xìnfēng [hsin-fung] envelope

xíng [hsing] all right

xìng surname

xìnggǎn [–gahn] sexy

xìngkuī [–kway] fortunately

xíngle [–lur] that's OK

xíngle awake

xíngli luggage, baggage

xīngqī [–chee] week

xīngqīèr [–chee-er] Tuesday

xīngqīliù [–lyoh] Saturday

xīngqīsān [–chee-sahn] Wednesday

xīngqītiān [–tyen] Sunday

xīngqīwǔ [–woo] Friday

xīngqīyī Monday

xìngqu [–chew] interest

xīngxing star

xìnhào [hsin-how] signal

xìnshǐ [hsin-shur] courier

xīnwén [hsin-wun] news (radio, TV etc)

xīnxiān [hsin-hsyen] fresh

xìnxiāng [hsin-hsyang] postbox, mailbox

Xīnxīlán [hsin-hshee-lahn] New Zealand

xìnyòng kǎ [hsin-yoong kah] credit card

xīnzàng [hsin-dzahng] heart

xiōng [hsyoong] chest

xiōngdì brother

xiōngkǒu [–koh] chest

xióngmāo [–mow] panda

xiōngzhào [–jow] bra

xiōngzhēn [–jun] brooch

xishéng [hshee-shung] string

xīshì [hshee-shur] Western-style

xiūlǐ [hsyoh-lee] repair

xiūxiéjiàng [–hsyeh-jyang] shoe repairer

xiūxiépù shoe repairer

xiūxishì [–hshee-shur] lounge

xiūxitīng foyer

xiùzhēn fàngyīnjī [–jun fahng-yin-jee] personal stereo

xiùzi [–dzur] sleeve

xīwàng [hshee-wahng] hope

xǐyīdiàn [–dyen] laundry (place)

xǐyiji washing machine

xīyǐnrén [–run] attractive

xīyǒu [–yoh] rare, uncommon

Xīzàng [–dzahng] Tibet

xízǎo [–dzow] bathe

xízǎojiān [–jyen] bathroom

xuǎn [hsyew-ahn] choose

xuányá [–yah] cliff

xǔduō [–dwor] a lot, lots, plenty of

xuě [hsyew-eh] snow

xuějiā [–jyah] cigar

xuéqī [–chur] term

xuésheng [–shung] student

xuéxí [–hshee] learn

xuéxiào [–hsyow] school

xuéyuàn [–yew-ahn] college

xuēzi [–dzur] boot (footwear)

xúkě zhèng [hsyew-kur jung] permit (noun)

xūyào [hsyew-yow] need

Y

yá [yah] tooth

yágāo [yah-gow] toothpaste

yājin [yah-jin] deposit

yákē dàifu [yah-kur] dentist

yákē yīshēng [yee-shung] dentist

yān [yen] smoke

  nǐ chōu yān ma? [choh yen

mah] do you smoke?

yāndǒu [yen-doh] pipe

yángguāng [yang-gwahng] sunshine

yángmáo [yang-mow] wool

yángsǎn [yang-sahn] sunshade

yángtái balcony

yángwáwa [yang-wah-wah] doll

yángyang itch

yànhuì [yen-hway] banquet

yǎnjing [yen-jing] eye

yǎnjing glasses, eyeglasses

yǎnjingdiàn [–dyen] optician

yǎnkē yīshēng [yen-kur yee-shung] optician

yánsè [yen-sur] colour

yǎo [yow] bite (by insect)

yāo waist; one

yào want; drug; Chinese medicine

  nǐ yào shénme? [shun-mur] what do you want?

yàobùrán [yow-boor-ahn] otherwise

yāodài [yow-dai] belt

yáodòng [yow-doong] cave (dwelling)

yàofāng [yow-fahng] prescription

yàofáng pharmacy

yàogāo [yow-gow] ointment

yàomián [yow-myen] cotton wool, absorbent cotton

yāoqǐng [yow-ching] invitation; invite

yǎoshāng [yow-shahhg] bite

yàoshi [yow-shur] key

yáshuā [yah-shwah] toothbrush

yáténg [yah-tung] toothache

yě [yur] also, too

yè night; page

yèli at night; p.m.

yéye [yur-yur] grandfather (paternal)

yèzǒnghuì [yur-dzoong-hway] nightclub

yi [yee] one

yìbǎi one hundred

yíbàn [yee-bahn] half

yìbāo [yee-bow] packet

yìbēi [yee-bay] cup

yìcéng [yee-tsung] ground floor, (US) first floor

yícì [yee-tsur] once

xià yícì [hsyah] next time

yìdá [yee-dah] dozen

yídàkuàir [–kwai-r] a big bit

yìděng [yee-dung] first class

yìdiǎnr [yee-dyenr] a little bit

... yìdiǎnr a bit more ...

yìdiǎnrdiǎnr tiny

yídìng definitely

yīfu dress; clothes

yíge [yee-gur] a, an

nǎ yíge? [nah yee-gur] which one?

yígerén [yee-gur-run] alone

yígòng [yee-goong] altogether

yí guànr [gwahnr] can; jug

yíhòu [yee-hoh] after; afterwards

yíhuìr [yee-hwayr] soon

yǐjing already

yíkè [yee-kur] quarter past

yíkuàir [yee-kwai-r] piece

yìlǐng collar

yī lóu [loh] ground floor, (US) first floor

yílù shùnfēng! [yee-loo shun-fung] have a good journey!

yímā [yee-mah] aunt (mother's sister)

yīmàojiān [yee-mow-jyen] cloakroom

yímǔ [yee-moo] aunt (mother's sister)

yín(zi) [yin(-dzur)] silver

Yìndu [yin-doo] India; Indian (adj)

yìng hard

yìngbàng [ying-bahng] pound sterling

yìngbì coin

yìng'ér [ying-er] baby

Yìngguó [ying-gwor] England; Britain; English; British

Yìngguóde [–dur] English; British

yìngwò [ying-wor] hard sleeper, second class sleeper

Yìngyǔ [ying-yew] English (language)

yìngzuò [ying-dzwor] hard seat, third class seat

yínháng [yin-hahng] bank

yínshuǐ lóngtóu [yin-shway loong-toh] fountain (for drinking)

yīnwèi [yin-way] because

yǐnyòngshuǐ [yin-yoong-shway] drinking water

yīnyuè [yin-yew-eh] music

yīnyuèhuì [–way] concert

yìqǐ [yee-chee] together

yǐqián: ... yǐqián [yee-chyen]

before ...
yìqiān one thousand
yìrìyóu [yee-rur-yoh] day trip
yīsheng [yee-shung] doctor
yìshù [yee-shoo] art
yíwàn [yee-wahn] ten thousand
yǐxià: zài ... yǐxià [dzai ...
  yee-hsyah] below, less than
yìxiē [yee-hsyeh] a few
yí yì [yur yee] a hundred
  million
yīyuàn [yee-yew-ahn] hospital
yīyuè [yee-yew-eh] January
yìzhí cháoqián [yee-jur
  chow-chyen] straight ahead
yǐzi [yee-dzur] chair
yòng [yoong] with; by means
  of; use; in
yōngjǐ [–jee] crowded
yǒu [yoh] have; there is; there
  are
yǒu ... ma? [mah] is
  there ...?; are there ...?
yòu right (not left)
yòubiānr [yoh-byenr] right
yòubìng [yoh-bing] ill, sick
yǒudúde [yoh-doo-dur]
  poisonous
yóuguǐ diànchē [yoh-gway
  dyen-chur] tram
yóuhǎo [yoh-how] friendly
yóujì [yoh-jee] post, mail (verb)
yóujiàn [yoh-jyen] post, mail
yóujú [yoh-jew] post office
yóulǎn [yoh-lahn] tour, visit
yǒu lǐmào [yoh lee-mow] polite
yǒu máobìng [yoh mow-bing]
  faulty
yǒumíng famous

yóunì greasy, oily (food)
yóupiào [yoh-pyow] stamp
yǒuqián [yoh-chyen] rich
yǒurén [yoh-run] somebody,
  someone; engaged,
  occupied
yǒushíhòu [yoh-shur-hoh]
  sometimes
Yóutàiren de [yoh-tai-run dur]
  Jewish
yóuxì [yoh-hshee] game
yǒuxiào [yoh-hsyow] valid
yòu yíge [yee-gur] another,
  one more
yǒu yìsi [yee-sur] interesting;
  funny, amusing
yóuyǒng [yoh-yoong] swim
yǒuyòng useful
yóuyǒngchí [–chur] swimming
  pool
yóuzhèng biānmǎ [yoh-jung
  byen-mah] postcode, zip
  code
yú [yew] fish
yù jade
yǔ rain
yuǎn [yew-ahn] far; far away
yuǎnchù: zài yuǎnchù [dzai
  yew-ahn-choo] in the distance
yuánlái de [dur] usual
yuánzhūbǐ [–joo-bee] ballpoint
  pen
yúchǔn [yew-chun] stupid
yùdìng [yew-ding] reservation;
  reserve
yuè [yew-eh] month
yuèfù [yew-eh] father-in-law
yuèfù yuèmǔ [yew-eh-moo]
  husband's parents-in-law

yuèliang [yew-eh-lyang] moon
Yuènán [yew-eh-nahn] Vietnam
yúkuài [yew-kwai] lovely
yúkuàide [yew-kwai-dur]
  enjoyable
yùndòng [yewn-doong] sport
yùndǒu [yewn-doh] iron
yùnqi [yewn-chee] luck
yǔsǎn [yew-sahn] umbrella
yùshì [yew-shur] bathroom
yǔyán [yew-yahn] language
yǔyán kè [yew-yahn kur]
  language course
yǔyī [yew-yee] raincoat
yùyuē [yew-yew-eh]
  appointment

Z

záhuòdiàn [dzah-hwor-dyen]
  grocer's
zài [dzai] in; at; on; be in/at a
  place; again
  zài nǎr? where is it?
zài … de shíhou [dur shur-hoh]
  during …
zài … hòumian [hoh-myen]
  behind …
zàijiàn [dzai-jyen] goodbye
zài nàr over there; up there
zájì acrobatics
zài …-li inside …
zài …-pángbiān [pahng-byen]
  beside the …, next to …
zài …-shàng [shahng] above …
zài …-shàngmian [shahng-myen]
  on …
zài …-xià [hsyah] under …
zài …-xiàmian [hsyah-myen]

below …
zài …-yǐxià [yee-hsyah]
  below …, less than …
zài …-zhījiān [jur-jyen]
  between …
zài …-zhōng [joong] among …
zāng [dzahng] dirty, filthy
zànglǐ funeral
zǎo [dzow] good morning;
  early
  yì zǎo early in the morning
zǎofàn [dzow-fahn] breakfast
zǎopén [dzow-pun] bathtub
zǎoshang [dzow-shahng]
  morning; in the morning;
  a.m. (up to 9 a.m.)
  jīntian zǎoshang [jin-tyen]
  this morning
zàoyin [dzow-yin] noise
zázhì [dzah-jur] magazine
zéi [dzay] thief
zěnme? [dzun-mur] how?
  zěnme huí shìr? [hway shur]
  what's happening?; what's
  up?, what's wrong?
  zěnme le? [lur] what's
  happening?
zěnmele? what's wrong?,
  what's the matter?
zhǎi [jai] narrow
zhāng [jahng] measure word*
  used for tables, beds, tickets
  and sheets of paper
zhàngdānr [–dahnr] bill, (US)
  check
zhàngfu husband
zhāngláng [–lahng] cockroach
zhàntái [jahn-tai] platform,
  (US) track

zhànxiàn [jahn-hsyen] engaged

zhànzhù [jahn-joo] stop

zhǎodào [jow-dow] find

zhàopiàn [jow-pyen] photo

zhāotiē [jow-tyeh] poster

zhàoxiàngjī [jow-hsyang-jee] camera

zhá tǔdòupiànr [jah too-doh-pyenr] crisps, (US) potato chips

zhè [jur] this; the

-zhe verb suffix indicating continuous action or two actions taking place at the same time

zhèi [jay] this; this one
zhèi? whose?

zhèicì [jay-tsur] this time

zhèige [jay-gur] this; this one

zhēn [jun] really

zhēnde [jun-dur] true; genuine, real; sure

zhèngcháng(de) [jung-chahng(-dur)] normal

zhèngfǔ [jung-foo] government

zhèngshì [jung-shur] formal

zhènguì(de) [jung-way(-dur)] valuable

zhěngzhěng whole, full

zhēnjiǔ [jun-jyoh] acupuncture

zhēn láijìn exciting

zhěnsuǒ [jun-swor] clinic

zhěntou [jun-toh] pillow

zhěnyù [jun-yew] shower

zhēnzhèng [jun-jung] genuine

zhèr [jer] here
zài zhèr [dzai] over here

zhī [jur] measure word* used for hands, birds, suitcases

and boats

zhīdao [jur-dow] know
wǒ bù zhīdao [wor] I don't know

zhífēi [jur-fay] direct flight

zhījiān: zài ... zhījiān [dzai ... jur-jyen] between ...

zhíjiē [jur-jyeh] direct

zhǐjīn [jur-jin] tissues, Kleenex®

zhìliàng [jur-lyang] quality

zhínǚ [jin-yew] niece

zhǐshi [jur-shur] only

zhǐténgyào [jur-tung-yow] painkillers

zhíwù [jur-woo] plant

zhíxuě gāobù [jur-hsyew-eh gow-boo] plasters, Bandaid®

zhíyǒu [jur-yoh] only

zhìzào [jur-dzow] make (verb)

zhízi [jur-dzur] nephew

zhì [jur] cure (verb)

zhǐ just, only; paper

zhōng [joong] clock

-zhōng in the middle; between
zài ...-zhōng [dzai] among ...

zhòng heavy

zhǒng type; swollen

zhōngdiǎnzhàn [–dyen-jahn] rail terminus

Zhōngguó [joong-gwor] China; Chinese (adj)
Zhōngguó rén [run] Chinese (person)
Zhōngguó rénmín [run-min] the Chinese

Zhōnghuá Rénmín Gònghéguó [–hwah run-min goong-hur-gwor]

People's Republic of China

zhōngjiān: zài zhōngjiān [dzai joong-jyen] in the middle

zhòngliàng [−lyang] weight

Zhōngshì [−shur] Chinese-style

Zhōngwén [−wun] Chinese (written language)

zhōngwǔ noon; at noon

zhōngxīn [−hsin] central; centre

zhòngyào [−yow] important

zhōngzhuǎn [−jwahn] connection

zhōumò [joh-mor] weekend

zhù [joo] live (verb)

nín zhù nǎr? what's your address?

zhuǎnxìn dìzhǐ [−hsin dee-jur] forwarding address

zhújiàn de [joo-jyen dur] gradually

zhǔnbèi hǎo le [jun-bay how lur] ready

zhù nǐ shùnlì! [joo nee shun-lee] good luck!

zhuōzi [jwor-dzur] table

zhǔyào de [joo-yow dur] main

zhǔyì [joo-yee] idea

zhúzi [joo-dzur] bamboo

zǐ [dzur] purple

zìdòng [dzur-doong] automatic

zìdòng qǔkuǎnjī [chew-kwahn-jee] cash dispenser, ATM

zìjǐ [dzur-jee] oneself

zìrán [dzur-rahn] natural

zìxíngchē [dzur-hsing-chur] bicycle

 zìyóu [dzur-yoh] free

zìzhù [dzur-joo] self-service

zǒng [dzoong] always

zǒng fúwùtái reception desk

zǒnggòng [−goong] total

zǒngjī operator

zōngjiào [−jyow] religion

zōngsè [−sur] brown

zǒngshì [−shur] always

zǒu [dzoh] leave, depart, go

zǒuláng [dzoh-lahng] corridor

zǒuzou go for a walk

zū [dzoo] hire, rent

zuǐ [dzway] mouth

zuì drunk

zuì ... ...-est, the most ...

zuǐba [-bah] mouth

zuì hǎo [how] best

zuìhòu [−hoh] eventually; last

zuì huài [hwai] worst

zuìjìn recently; last, latest

zuò [dzwor] by; do

zuò fēijī [fay-jee] by air

zuò huǒchē [hwor-chur] by rail

zuǒ left

zuǒbiānr [−byenr] left

zuò fānyì [fahn-yee] interpret

zuótiān [−tyen] yesterday

zuótiān wǎnshàng [wahn-shahng] last night

zuótian zǎoshang [dzow-shahng] yesterday morning

zuòwei [−way] seat

zuòxià [−hsyah] sit down

zuǒyòu [−yoh] about

zúqiúsài football

Chinese-English:

Signs and Notices

Contents

General Signs 237
Airport, Planes 237
Banks, Money 238
Bus and Taxi Travel 238
Chinese Culture 239
Countries, Nationalities 240
Customs 241
Emergencies 241
Entertainment 242
Forms 242
Geographical Terms 242
Health 243
Hiring, Renting 243
Hotels 243
Lifts (Elevators) 243
Medicines 243
Notices on Doors 244
Phones 244
Place Names 244
Post Office 245
Public Buildings 245
Restaurants, Cafés, Bars 245
Shopping 246
Streets and Roads 247
Toilets 247
Train and Underground Travel 248

GENERAL SIGNS

危险 wēixiǎn danger

请勿乱踏草地 qǐng wù luàntā cǎodì keep off the grass

军事要地请勿靠近 jūnshì yàodì, qǐng wù kàojìn military zone, keep out

禁止入内 jìnzhǐ rù nèi no entry

外国人未经许可禁止超越 wàiguórén wèi jīng xúkě, jìnzhǐ chāoyuè no foreigners beyond this point without permission

请勿随地乱扔果皮纸屑 qǐng wù suídì luànrēng guǒpí zhǐxiè no litter

请勿大声喧哗 qǐng wù dàshēng xuānhuá no noise, please

禁止拍照 jìnzhǐ pāizhào no photographs

请勿吸烟 qǐng wù xī yān no smoking

请勿随地吐痰 qǐng wù suídì tǔtán no spitting

人行横道 rénxíng héngdào pedestrian crossing

肃静 sùjìng quiet

一慢二看三通过 yī màn, èr kàn, sān tōngguò slow down, look and then cross

闲人免进 xiánrén miǎn jìn staff only

楼下 lóuxià downstairs

楼上 lóushàng upstairs

AIRPORT, PLANES

机场 jīchǎng airport

机场班车 jīchǎng bānchē airport bus

来自 láizì arriving from

前往 qiánwǎng departing to

起飞时间 qǐfēi shíjiān departure time

终点站 zhōngdiǎnzhàn destination

变更时间 biàngēng shíjiān estimated time of arrival

行班号 hángbānhào flight number

预计时间 yùjì shíjiān scheduled time

延误 yánwù delayed

经停站 jīngtíngzhàn via

国内行班进站 guónèi hángbān jìnzhàn domestic arrivals

国内行班出站 guónèi hángbān chūzhàn domestic departures

国际行班进站 guójì hángbān jìnzhàn international arrivals

国际行班出站 guójì hángbān chūzhàn international departures

登记牌 dēngjìpái boarding pass

日期 rìqī date

行李牌儿 xínglipáir baggage check

行李领取处 xíngli lǐngqǔchù baggage claim

办理登机手续 bànlǐ dēngjī shǒuxù check-in

问讯处 wènxùnchù information desk

登机口 dēngjīkǒu gate

安全检查 ānquán jiǎnchá security control

中转旅客 zhōngzhuǎn lǚkè transfer passengers

中转 zhōngzhuǎn transfers

过境旅客 guòjìng lǚkè transit passengers

侯机室 hòujīshì departure lounge

免税商店 miǎnshuì shāngdiàn duty-free shop

系好安全带 jìhǎo ānquándài fasten seat belts

救生衣 jiùshēngyī life jacket

请勿吸烟 qǐng wù xīyān no smoking

座位号 zuòwèihào seat number

BANKS, MONEY

帐户 zhànghù account

帐号 zhànghào account no.

银行 yínháng bank

中国银行 Zhōngguó
Yínháng Bank of China

分行 fēnháng branch

营业时间 yíngyè shíjiān business hours

买价 mǎijià buying rate

交款处 jiāokuǎnchù cashier

信用卡 xìnyòng kǎ credit card

外币对换 wàibì duìhuàn foreign exchange

中国人民银行 Zhōngguó Rénmín Yínháng People's Bank of China

卖价 màijià selling rate

今日牌价 jīnrì páijià today's exchange rate

旅行支票 lǚxíng zhīpiào traveller's cheque

元 yuán unit of currency

澳元 Àoyuán Australian dollar

加拿大元 Jiānádà yuán Canadian dollar

人民币 Rénmínbì Chinese currency

港币 Gǎngbì Hong Kong dollar

英镑 Yīngbàng pound sterling

美元 Měiyuán US dollar

BUS AND TAXI TRAVEL

长途汽车站 chángtú qìchē zhàn long-distance bus station

夜班车 yèbān chē all-night bus

公共汽车 gōnggòng qìchē bus

快车 kuàichē express bus

小公共汽车 xiǎo gōnggòng qìchē minibus

区间车 qūjiānchē part-route shuttle bus

无轨电车 wúguǐ diànchē trolley bus

游览车 yóulǎnchē tourist bus

售票处 shòupiàokǒu booking office

长途汽车时刻表 chángtú qìchē shíkèbiǎo long-distance bus timetable/schedule

城市交通图 chéngshì jiāotōngtú city transport map

始发 shǐfā departure point

票价 piàojià fare

问讯处 wènxùnchù information office

月票 yuèpiào monthly ticket

一日游 yí rì yóu one-day tour

就近下车 jiùjìn xiàchē alight on request

先下后上 xiān xià hòu shàng allow passengers to alight before boarding

保持车内清洁 bǎochí chēnèi qīngjié keep the bus tidy

请勿与司机谈话 qǐng wù yǔ sījī tánhuà please do not speak to the driver

老弱病残孕专座 lǎoruò bìngcānyùn zhuānzuò seats for the elderly or disabled and for pregnant women

招手上车 zhāoshǒu shàngchē stop on request

小卖部 xiǎomàibù kiosk

小吃店 xiǎochīdiàn snack bar

候车室 hòuchēshì waiting room

出租汽车 chūzū qìchē taxis

CHINESE CULTURE

寺 sì Buddhist temple

文化大革命 Wénhuà Dàgémìng Cultural Revolution (1966-1976)

天安门 Tiān'ānmén Gate of Heavenly Peace

长城 Chángchéng the Great Wall

五四运动 Wǔsì Yùndòng May 4th Movement (1919)

明 Míng Ming Dynasty (1368-1644)

十三陵 Shísānlíng Ming Tombs

年画 niánhuà New Year prints

塔 tǎ pagoda

故宫 Gùgōng Forbidden City

八达岭　Bādálǐng pass at Great Wall

京剧　Jīngjù Peking opera

木偶戏　mù'ǒuxì puppet show

清　Qīng Qing Dynasty (1644-1911)

宋　Sòng Song Dynasty (960-1279)

颐和园　Yíhéyuán Summer Palace

唐　Táng Tang Dynasty (618-907)

宫　gōng Taoist temple

观　guàn Taoist temple

庙　miào temple

天坛　Tiāntán Temple of Heaven

兵马俑　Bīngmáyǒng Terracotta Army

辛亥革命　Xīnhài Gémìng Xinhai Revolution (1911)

COUNTRIES, NATIONALITIES

美国　Měiguó America; American

澳大利亚　Àodàlìyà Australia; Australian

缅甸　Miǎndiàn Burma; Burmese

加拿大　Jiānádà Canada; Canadian

中国　Zhōngguó China; Chinese

英国　Yīngguó England; English; UK

法国　Fǎguó France; French

德国　Déguó Germany; German

香港　Xiānggǎng Hong Kong

印度尼西亚　Yìndùníxīyà Indonesia; Indonesian

爱尔兰　Ài'ěrlán Ireland; Irish

日本　Rìběn Japan; Japanese

朝鲜　Cháoxiǎn Korea; Korean

老挝　Lǎowō Laos

马来西亚　Mǎláixīyà Malaysia; Malaysian

满　Mǎn minority people from North-East China

维吾尔　Wéiwú'ěr minority people from North-West China

傣　Dǎi minority people from South-West China

苗　Miáo minority people from South-West China

彝　Yí minority people from South-West China

僮　Zhuàng minority people from South-West China

蒙　Měng Mongol

蒙古　Ménggǔ Mongolia

回　Huí Muslim minority people

尼泊尔　Níbó'ěr Nepal;

Nepali

中华人民共和国
Zhōnghuá Rénmín Gònghéguó
People's Republic of China

菲律宾 Fēilǜbīn Philippines;
Filipino

俄国 Éguó Russia; Russian

苏格兰 Sūgélán Scotland;
Scottish

新加坡 Xīnjiāpō Singapore;
Singaporean

西藏 Xīzàng Tibet

藏 Zàng Tibetan

台湾 Táiwān Taiwan;
Taiwanese

泰国 Tàiguó Thailand; Thai

威尔士 Wēi'ěrshì Wales;
Welsh

CUSTOMS

中国海关 Zhōngguó
hǎiguān Chinese Customs

海关 hǎiguān Customs

边防检查站 biānfáng
jiǎncházhàn frontier
checkpoint

免疫检查 miǎnyì jiǎnchá
health inspection

护照检查 hùzhào jiǎnchá
passport control

报关 bàoguān goods to
declare

不用报关 búyòng bàoguān
nothing to declare

绿色通道 lǜsè tōngdào

green channel, nothing to
declare

红色通道 hóngsè tōngdào
red channel, goods to
declare

入境签证 rùjìng qiānzhèng
entry visa

出境签证 chūjìng qiānzhèng
exit visa

护照 hùzhào passport

过境签证 guòjìng qiānzhèng
transit visa

旅行证 lǚxíngzhèng travel
permit

免税物品 miǎnshuì wùpǐn
duty-free goods

EMERGENCIES

救护车 jiùhùchē ambulance

太平门 tàipíngmén
emergency exit

火警匪警 huǒjǐng, féijǐng
emergency telephone
number: fire, robbery

消防队 xiāofángduì fire
brigade, fire department

急诊室 jízhěnshì first-aid
room

派出所 Pàichūsuǒ local
police station

警察 jǐngchá police

公安局 gōng'ānjú Public
Security Bureau

ENTERTAINMENT

售票处 shòupiàochù box office

入场院 rùchǎngyuàn cinema ticket

电影院 diànyǐngyuàn cinema

迪斯科 dísīkē disco

夜场 yèchǎng evening performance

全满 quánmǎn house full

休息 xiūxi interval

京剧 Jīngjù Peking Opera

节目单 jiémùdān programme

排 ... pái row ...

号 ... hào seat number ...

票已售完 piào yǐ shòu wán sold out

剧场 jùchǎng theatre

剧院 jùyuàn theatre

戏院 xìyuàn theatre

表演时间 biáoyǎn shíjiān times of performance

FORMS

从何处来 cóng héchù lái arriving from

出生年月 chūshēng niányuè date of birth

籍贯 jíguàn father's place of birth

到何处去 dào héchù qù heading for

拟住天数 nǐ zhù tiānshù length of stay

姓名 xìngmíng full name

国籍 guójí nationality

性别 xìngbié (nán/nǚ) sex (male/female)

护照号码 hùzhào hàomǎ passport number

永久地址 yóngjiǔ dìzhǐ permanent address

旅客登记表 lǚkè dēngjìbiǎo registration form

签名 qiānmíng signature

GEOGRAPHICAL TERMS

自治区 zìzhìqū autonomous region

运河 yùnhé canal

市 shì city

国家 guójiā country

县 xiàn county

森林 sēnlín forest

岛 dǎo island

湖 hú lake

江 jiāng large river

地图 dìtú map

山 shān mountain, hill

山脉 shānmài mountains

海洋 hǎiyáng ocean

省 shěng province

河 hé river

海 hǎi sea

镇 zhèn town

山谷 shāngǔ valley

村 cūn village

树林 shùlín woods

HEALTH

中医科 zhōngyīkē Chinese
medicine department
中药房 zhōngyàofáng
Chinese medicine
dispensary
牙科 yákē dental
department
急诊室 jízhěnshì emergency
外宾门诊部 wàibīn
ménzhěnbù foreign
outpatients
医院 yīyuàn hospital
住院处 zhùyuànchù hospital
admissions office
内科 nèikē medical
department
门诊部 ménzhěnbù
outpatients
挂号 guàhào registration
西药房 xīyàofáng Western
medicine dispensary

HIRING, RENTING

出租自行车 chūzū
zìxíngchē bikes to rent
租船 zū chuán boats to rent
出租 chūzū for hire, to rent

HOTELS

中国国际旅行社
Zhōngguó Guójì Lǚxíngshè
China International Travel
Service
中国旅行社 Zhōngguó
Lǚxíngshè China Travel
Service
宾馆 bīnguǎn hotel
饭店 fàndiàn hotel
小卖部 xiǎomàibù kiosk
总服务台 zǒng fúwùtái
reception
游艺室 yóuyìshì recreation
room
电传室 diànchuánshì telex
office

LIFTS (ELEVATORS)

关 guān close
下 xià down
电梯 diàntī lifts, elevators
开 kāi open
上 shàng up

MEDICINES

抗菌素 kàngjūnsù
antibiotics
阿斯匹林 āsīpǐlín aspirin
咳鼻清 kébíqīng cough
lozenges
棕色合剂 zōngsè héjì cough
mixture
止咳糖浆 zhǐké tángjiāng
cough syrup
止疼片儿 zhǐténgpiànr
painkillers
青霉素 qīngméisù penicillin
含碘片 hándiǎnpiàn throat
pastilles
剂量 jìliàng dosage

失效期 shīxiàoqī expiry date

初诊 chūzhěn first treatment

外用 wàiyòng for external use

一日三次 yírì sān cì four times a day

胃炎 wèiyán gastritis

饭前/后温开水送服 fàn qián/hòu wēnkāishuǐ sòngfú to be taken with warm water before/after food

每四/六小时服一次 měi sì/liù xiǎoshí fú yícì one dose every four/six hours

一日四次 yírì sāncì three times a day

内服 nèifú to be taken orally

每次一个 měi cì yì gé one measure at a time

每次一丸 měicì yì wán one pill at a time

每次一片儿 měicì yí piànr one tablet at a time

必要时服 bìyào shí fú when necessary

NOTICES ON DOORS

太平门 tàipíngmén emergency exit

入口 rùkǒu entrance

出口 chūkǒu exit

顾客止步 gùkè zhǐ bù no entry for customers

未经许可禁止入内 wèi jīng xúkě, jìnzhǐ rù nèi no entry without permission

拉 lā pull

推 tuī push

闲人免进 xiánrén miǎn jìn staff only

PHONES

长途区号 chángtú qūhào area code

用卡电话亭 yòng kǎ diànhuà tíng cardphone

查号台 cháhàotái directory enquiries

分机 fēnjī extension

国际长途 guójì chángtú international call

长途电话 chángtú diànhuà long-distance call

电话卡 diànhuàkǎ phonecard

公用电话 gōngyòng diànhuà public telephone

总机 zǒngjī switchboard

电话簿 diànhuàbù telephone directory

一次一角(毛) yícì yìjiǎo (máo) ten fen per call

磁卡电话 cíkǎ diànhuà cardphone

PLACE NAMES

北京 Běijīng Beijing

成都 Chéngdū Chengdu

敦煌 Dūnhuáng Dunhuang

峨嵋山 Éméishān Emei

Mountains
广州 Guǎngzhōu Canton
长城 Chángchéng the Great Wall
桂林 Guìlín Guilin
杭州 Hángzhōu Hangzhou
昆明 Kūnmíng Kunming
拉萨 Lāsā Lhasa
洛阳 Luòyáng Luoyang
南京 Nánjīng Nanjing
深圳 Shēnzhèn Shenzhen
天津 Tiānjīn Tientsin
西湖 Xīhú West Lake
西安 Xī'ān Xi'an
长江三峡 Chángjiāng Sānxiá Yangtze Gorges

POST OFFICE

邮局 yóujú post office
开箱时间 kāixiāng shíjiān collection times
信封 xìnfēng envelope
邮筒 yóutǒng letterbox, mailbox
信函 xìnhán letters
杂志报刊 zázhì bàokān magazines and newspapers
包裹单 bāoguǒdān parcel form
包裹印刷品 bāoguǒ - yìnshuāpǐn parcels, printed matter
邮电局 yóudiànjú post and telecommunications office
信箱电报 xìnxiāng postbox

邮政编码 yóuzhèng biānmǎ postcode, zip code
邮票挂号 yóupiào - guàhào stamps, registered mail
电报纸 diànbàozhǐ telegram form
电报 diànbào telegram
电报大楼 diànbào dàlóu telegraph building

PUBLIC BUILDINGS

浴池 yùchí baths
学院 xuéyuàn college
领事馆 lǐngshìguǎn consulate
大使馆 dàshǐguǎn embassy
工厂 gōngchǎng factory
游泳馆 yóuyǒngguǎn indoor swimming pool
图书馆 túshūguǎn library
博物馆 bówùguǎn museum
中学 zhōngxué secondary school
体育馆 tǐyùguǎn sports hall, indoor stadium
体育场 tǐyùchǎng stadium
大学 dàxué university

RESTAURANTS, CAFÉS, BARS

酒吧 jiǔbā bar
咖啡店 kāfēidiàn café, coffee house
茶楼 chálóu café, teahouse
茶馆 cháguǎn café, teahouse

茶室 cháshì café, teahouse

收款台 shōukuǎntái cashier

冷饮店 léngyǐndiàn cold drinks bar

中餐厅 Zhōng cāntīng Chinese dining room

清真饭店 qīngzhēn fàndiàn Muslim restaurant

面馆 miànguǎn noodle shop

菜馆 càiguǎn large restaurant

饭店 fàndiàn large restaurant

酒家 jiǔjiā large restaurant

酒楼 jiǔlóu large restaurant

餐厅 cāntīng restaurant; dining room

快餐 kuàicān snack bar

小吃店 xiǎochīdiàn snack bar

今日供应 jīnrì gòngyìng today's menu

素菜馆 sùcàiguǎn vegetarian restaurant

西餐厅 xī cāntīng Western dining room

西菜馆 xīcàiguǎn Western restaurant

SHOPPING

文物商店 wénwù shāngdiàn antique shop

工艺美术商店 gōngyì měishù shāngdiàn arts and crafts shop

自行车 zìxíngchē bicycles

收款台 shōukuǎntái cashier

烟酒糖茶 yān jiǔ táng chá cigarettes, wine, confectionery, tea

服装店 fúzhuāngdiàn clothes shop

男女服装 nánnǚ fúzhuāng clothing

化妆用品 huàzhuāng yòngpǐn cosmetics

百货商店 bǎihuò shāngdiàn department store

家用电器 jiāyòng diànqì domestic appliances

食品商店 shípǐn shāngdiàn food shop

食品糕点 shípǐn gāodiǎn food and confectionery

自由市场 zìyóu shìchǎng free market

友谊商店 yǒuyí shāngdiàn Friendship store

菜市场 càishìchǎng greengrocer

副食品商店 fùshípǐn shāngdiàn grocery store

五金交电 wǔjīn jiāodiàn hardware and electrical goods

袜子鞋帽 wàzi xiémào hosiery, shoes, hats

日用杂品 rìyòng zápǐn household goods

橱房用品 chúfáng yòngpǐn

kitchenware

妇女用品 fùnǚ yòngpǐn
ladies' accessories

女装 nǚzhuāng ladies' wear

洗衣店 xǐyīdiàn laundry

皮革制品 pígé zhìpǐn
leather goods

市场 shìchǎng market

男装 nán zhuāng menswear

乐器行 yuèqì háng musical
instruments section

新华书店 xīnhuá shūdiàn
New China bookshop

夜市 yèshì night market

眼镜店 yǎnjìngdiàn optician

复印 fùyìn photocopying

照相器材 zhàoxiàng qìcái
photographic equipment

钱票当面点清过后该不
负责 qián piào dāngmiàn
diǎnqīng, guòhòu gài bù fùzé
please check your change
before leaving as mistakes
cannot be rectified

雨伞雨具 yǔsǎn yǔjù
rainwear

大减价 dàjiǎnjià sale

古旧书店 gǔjiù shūdiàn
secondhand bookshop

购物中心 gòuwù zhōngxīn
shopping centre

体育用品 tǐyù yòngpǐn
sports goods

文具商店 wénjù shāngdiàn
stationery

文具用品 wénjù yòngpǐn
stationery

牙膏牙刷 yágāo yáshuā
toothpaste and tooth-
brushes

儿童玩具 értóng wánjù toys

针织用品 zhēnzhī yòngpǐn
underwear

STREETS AND ROADS

大街 dàjiē avenue

胡同 hútòng lane

巷 xiàng lane

路 lù road

广场 guángchǎng square

街 jiē street

TOILETS

有人 yǒurén engaged,
occupied

男厕所 náncèsuǒ gents'
toilet, men's room

男厕 náncè gents' toilet,
men's room

女厕所 nǚcèsuǒ ladies'
toilet, ladies' room

女厕 nǚcè ladies' toilet,
ladies' room

公厕 gōngcè public toilets,
rest rooms

盥洗室 guànxǐshì toilet,
rest room

无人 wúrén vacant, free

TRAIN AND UNDERGROUND TRAVEL

火车站 huǒchēzhàn station

火车 huǒchē train

列车到站时刻表 lièchē dàozhàn shíkèbiǎo arrival times

列车离站时刻表 lièchē lízhàn shíkèbiǎo departure times

开往...方向... kāiwǎng ... fāngxiàng to ...

车次 chēcì train number

检票处 jiǎnpiàochù barrier

站台 zhàntái platform, (US) track

站台票 zhàntáipiào platform ticket

问讯处 wènxùnchù information desk

火车时刻表 huǒchē shíkèbiǎo timetable, (US) schedule

天 tiān day

特快 tèkuài express

直快 zhíkuài through train

快车 kuàichē fast train

客车 kèchē ordinary passenger train

站名 zhànmíng station name

开往... kāiwǎng ... to ...

旅车 lǚyóuchē tourist train

车次 chēcì train number

星期 xīngqī week

行李寄存处 xíngli jìcúnchù left luggage, baggage checkroom

乘警 chéngjǐng railway police

售票处 shòupiàochù ticket office

候车室 hòuchēshì waiting room

餐车 cānchē dining car

硬席 yìngxí hard seat

硬席车 yìngxíchē hard seat carriage

硬卧 yìngwò hard sleeper

硬卧车 yìngwòchē hard sleeper carriage

软席 ruǎnxí soft seat

软席车 ruǎnxíchē soft seat carriage

软卧 ruǎnwò soft sleeper

软卧车 ruǎnwòchē soft sleeper carriage

紧急制动闸 jǐnjí zhìdòngzhá emergency brake

乘务员 chéngwùyuán train attendant

地铁 dìtiě underground, (US) subway

Menu Reader:

Food

ESSENTIAL TERMS

bowl diézi [dyeh-dzur]
碟子

chopsticks kuàizi [kwai-dzur]
筷子

cup bēizi [bay-dzur]
杯子

dessert tiánpǐn [tyen-pin]
甜品

fork (for eating) chā [chah]
叉

fried noodles chǎomiàn [chow-myen]
炒面

fried rice chǎofàn [chow-fahn]
炒饭

glass bōli bēi [bor-lee bay]
玻璃杯

knife dāozi [dow-dzur]
刀子

menu càidānr [tsai-dahnr]
菜单儿

noodles miàntiáo [myen-tyow]
面条

plate pánzi [pahn-dzur]
盘子

rice mǐfàn [mee-fahn]
米饭

soup tāng [tahng]
汤

soy sauce jiàngyóu [jyahn-gyoh]
酱油

spoon sháozi [show-dzur]
勺子

table zhuōzi [jwor-dzur]
卓子

excuse me ... máfan nín, qǐng wèn ... [mah-fahn nin ching wun]
麻烦您请问...

could I have the bill, please? qǐng bāng wǒ jiézhàng, hǎo ma? [ching bahng wor jyeh-jahng how mah]
请帮我结帐好吗?

BASIC FOODS

黄油 huángyóu [hwahng-yoh]
butter

奶酪 nǎilào [nai-low] cheese

辣椒油 làjiāo yóu [lah-jyow
yoh] chilli oil

辣椒酱 làjiāo jiàng [jyang]
chilli paste

椰子油 yēzi yóu [yur-dzur yoh]
coconut milk

奶油 nǎiyóu [nai-yoh] cream

豆腐干儿 dòufu gānr [doh-
foo gahnr] dried bean curd

大蒜 dàsuàn [dah-swahn]
garlic

黄米 huángmǐ [hwahng-mee]
glutinous millet

豆瓣儿辣酱儿 dòubànr
làjiàngr [doh-bahnr lah-jyengr]
hot soya bean paste

玉米 yùmǐ [yoo-mee] maize

小米 xiáomǐ [hsyah-mee]
millet

蚝油 háoyóu [how-yoh]
oyster sauce

花生油 huāshēng yóu [hwah-
shung yoh] peanut oil

咸菜 xiáncài [hsyen-tsai]
pickles

松花蛋 sōnghuādàn [soong-
hwah-dahn] preserved eggs

菜籽油 càizi yóu [tsai-dzur
yoh] rape oil

大米 dàmǐ [dah-mee] rice

芝麻油 zhīma yóu [jur-mah
yoh] sesame oil

盐 yán [yahn] salt

高梁 gāoliáng [gow-lyang]
sorghum (similar to corn)

豆油 dòuyóu [doh-yoh] soya
bean oil

酱油 jiàngyóu [jyang-yoh] soy
sauce

糖 táng [tahng] sugar

番茄酱 fānqié jiàng [fahn-
chyeh jyang] tomato paste

素鸡 sùjī [soo-jee]
'vegetarian chicken' (rolled
dried soya bean milk cream)

小麦 xiǎomài [hsyow-mai]
wheat

面粉 miànfěn [myen-fun]
wheat flour

BASIC PREPARATION AND COOKING METHODS

什锦... shíjǐn ... [shur-jin]
assorted ...

... 丸 ... wán [wahn] ... balls

... 圆 ... yuán [yew-ahn] ...
balls

叉烧... chāshāo ... [chah-
show] barbecued ...

煮... zhǔ ... [joo] boiled ...

烧... shāo ... [show]
braised ...

... 块儿 ... kuàir ... [kwair] ...
chunks, pieces

香酥... xiāngsū ... [hsyang-
soo] crispy deep-fried ...

咖喱 … gālí … [gah-lee]
curried …

炸 … zhá … [jah] deep-
fried …

… 丁 … dīng diced …

家常 … jiācháng … [jyah-
chahng] home-style … (plain)

火锅 … huǒguō … [hwor-
gwor] … in hot pot, i.e.
served with a pot of boiling
water in which the meat or
fish is cooked, also creating
a soup

烤 … kǎo … [kow] roasted,
baked

… 片儿 … piànr [pyenr] …
slices

蒸 … zhēng … [jung]
steamed …

清蒸 … qīngzhēng … [ching-
jung] steamed …

烩 … huì … [hway] stewed
…

炒 … chǎo … [chow]
stir-fried …

糖醋 … tángcù … [tahng-
tsoo] sweet and sour …

三鲜 … sānxiān … [sahn-
hsyen] 'three-fresh' … (with
three ingredients which vary)

BEAN CURD DISHES

麻婆豆腐 mápó dòufu [mah-
por doh-foo] bean curd with
minced beef in spicy sauce

三鲜豆腐 sānxiān dòufu
[sahn-hsyen] 'three-fresh'
bean curd (made with three
ingredients)

沙锅豆腐 shāguō dòufu
[shah-gwor] bean curd served
with a pot of boiling water
in which the bean curd is
cooked, also creating a soup

麻辣豆腐 málà dòufu [mah-
lah] bean curd with chilli
and wild pepper

虾仁豆腐 xiārén dòufu
[hsyah-run] bean curd with
shrimps

家常豆腐 jiācháng dòufu
[jyah-chahng] home-style
bean curd

BEEF DISHES

红烧牛肉 hóngshāo niúròu
[hoong-show nyoh-roh] beef
braised in brown sauce

麻酱牛肉 májiàng niúròu
[mah-jyang] beef quick-fried
in sesame paste

酱爆牛肉 jiàngbào niúròu
[jyang-bow] beef quick-fried
with black bean sauce

葱爆牛肉 cōngbào niúròu
[tsoong-bow] beef quick-fried
with spring onions

咖喱牛肉 gālí niúròu [gah-
lee] curried beef

时菜牛肉片儿 shícài

niúròupiànr [shur-tsai nyoh-roh-pyenr] shredded beef with seasonal vegetables

鱼香牛肉 yúxiāng niúròu [yoo-hsyang nyoh-roh] stir-fried beef in hot spicy sauce

笋炒牛肉 súnchǎo niúròu [sun-chow] stir-fried beef with bamboo shoots

麻辣牛肉 málà niúròu [mah-lah] stir-fried beef with chilli and wild pepper

蚝油牛肉 háoyóu niúròu [how-yoh] stir-fried beef with oyster sauce

宫保牛肉 gōngbǎo niúròu [goong-bow] stir-fried beef with peanuts and chilli

茄汁牛肉 qiézhī niúròu [chyeh-jur] stir-fried sliced beef with tomato sauce

BREAD, DUMPLINGS etc

葱油饼 cōngyóubǐng [tsoong-yoh-bing] spring onion pancake

水饺 shuǐjiǎo [shway-jyow] Chinese ravioli

饺子 jiǎozi [jyow-dzur] dumplings

锅贴 guōtiē [gwor-tyeh] fried Chinese ravioli

馄饨 húntun small Chinese ravioli in soup

馒头 mántou [mahn-toh] steamed bread containing various fillings

蒸饺 zhēngjiǎo [jung-jyow] steamed Chinese ravioli

烧卖 shāomài [show-mai] steamed dumplings open at the top

包子 bāozi [bow-dzur] steamed dumplings with various fillings, usually minced pork

花卷儿 huājuǎnr [hwah-jwahnr] steamed rolls

三鲜水饺 sānxiān shuǐjiǎo [sahn-hsyen shoo-jyow] 'three-fresh' Chinese ravioli (pork, shrimps and chives)

面包 miànbāo [myen-bow] white bread

COLD PLATTERS

什锦冷盘儿 shíjǐn lěngpánr [shur-jin lung-pahnr] assorted cold platter

海杂拌儿 hǎi zábànr [hai zah-bahnr] seafood cold platter

七菜冷拼盘儿 qīcǎi lěng pīnpánr [chee-tsai lung pin-pahnr] 'seven colours' cold platter

DESSERTS

西瓜盅 xīgua zhōng [hshee-gwah joong] assorted fruit and water melon

什锦水果羹 shíjǐn shuǐguo
gēng [shur-jin shway-gwor gung]
fruit salad

莲子羹 liánzi gēng [lyen-dzur]
lotus-seed in syrup

酸奶 suānnǎi [swahn-nai]
yoghurt

FISH AND SEAFOOD

鲈鱼 lúyú [loo-yoo] bass

螃蟹 pángxiè [pahng-hsyeh]
crab

鱼 yú [yoo] fish

鲳鱼 chāngyú [chahng-yoo] pomfret

虾 xiā [hsyah] prawns

加级鱼 jiājí [jyah-jee] red
snapper

鱿鱼 yóuyú [yoh-yoo] squid

FISH AND SEAFOOD
DISHES

红烧鲤鱼 hóngshāo lǐyú
[hoong-show lee-yoo] carp
braised in brown sauce

干烧桂鱼 gānshāo guìyú
[gahn-show gway-yoo] Chinese
perch braised with chilli and
black bean sauce

咖喱鱿鱼 gāli yǒuyú [gah-lee
yoh-yoo] curried squid

茄汁石斑块儿 qiézhī
shíbānkuàir [chyeh-jur shur-
bahn-kwair] deep-fried
grouper with tomato sauce

火锅鱼虾 huǒguō yúxiā
[hwor-gwor yoo-hsyah] fish and
prawns served with a pot of
boiling water in which they
are cooked, creating a soup

家常鱼块儿 jiācháng yúkuàir
[jyah-chahng yoo-kwair] home-
style fish

干烧黄鳝 gānshāo
huángshàn [gahn-show hwahng-
shahn] paddyfield eel
braised with chilli and black
bean sauce

时菜虾球 shícài xiāqiú [shoo-
tsai hsyah-chew] prawn balls
with seasonal vegetables

虾仁干贝 xiārén gānbèi
[hsyah-run gahn-bay] scallops
with shrimps

葱爆海参 cōngbào hǎishēn
[tsoong-bow hai-shun] sea
cucumber quick-fried with
spring onions

蚝鱿鲍鱼 háoyóu bāoyú
[how-yoh bow-yoo] stir-fried
abalone with oyster sauce

滑溜鱼片儿 huáliū yúpiànr
[hwah-lyoh yoo-pyenr] stir-fried
fish slices with thick sauce

鱼香龙虾 yúxiāng lóngxiā
[yoo-hsyang loong-hsyah]
stir-fried lobster in hot spicy
sauce

冬笋炒海参 dōngsǔn cháo
hǎishēn [doong-sun chow hai-
shun] stir-fried sea

cucumber with bamboo
shoots

糖醋鱼块儿 tángcù yúkuàir
[tahng-tsoo yoo-kwair] sweet
and sour fish

FRUIT

萍果 píngguǒ [ping-gwor]
apple

杏 xìng [hsing] apricot

香蕉 xiāngjiāo [hsyang-jyow]
banana

椰子 yēzi [yur-dzur] coconut

海棠果 hǎitángguǒ [hai-tahng-
gwor] crab apple

枣 zǎo [dzow] date

葡萄 pútao [poo-tow] grape

广柑 guǎnggān [gwahng-gahn]
Guangdong orange

哈密瓜 hāmìgua [hah-mee-
gwah] honeydew melon

龙眼 lóngyǎn [loong-yahn]
longan (similar to lychee)

荔枝 lìzhī [lee-jur] lychee

柑子 gānzi [gahn-dzur]
orange

桔子 júzi [joo-dzur] orange

桃子 táozi [tow-dzur] peach

梨 lí [lee] pear

柿子 shìzi [shur-dzur]
persimmon, sharon fruit

菠萝 bōluó [bor-lwor]
pineapple

李子 lǐzi [lee-dzur] plum

石榴 shíliu [shur-lyoh]

pomegranate

沙田柚 shātiányòu [shah-tyen-
yoh] pomelo

橘子 júzi [joo-dzur] tangerine

蜜桔 mìjú [mee-joo]
tangerine

西瓜 xīguā [hshee-gwah]
water melon

LAMB AND MUTTON DISHES

咖喱羊肉 gālí yángròu [gah-
lee yahn-roh] curried mutton

烤羊肉串儿 kǎo
yángròuchuànr [kow yahng-roh-
chwahnr] lamb kebabs

涮羊肉 shuàn yángròu
[shwahn yang-roh] Mongolian
lamb served with a pot of
boiling water in which the
meat is cooked, also
creating a soup

红烧羊肉 hóngshāo yángròu
[hoong-show] mutton braised
in brown sauce

火锅羊肉 huǒguō yángròu
[hwor-gwor] mutton served
with a pot of boiling water
in which the meat is cooked,
also creating a soup

酱爆羊肉 jiàngbào yángròu
[jyang-bow] mutton
quick-fried with black bean
sauce

葱爆羊肉 cōngbào yángròu [tsoong-bow] mutton quick-fried with spring onions

时菜羊肉片儿 shícài yángròupiànr [shur-tsai yang-roh-pyenr] shredded mutton with seasonal vegetables

麻辣羊肉 málà yángròu [mah-lah] stir-fried mutton with chilli and wild pepper

蚝油羊肉 háoyóu yángròu [how-yoh] stir-fried mutton with oyster sauce

MEATS

牛肉 niúròu [nyoh-roh] beef

鸡 jī [jee] chicken

鸭 yā [yah] duck

羊肉 yángròu [yahng-roh] lamb; mutton

肉 ròu [roh] meat (usually pork)

猪肉 zhūròu [joo-roh] pork

NOODLES

炒面 chǎomiàn [chow-myen] fried noodles

鸡丝炒面 jīsī chǎomiàn [jee-sur] fried noodles with shredded chicken

肉丝炒面 ròusī chǎomiàn [roh-sur] fried noodles with shredded pork

虾仁炒面 xiārén chǎomiàn [hsyah-run chow-myen] fried noodles with shrimps

炒米粉 chǎomǐfěn [chow-mee-fun] fried rice noodles

面条 miàntiáo [myen-tyow] noodles

PORK DISHES

叉烧肉 chāshāo ròu [chah-show roh] barbecued pork

咖喱肉丸 gālí ròuwán [gah-lee roh-wahn] curried meatballs

狮子头 shīzi tóu [shur-dzur toh] a large meatball stewed with cabbage

火锅猪排 huǒguō zhūpái [hwor-gwor joo-pai] pork chop served with a pot of boiling water in which the meat is cooked, also creating a soup

酱爆三样 jiàngbào sānyàng [jyang-bow sahn-yang] pork, pig's liver and kidney quick-fried with black bean sauce

烤小猪 kǎo xiǎozhū [kow hsyow-joo] roast sucking pig

米粉蒸肉 mǐfěn zhēngròu [mee-fun jung-roh] steamed pork with rice

宫保肉丁 gōngbǎo ròudīng [goong-bow roh-ding] stir-fried diced pork with peanuts and chilli

鱼香肉丝 yúxiāng ròusī [yoo-hsyang roh-sur] stir-fried

shredded pork in hot sauce

冬笋肉丝 dōngsǔn ròusī
[doong-sun] stir-fried
shredded pork with bamboo
shoots

榨菜炒肉丝 zhàcài chǎo
ròusī [jah-tsai chow] stir-fried
shredded pork with pickled
mustard greens

笋炒肉片儿 súnchǎo
ròupiànr [sun-chow roh-pyenr]
stir-fried sliced pork with
bamboo shoots

芙蓉肉片儿 fúróng ròupiànr
[foo-roong] stir-fried sliced
pork with egg white

青椒炒肉片儿 qīngjiāo chǎo
ròupiànr [ching-jyow chow]
stir-fried sliced pork with
green pepper

时菜炒肉片儿 shícài chǎo
ròupiànr [shur-tsai] stir-fried
sliced pork with seasonal
vegetables

滑溜肉片儿 huáliū ròupiànr
[hwah-lyoh] stir-fried sliced
pork with thick sauce

回锅肉 huíguō ròu [hway-gwor
roh] boiled then stir-fried
pork

POULTRY AND POULTRY DISHES

时菜扒鸭 shícài páyā [shur-
tsai pah-yah] braised duck

with seasonal vegetables

佛跳墙 fó tiào qiáng [for tyow
chyang] chicken with duck,
pig's trotters and seafood
stewed in rice wine (literally:
Buddha leaps the wall)

茄汁鸡脯 qiézhī jīpú [chyeh-
jur jee-poo] chicken breast
with tomato sauce

咖喱鸡块儿 gāli jīkuàir [gah-
lee jee-kwair] curried chicken
pieces

酱爆鸡丁 jiàngbào jīdīng
[jyang-bow jee-ding] diced
chicken quick-fried with
black bean sauce

冬笋鸡片儿 dōngsǔn jīpiànr
[doong-sun jee-pyenr] chicken
slices with bamboo shoots

冬菇鸡片儿 dōnggū jīpiànr
[doong-goo] chicken slices
with mushrooms

香酥鸡 xiāngsū jī [hsyang-soo
jee] crispy deep-fried whole
chicken

香酥鸭 xiāngsū yā [yah]
crispy deep-fried whole
duck

辣子鸡丁 làzi jīdīng [lah-dzur
jee-ding] diced chicken with
chilli

麻辣鸡丁 málà jīdīng [mah-
lah] diced chicken with
chilli and wild pepper

香菇鸭掌 xiānggū yāzhǎng

[hsyang-goo yah-jahng] duck's
foot with mushroom

茄汁煎软鸭 qiézhī jiān
ruǎnyā [chyeh-jur jyen rwahn-
yah] fried duck with tomato
sauce

家常焖鸡 jiācháng mènjī
[jyah-chahng mun-jee]
home-style braised chicken

北京烤鸭 Běijīng kǎoyā [bay-
jing kow-yah] Peking duck

酱爆鸭片儿菜心 jiàngbào
yāpiànr càixīn [jyang-bow yah-
pyenr tsai-hsin] sliced duck
and green vegetables
quick-fried with black bean
sauce

葱爆烧鸭片儿 cōngbào
shāoyāpiànr [tsoong-bow show-
yah-pyenr] sliced duck
quick-fried with spring
onions

宫保鸡丁 gōngbǎo jīdīng
[goong-bow jee-ding] stir-fried
diced chicken with peanuts
and chilli

怪味儿鸡 guàiwèirjī [gwai-
wayr-jee] whole chicken with
peanuts and pepper (literally:
strange-tasting chicken)

汽锅蒸鸡 qìguō zhēngjī
[chee-gwor jung-jee] whole
chicken steamed in a pot

红烧全鸭 hóngshāo quányā
[hoong-show choo-en-yah]

whole duck braised in
brown sauce

红烧全鸡 hóngshāo quánjī
[choo-en-jee] whole chicken
braised in brown sauce

RICE

炒饭 chǎofàn [chow-fahn]
fried rice

蛋炒饭 dàn chǎofàn [dahn]
fried rice with eggs

鸡丝炒饭 jīsī chǎofàn [jee-
sur] fried rice with shredded
chicken

肉丝炒饭 ròusī chǎofàn [roh-
sur] fried rice with shredded
pork

虾仁炒饭 xiārén chǎofàn
[hsyah-run] fried rice with
shrimps

米饭 mǐfàn [mee-fahn] rice

稀饭 xīfàn [hshee-fahn] rice
porridge

叉烧包 chāshāobāo [chah-
show-bow] steamed
dumplings with pork filling

SEASONINGS, SPICES

桂皮 guìpí [gway-pee]
Chinese cinnamon

丁香 dīngxiāng [ding-hsyang]
cloves

茴香 huíxiāng [hway-hsyang]
fennel seed

五香面儿 wǔxiāng miànr

[woo-hsyang myenr] 'five
spice' powder

生姜 **shēngjiāng** [shung-jyang]
ginger

辣椒 **làjiāo** [lah-jyow] chilli,
chilli peppers

辣椒粉 **làjiāo fěn** [fun] chilli
powder

胡椒 **hújiāo** [hoo-jyow]
pepper

盐 **yán** [yahn] salt

醋 **cù** [tsoo] vinegar

SNACKS

豆沙酥饼 **dòushā sūbǐng**
[doh-shah soo-bing] baked
flaky cake with sweet bean
paste filling

火烧 **huǒshāo** [hwor-show]
baked wheaten bun

糖火烧 **táng huǒshāo** [tahng]
baked wheaten bun with
sugar

油饼 **yóubǐng** [yoh-bing]
deep-fried savoury pancake

柚炸糕 **yóuzhágāo** [yoh-jah-
gow] deep-fried sweet
pancake

馅儿饼 **xiànrbǐng** [hsyenr-bing]
savoury fritter

烧饼 **shāobǐng** [show-bing]
sesame pancake

春卷儿 **chūnjuǎnr** [chun-
jwahnr] spring rolls

豆沙包 **dòushābāo** [doh-shah-
bow] steamed dumpling with
sweet bean paste filling

油跳 **yóutiáo** [yoh-tyow]
unsweetened doughnut
sticks

SOUPS

开水白菜 **kāishuǐ báicài** [kai-
shway bai-tsai] Chinese
cabbage in clear soup

酸辣汤 **suān là tāng** [swahn
lah tahng] hot and sour soup

汤 **tāng** soup

竹笋鲜蘑汤 **zhúsǔn xiānmó
tāng** [joo-sun hsyen-mor] soup
with bamboo shoots and
mushrooms

西红柿鸡蛋汤 **xīhóngshì
jīdan tāng** [hshee-hoong-shur
jee-dahn] soup with eggs and
tomato

榨菜肉丝汤 **zhàcài ròusī
tāng** [jah-tsai roh-sur] soup
with shredded pork and
pickled mustard greens

时菜肉片儿汤 **shícài
ròupiànr tāng** [shur-tsai roh-
pyenr] soup with sliced pork
and seasonal vegetables

菠菜粉丝汤 **bōcài fěnsī tāng**
[bor-tsai fun-sur] soup with
spinach and vermicelli

三鲜汤 **sānxiān tāng** [sahn-
hsyen] 'three-fresh' soup
(prawns, meat and a vegetable)

圆汤素烩 **yuántāng sùhuì**
[ywahn-tahng soo-hway]
vegetable chowder

TYPICAL COMBINATIONS

红烧... **hóngshāo** ... [hoong-
show] ... braised in brown
sweet and soy sauce

干烧... **gānshāo** ... [gahn-
show] ... braised with chilli
and black bean sauce

麻酱... **jiàngbào** ... [jyang-
bow] ... quick-fried with
black bean sauce

葱爆... **cōngbào** ... [tsoong-
bow] ... quick-fried with
spring onions

鱼香... **yúxiāng** ... [yoo-
hsyang] stir-fried ... in hot
spicy sauce (literally: fish
fragrance; not always with fish)

笋炒... **súnchǎo** ... [sun-
chow] stir-fried ... with
bamboo shoots

宫保... **gōngbǎo** ... [goong-
bow] stir-fried ... with
peanuts and chilli

滑溜... **huáliū** ... [hwah-lyoh]
stir-fried ... with sauce

冬笋... **dōngsǔn** ... [doong-
sun] ... with bamboo shoots

辣子... **làzi** ... [lah-dzur] ...
with chilli

麻辣... **málà** ... [mah-lah] ...
with chilli and wild pepper

蟹肉... **xièròu** ... [hsyeh-roh]
... with crab

火腿... **huótuǐ** ... [hwor-tway]
... with ham

冬菇... **dōnggū** ... [doong-
goo] ... with mushrooms

香菇... **xiānggū** ... [hsyang-
goo] ... with mushrooms

蚝油... **háoyóu** ... [how-yoh]
... with oyster sauce

榨菜... **zhàcài** ... [jah-tsai]
... with pickled mustard
greens

时菜... **shícài** ... [shur-tsai]
... with seasonal vegetables

虾仁... **xiārén** ... [hsyah-run]
... with shrimps

茄汁... **qiézhī** ... [chyeh-jur]
... with tomato sauce

番茄... **fānqié** ... [fahn-chyeh]
... with tomato sauce

VEGETABLES

茄子 **qiézi** [chyeh-dzur]
aubergine, eggplant

竹笋 **zhúsǔn** [joo-sun]
bamboo shoots

豆芽 **dòuyá** [doh-yah] bean
sprouts

卷心菜 **juǎnxīncài** [jwahn-
hsin-tsai] cabbage

胡萝卜 **húluóbo** [hoo-lwor-
bor] carrots

白菜 **báicài** [bai-tsai] Chinese
cabbage

青豆 qīngdòu [ching-doh]
green beans

蘑菇 mógu [mor-goo]
mushrooms

菠菜 bōcài [bor-tsai] spinach

红薯 hóngshǔ [hoong-shoo]
sweet potato

西红柿 xīhóngshì [hshee-
hoong-shur] tomato

蔬菜 shūcài [shoo-tsai]
vegetables

VEGETABLE DISHES

烧茄子 shāo qiézi [show
chyeh-dzur] stewed
aubergine/eggplant

烧胡萝卜 shāo húluóbo
[hoo-lwor-bor] stewed carrot

烧三鲜 shāo sānxiān [sahn-
hsyen] stewed 'three-fresh'
vegetables

炒玉兰片儿 chǎo yùlánpiànr
[chow yoo-lahn-pyenr]
stir-fried bamboo shoots

炒豆芽 chǎo dòuyá [doh-yah]
stir-fried bean sprouts

炒白菜 chǎo báicài [bai-tsai]
stir-fried Chinese cabbage

海米白菜 háimǐ báicài [hai-
mee] stir-fried Chinese
cabbage with dried shrimps

韭菜炒鸡蛋 jiǔcài chǎo jīdàn
[jyoh-tsai-chow jee-dyen] stir-
fried chives with eggs

黄瓜炒鸡蛋 huángguā chǎo
jīdàn [hwahng-gwah chow jee-
dahn] stir-fried cucumber
with eggs

鱼香茄子 yúxiāng qiézi [yoo-
hsyang chyeh-dzur] stir-fried
aubergine in hot spicy sauce

冬笋扁豆 dōngsǔn biǎndòu
[doong-sun byen-doh] stir-fried
French beans with bamboo
shoots

烧二冬 shāo èr dōng [show er
doong] stir-fried mushrooms
and bamboo shoots with
vegetables

鲜蘑豌豆 xiānmó wāndòu
[hsyen-mor wahn-doh]
stir-fried peas with
mushrooms

炒土豆丝 chǎo tǔdòusī
[chow too-doh-sur] stir-fried
shredded potato

炒萝卜丝 chǎo luóbosī [lwor-
bor-sur] stir-fried shredded
turnip

菠菜炒鸡蛋 bōcài chǎo jīdàn
[bor-tsai —jee-dahn] stir-fried
spinach with eggs

西红柿炒鸡蛋 xīhóngshì
chǎo jīdàn [hshee-hoong-shur]
stir-fried tomato with eggs

MENU READER: FOOD

Menu Reader:

Drink

ESSENTIAL TERMS

beer píjiǔ [pee-jyoh]
啤酒

bottle píngzi [ping-dzur]
瓶子

coffee kāfēi [kah-fay]
咖啡

cup bēizi [bay-dzee]
杯子

glass bolibēi [bor-lee-bay]
玻璃杯

milk niúnǎi [nyoh-nai]
牛奶

mineral water kuàngquánshuǐr
[kwahng-choo-en-shwayr]
矿泉水儿

orange juice xiānjúzhī [hsyen-
jyew-jur]
鲜橘汁

rice wine míjiǔ [mee-jyoh]
米酒

soft drink qìshuǐr [chee-shwayr]
汽水儿

sugar táng [tahng]
糖

tea chá [chah]
茶

water shuǐ [shway]
水

whisky wēishìjì [way-shur-jee]
威士忌

酒水在外 jiǔshuǐ zài wài
drinks not included

a cup of tea/coffee, please yì bēi
chá/kāfēi [bay]
一杯茶／咖啡

another beer, please qǐng zài lái
yì bēi píjiǔ [ching dzai lai yee bay
pee-jyoh]
请再来一杯啤酒

a glass of Maotai (lái) yì bēi
Máotáijiǔ [yee bay mow-tai-jyoh]
（来）一杯茅台酒

BEER

啤酒 píjiǔ [pee-jyoh] beer

冰镇啤酒 bīngzhèn píjiǔ [bing-jun] iced beer

青岛啤酒 Qīngdǎo píjiǔ [ching-dow] most famous type of Chinese beer

COFFEE, TEA etc

红茶 hóngchá [hoong-chah] black tea

菊花茶 júhuāchá [joo-hwah-chah] chrysanthemum tea

咖啡 kāfēi [kah-fay] coffee

绿茶 lǜchá [lyew-chah] green tea

茉莉花茶 mòli huāchá [mor-lee hwah-chah] jasmine tea

乌龙茶 wūlóngchá [woo-loong-chah] oolong tea, famous semi-fermented tea, half green, half black

花茶 huāchá [hwah-chah] scented tea

牛奶咖啡 niúnǎi kāfēi [nyoh-nai kah-fay] white coffee, coffee with milk

SOFT DRINKS

可口可乐 kékou kělè [kur-koh kur-lur] Coke®

果子汁 guǒzizhī [gwor-dzur-jur] fruit juice

冰水 bīngshuǐ [bing-shway] iced water

崂山可乐 Láoshān kělè [low-shahn kur-lur] Chinese variety of cola made from Laoshan water

柠檬汽水儿 níngméng qìshuǐr [ning-mung chee-shwayr] lemonade

牛奶 niúnǎi [nyoh-nai] milk

矿泉水儿 kuàngquánshuǐr [kwahng-chwahn-shwayr] mineral water

橘子汽水儿 júzi qìshuǐr [joo-dzur chee-shwayr] orangeade

橘子汁 júzizhī [joo-dzur-jee] orange juice

菠萝汁 bōluozhī [bor-lwor-jur] pineapple juice

酸梅汤 suānméitāng [swahn-may-tahng] sweet-sour plum juice

WINE, SPIRITS etc

白兰地 báilándì [bai-lahn-dee] brandy

香槟酒 xiāngbīnjiǔ [hsyang-bin-jyoh] champagne

白干儿 báigānr [bai-gahnr] clear spirit, distilled from sorghum grain

白酒 báijiǔ [bai-jyoh] clear spirit, distilled from sorghum grain

法国白兰地 fǎguó báilándì [fah-gwor bai-lahn-dee] cognac

干红葡萄酒 gān hóng pútaojiǔ [gahn hoong poo-tow-jyow] dry red wine

干白葡萄酒 gān bái pútaojiǔ dry white wine

金酒 jīnjiǔ [jin-jyoh] gin

果子酒 guǒzijiǔ [gwor-dzur-jyoh] liqueur

茅台酒 Máotáijiǔ [mow-tai-jyoh] Maotai spirit

红葡萄酒 hóng pútaojiǔ [hoong poo-tow-jyoh] red wine

黄酒 huángjiǔ [hwahng-jyoh] rice wine

老酒 láojiǔ [low-jyoh] rice wine

朗姆酒 lángmújiǔ [lahng-moo-jyoh] rum

苏格兰威士忌 Sūgélán wēishìjì [soo-gur-lahn] Scotch whisky

汽水儿 qìshuǐr [chee-shwayr] soda water

汽酒 qìjiǔ [chee-jyoh] sparkling wine

味美思 wèiměisī [way-may-sur] vermouth

俄得克酒 édékèjiǔ [ur-dur-kur-jyoh] vodka

威士忌 wēishìjì [way-shur-jur] whisky

白葡萄酒 bái pútaojiǔ [poo-tow-jyoh] white wine

葡萄酒 pútaojiǔ [] wine